W9-DEA-808

THE UPPER ROOM DISCIPLINES

1989

of Christmas 1988
Maureen

THE UPPER ROOM

Disciplines

1989

Coordinating Editor
Tom Page

Edited by
Janet McNish Bugg
Mary Ruth Coffman
Lynn W. Gilliam
John S. Mogabgab
Tom Page
Shirley H. Paris
Jill S. Reddig
Mary Lou Redding
Beth A. Richardson
Willie S. Teague
Douglas Tonks

The Upper Room Disciplines 1989

ISBN 0-8358-0572-7

The scripture quotations not otherwise identified are from the Revised Standard Version of the Bible, copyrighted 1946, 1952, and © 1971 by the Division of Christian Education, National Council of the Churches of Christ in the United States of America, and are used by permission.

Scripture quotations designated NEB are from *The New English Bible,* © The Delegates of the Oxford University Press and the Syndics of the Cambridge University Press 1961 and 1970, and are reprinted by permission.

Scripture quotations designated TEV are from the *Good News Bible, The Bible in Today's English Version,* copyright by American Bible Society 1966, 1971, © 1976, and are used by permission.

Scripture quotations designated NKJV are from the *Holy Bible, The New King James Version.* Copyright 1972, 1984 by Thomas Nelson, Inc., Publishers.

Scripture quotations designated NIV are from the *Holy Bible: New International Version.* Copyright © 1973, 1978, 1984 International Bible Society. Used by permission of Zondervan Bible Publishers.

Scripture quotations designated NJB are from the *New Jerusalem Bible,* copyright © 1985 by Darton, Longman & Todd, Ltd. and Doubleday & Company, Inc. Used by permission of the publisher.

The designation KJV is used throughout this book to identify quotations from the King James Version of the Bible.

Any scripture quotation designated AP is the author's paraphrase.

Cover photo: The World Christian Fellowship Window at The Upper Room Chapel, Nashville, Tennessee.

CONTENTS

FOREWORD

This is the thirtieth anniversary edition of *Disciplines*. Originally intended to be a companion to *The Upper Room* magazine, *Disciplines* soon revealed that it had its own quite distinctive identity. Whereas *The Upper Room* offers daily spiritual guidance through faith-inspired stories gleaned from personal experience, *Disciplines* nourishes the spirit through meditations on scripture rooted in biblical exegesis and organized according to the Common Lectionary. In *Disciplines* the focus shifts from the faith of the believer to the word of God which elicits, challenges, and sustains that faith.

Solid exegesis, faithful reflection, and guidance for prayer make *Disciplines* an ideal resource for the cultivation of an informed imagination. Each meditation offers biblical images which can transform our vision of life from a black-and-white "rerun" into a sparkling color live performance. Yet this is no unbridled imagination racing off into fantasy or self-delusion. Rather, it is imagination harnessed and guided by the best insights of contemporary theology and biblical scholarship.

Borne beyond our own time and place by imagination, we enter what Karl Barth called "the strange new world within the Bible." Once there, we discover people and events that, as Thomas Merton once wrote, are "extremely and mysteriously relevant to us." Through the many contours of God's faithful relationship with the fitful people of Israel depicted in scripture, we begin to discern God's word addressing us in our own time and place. How urgently our world needs to hear this word creatively represented through the informed imagination of faithful men and women!

Peter of Celle, a twelfth-century Benedictine abbot, observed that "the nourishment of holy books is so fruitful and abundant that in them our every weariness will be countered by as many varieties of readings as there are moments in our lives, however

11

long we live."[1] It is the hope of all of us at The Upper Room that through the pages of *Disciplines* you will find your imagination nourished and every weariness transformed into energetic witness to the kingdom of God already in our midst.

John S. Mogabgab

John S. Mogabgab
Editor
Weavings

---

[1]Peter of Celle, *Selected Works*, trans. by Hugh Feiss, O.S.B. (Kalamazoo, MI: Cistercian Pubns., 1987), p. 136.

The Wisdom and Power of Faithful Love

Sunday, January 1, 1989

Earl F. Barfoot†
Read Colossians 3:15-17;
Acts 3:1-7.

We shorten our greetings to "hi!" and "bye!" because we live in an informal age. No one would want to return to flowery formalities, and yet we do miss the import of those greetings in their shortened form.

In saying "Good-bye," we mean to say, "God be with you," or as the Spanish *Vaya con Dios* says it, "Go with God." Perhaps that is more accurate, for we discover in life that we do not take God along simply as a traveling companion. The One who gives us life is there before us. It is we who put our hand into the hand of God, to be guided along pathways that are not yet known to us as we face each new year.

It is in this sense that Paul urges that we do everything in the name of Jesus, for we must know that he is there before us, already present in situations that need healing and redeeming.

To know that healing and restoring are already God's purpose and that this purpose is actively abroad in the world is to relieve us of an enormous burden. It is not we who must change the world. Our role is to love, to teach and admonish in order that Christ may dwell in us richly. To act in the name of Christ is to go with Christ and participate in what he is already doing, even in the most difficult arenas of life.

Prayer: *I place my hand in yours this day, Lord, confident that your love will lead me into paths of usefulness. Amen.*

---

†United Methodist minister (retired); Family Ministries staff, General Board of Discipleship, The United Methodist Church (retired), Horseheads, New York.

Incarnating Holy Spirit

January 2-8, 1989   **Walter Wink†**
Monday, January 2   Read Isaiah 61:1-4.

Before we dare hope, optimism must be killed. Before we dare make ourselves vulnerable to the new thing God wants to do through us, we must let all our expectations of gradual improvement and better days turn to ashes. We would like to believe that things will get better by themselves. That dictators will get soft hearts. That militarists will ask for reduced budgets. That politicians will look after our best long-term interests. That pesticide merchants will voluntarily stop producing products they know to be humanly lethal and ecologically suicidal. That a cure will be found for cancer and AIDS. We would like to believe all this because we would be thrown into despair if we did not. So we deliberately foster illusions, or evade and repress knowledge of our plight. We try to be optimistic.

And to all these evasions the word of hope comes, in the first place, to smash our evasions to bits. Things do not get better. They are *made* better, when the Spirit of the Lord comes upon people. Then the brokenhearted and afflicted are nurtured, the oppressed are liberated, prisoners freed, ruined cities restored.

Hope in God. The evil of human society will not heal itself. God, however, offers a garland instead of ashes. What if, like Jesus, we let the Spirit of God anoint us, and staked everything on the new world of God?

Prayer: *God, what if I were to go for broke and put my whole being and resources in your hands? What could you do with me? Amen.*

---

† Professor of Biblical Interpretation, Auburn Theological Seminary (New York City), Sandisfield, Massachusetts.

Tuesday, January 3   Read Psalm 29.

This psalm begins curiously, so curiously that few readers today even register the words. The psalmist commands the heavenly beings (literally, the "sons of gods") to worship God and acknowledge Yahweh's glory and strength, manifested in this psalm by a dazzling thunderstorm. Who are these sons of gods? They are the powers of heaven. They form Yahweh's heavenly council. They are God's messengers, sending rain, hail, snow, and sleet. They are the angels that preside over nations, nature, and individuals.

What are we to make of them? Can we not regard them as the determining powers that rule the universe—the laws of nature, the archetypal forms, the perennial elements that constitute the world? They are the "angels" or spirituality of nations, worshiped falsely as gods by their peoples. They are the fundamental forces of nature, falsely ascribed ultimacy by scientists then (Democritus) and now. They are the raw, untamed, uncanny forces of nature that prompt adoration, terror, and sacrifice in peoples around the globe.

And the psalmist is ordering all these powers to worship God alone. When we fail to command the gods to worship thus, we ourselves forget and worship them. Then they possess us with all the irresistible force of a neurotic complex or a political obsession. The gods are real. That is why we must remind them that they are not ultimate. They are mere creatures. What better way to bring them to heel than to command them to worship the Truly Ultimate? What a magnificent task!

Suggestion for prayer: *Which of these gods needs your admonishment today to worship the true God? What "spiritual warfare" is required of you to make this admonishment effective in the world?*

Wednesday, January 4   Read Luke 3:15.

It is a matter of rare spiritual maturity to know that one is not the Messiah. No one all through my seminary training ever warned me against a messianic complex. On the contrary, I was encouraged to take Jesus as my model, to be a servant of God to the people. In subsequent decades of working with clergy, many of them exhausted trying to meet the expectations of others and themselves or crushed under the sheer need of their parishioners, I have observed that having a messianic complex is, for many people, indistinguishable from commitment to Christ.

John the Baptist knew better. Though he was far more famous than Jesus ever was, in his lifetime, John was never tempted by popular accolades or by his indisputable sense of calling to think of himself as the Messiah. He had a magnificent role to play for God, but he never edged over into identifying his role with the Messiah.

Martin Buber once commented that there is something incommensurate between thinking oneself a messiah and being a messiah. It may be that many of us fall into messianic roles because we haven't died to our egocentric need to "be" somebody. It is just possible that Jesus himself refused the messianic role later generations laid on him. His temptations in the wilderness seem explicitly to have been rejections of the current messianic hopes. Rather than identify with God, he related to God. He found his calling and followed precisely that, whatever later generations would call him.

Can we relate to the same divine powers within us that Jesus related to? Can we be vessels of divine healing without identifying ourselves with the Healer?

Prayer: *Grant me, O God, to be only myself and do only what you call me to do. Amen.*

Thursday, January 5   Read Luke 3:16.

The Holy Spirit wants to be incarnated. The prophets had declared this, beginning over 600 years before Jesus (see Isa. 11:2; Ezek. 37:14; Isa. 61:1). At first the Hebrews looked for a single leader who would receive or be anointed by the Spirit, a benevolent leader or king or high priest who would incarnate God's will for God's people. Gradually, however, this was perceived to be inadequate. The Spirit of God would have to be on *all* the people, not just on one person sitting at the top of the pyramid of power. What God wants is a whole people who can respond from the heart to God's purposes.

Joel 2:28-29 is perhaps the most astonishing of these later prophecies (around 400 B.C.). Even women, even servants, everyone, in a total democratization of religious authority and power, will be able to find the Spirit at their heart's core, if they only inquire.

God wants us spirited. The Spirit longs to be enfleshed. God's will can only be done through people willing to shoulder God, to free God from the captivity of invisibility, to give God bodies through which to act.

John the Baptist sensed that an evolutionary leap was at hand. The Spirit-receiver was coming, who would become Spirit-baptizer, the first of many brothers and sisters, incandescent with God.

How much Spirit have you been willing to infuse into flesh?

Prayer: *Spirit of God, make us God's bodies, that we might spirit life into the world. Amen.*

Friday, January 6 (Epiphany)

Read Luke 3:17.

The sharpest point of difference between Jesus and John concerned divine judgment. John divided people into "wheat" and "chaff," good trees and bad (see Luke 3:9). The fire of divine judgment was at hand, and it would destroy "chaffy" people.

Jesus, on the other hand, saw the line running not between groups of people but within the self. Each of us contains wheat *and* chaff. There is no percentage of chaff so high as to discount the tiny bit of wheat still there. He saw the image of God in everyone. No one was so evil as to be beyond the pale of God's redemptive power. So Jesus reversed John's message. Instead of John's "repent, and be baptized for the forgiveness of sins," Jesus proclaimed a whole new order: "You have been forgiven! Now you can repent. God loves you unconditionally, despite all you have done. Respond to that love, not after you've tidied yourselves up but right now, as you are. You are blessed: now you can live the lifestyle of the new reality, even in the bosom of the old." It was this insight that enabled him to eat with tax collectors and harlots.

So also for Jesus, judgment is not the end but the beginning. Not the death of sinners but awakening to sin. Not apocalypse but rebirth. Not rejection by God but recognition of the incomprehensible love of God and of our own miserliness beside it. Funny, how the churches have gone back to that old order: if you repent, then you may be forgiven.

Suggestion for meditation: *What is the chaff in me that needs to be consumed by fire? What is the wheat in others whom I have dismissed as chaff?*

Saturday, January 7   Read Luke 3:21-22.

John had warned people to flee the fire of the wrath to come by entering the waters of baptism. Jesus entered the waters, believing John's report, and experienced the fire nonetheless—internalized. The fire moved within. The last judgment happened, and he was spared. Not spared only, but pronounced beloved. Not beloved only, but kin. The divine Son had been birthed in him. The voice of the Father, the dove-like gentleness of "his Mother, the Holy Spirit" (Jerome), came together to form a new holy family. It was a natural trinity, mother-father-child, not the unnatural all-male trinity of the later all-male councils.

Jesus came to a new level of consciousness, however much he may have been aware before, that God was at the core of his self. The fire was inside. The gospel of the Ebionites put this all symbolically: "When Jesus went down into the water, fire was kindled in the Jordan." Now he saw his task as casting that fire on earth (Luke 12:49—and even here it is associated with baptism!), not to destroy sinners but to light a fire in the self of others. That fire licked at his own heels and sent him tearing through Galilee and Judea and finally landed him on the cross. But the powers could not put the fire out. It had burned all the way through to the Godhead and now burst out in hearts everywhere.

That fire—can people lean close and catch it from me? Am I incendiary?

Prayer: *Our Son—fire-starter—blowtorch of God—how can I let myself be a conflagration like you? Amen.*

Sunday, January 8   Read Luke 3:21-22.

The evolution of the world, Carl Jung once remarked, seems to be the progressive incarnation of deity. What momentus new step is being taken then at Jesus' baptism? Why did he submit to the baptismal waters? Waters of cleansing, repentance, new life, womb-waters, the matrix of new birth, the tomb of the old life, drowning, suffocation, resurrection—Jesus arose from the waters into a new world, as an old-new being, given to God. And God bent down, dovish, maternal, and took him to her breast and breathed into him the Holy Spirit. Then, like a proud father, wreathed in smiles, God spoke the words of the new creation: "This is my beloved son; I'm just crazy about him!" (AP)

What has been born of God and the Holy Spirit in Jesus? Is this "son" someone who Jesus is, or is it a process within him? What happens when this holy child is identified with Jesus? In Paul, the Holy Spirit (feminine in Hebrew, neuter in Greek) becomes the Spirit of Jesus, hence masculine (Gal. 4:6; Rom. 8:9). At the baptism, however, the water-womb and the dove-like Spirit are feminine. Why did the later church theologians develop an all-male trinity, instead of a holy family of mother-father-child? Is their formulation binding on us? What is the psychic, spiritual, and political cost of excluding the feminine from the Godhead?

Is this experience of Jesus at his baptism confined to him, or is it the prototype for our re-creation as well? Is what comes to birth in us Jesus, or is it what came to birth in Jesus? Is it Jesus' intent to become my inner life, or to help me incarnate the Holy Spirit as he did, in order to find my own selfhood?

Suggestion for meditation: *If I really knew how beloved I was of God, would I just* sit *here like this?*

20

THE GIFTS OF GOD FOR THE PEOPLE OF GOD

January 9-15, 1989   **Anne Broyles†**
Monday, January 9   Read Psalm 36:5-6.

Our three-year-old son's prayer burst upon the air like a shimmer of sunshine:

"Dear God, I like you a lot!"

Justus' beaming face said more than long theological phrases could ever express: he was responding to the God whose love he deeply felt.

"Lord, your constant love reaches the heavens" (TEV). For the psalmist, the only images large enough to encompass such incredible love are those of natural phenomenon beyond our intellectual comprehension—the skies, mountains, seas.

The landscape of God's love is painted in Psalm 36. We are in awe of the blue vaulting heavens; we feel very small as we gaze up at snow-capped peaks; we cannot begin to imagine how deep the oceans really are. Yet we feel a power in nature that reaches deep within us, reminding us that the earth on which we stand is indeed "holy ground." And, then, in the presence of all that powerful beauty, the psalmist adds, "All creatures are in your care."

God's greatest gift to us is the assurance that we are loved and cared for. As we see and marvel at the beauties of nature, so God sees us, knows us through and through, and loves us as we are.

Prayer: *God of mountain, sea, and sky, how incredible it is that you should care for me! Remind me again and again that you care for me in a steadfast love that is more than I can ever imagine. For this love and all your good gifts, I give you thanks and praise! Amen.*

---

† Co-pastor, Malibu United Methodist Church; author and retreat leader; editorial advisor to *Weavings;* Malibu, California.

Tuesday, January 10   Read Psalm 36:7-10.

Our God is more than the grandeur of nature. God is one who knows us personally, who is available as a good friend in times of crisis. "How precious, O God, is your constant love!" (TEV)

God's love is made manifest to us in many ways. We feel security as we find refuge in the shelter of the wings of the Most High. We are gifted with abundant food; our thirst is quenched from an everflowing stream. And, most amazingly, God's love meets much more than our physical needs for shelter, security, food, and drink. We are surrounded by God's presence and can proclaim with the psalmist, "You are the source of all life, and because of your light we see the light" (TEV).

I arrived in high spirits at the quadrennial Consultation of United Methodist Clergywomen. I looked forward to being with friends from my own area, seminary friends, and many others I knew through a variety of networks. I was ready for a week of long conversations and feeling loved and affirmed. My expectations were more than met during the week, but the first day I found myself unable to link up with anyone I knew. I felt extremely lonely among one thousand vivacious and active clergywomen.

God's gift of life and light came to me in a small group setting where I was able to reflect on my present loneliness. I realized that, as I felt more and more miserable, I had been carrying on long talks with God. Even when I felt lonely on the outside, God was present to me on the inside. This "re-membering" filled me with a joy that continued throughout all of the experiences of the week. God loved and cared for me past all human caring!

Prayer: *Gracious God, I thank you that you are always there for me, that your love is personal and meets me where I am. Let me carry you always in my heart. Amen.*

Wednesday, January 11   Read 1 Corinthians 12:1-11.

"But it won't do any good for me to sign up for the church work day. I don't know how to do anything!"

"Oh, come join us. We'll find something for you to do. Working together at church is a great fellowship experience."

For most churches, the occasional work days are wonderful opportunities for people of various interests and skills to join together in a common goal: fixing up and beautifying the church plant. Some lend their skills as electricians or plumbers; others paint walls or scrub floors. Volunteers soon discover that everyone can be helpful: someone needs to coordinate the job list, prepare a meal, be a "gofer," lend a helping hand. People of all ages and capabilities have special gifts that can be shared in a common effort.

In writing to the church at Corinth, Paul reminds those Christians of the variety of gifts available through the Spirit of Jesus Christ. "There are different kinds of spiritual gifts, but the same Spirit gives them. There are different ways of serving, but the same Lord is served" (TEV).

The gifts do not come in a hierarchical listing, with some gifts being more spiritual, better than others. Rather, says Paul, "The same Spirit . . . gives a different gift to each person" (TEV).

Just as the church work day benefits from a variety of people lending their time and skills, so the community of Christ flourishes when individuals discover their particular gifts of the Spirit and feel empowered to dedicate those gifts to God's work.

Prayer: *Thank you, Giver of all good gifts, that each of us can receive the gift appropriate for us and can dedicate ourselves—time, energy, skills, spiritual gifts—to the building of your reign to come. Amen.*

23

Thursday, January 12   Read John 2:1-11.

Mary faced her son. Gesturing toward the stone waterpots, she said, "They are out of wine" (TEV). Then, even as her son responds "You must not tell me what to do," Mary instructs the servants to listen and heed Jesus.

Mary knew how important it was to the bride and bridegroom that there be an adequate supply of wine for all the wedding guests. She faced the reality of the present situation and instinctively knew that Jesus had the power to help.

Mary exhibited two gifts of God in this simple encounter. First, she had the discernment to know that Jesus would be able to make more wine. This insight came from many years of loving her son, nurturing him, praying for guidance as she raised this very special child. No one told her that he could perform miracles. Yet something deep within her confirmed what she had perhaps known from the angel's visitation many years earlier: Jesus was no ordinary person.

Mary's second gift was that of faith. She believed in the power of God working within her son. She knew without a doubt that whatever needed to be done, Jesus could do. She watched him carefully as he gave commands to the servants. Perhaps her eyes met his across the courtyard as the steward proclaimed, "You have kept the best wine until now!" (TEV)

Mary, discerning mother and faithful believer, reminds us that we are called to develop discernment and faith. Mary was able to witness the first miracle of Jesus. What miracles may we yet see and experience as we live in faith and discernment?

Prayer: *Divine Author of history, I give you thanks for the way you worked in Mary and Jesus. I ask that you work also in me that I might further develop discernment of your will and faith to act on what I understand your call to be. Amen.*

Friday, January 13   Read John 2:11.

The magician captivated the audience with incredible tricks and sleight of hand. Pamela turned to Mason and whispered, "I just love to try to figure out how he does that. I'm not going to let him trick me!"

Never taking his eyes away from the magician's captivating gaze, Mason shook his head. "Not me. I like being fooled. There's little enough real magic in the world. I want miracles however I can get them."

With advanced technology and scientific exploration expanding the walls of our knowledge and comprehension, it does sometimes seem as if there are no miracles. So when we read about Jesus changing water into wine at the wedding in Cana, we are unsure how to react. The Gospel writer reminds us that "Jesus performed this first miracle in Cana in Galilee; there he revealed his glory, and his disciples believed in him" (TEV).

One of the gifts of the Spirit which Paul lifts up in First Corinthians is the gift of "working miracles." As incredible as it is to think of Jesus turning water into wine (and performing even greater miracles than this), it is beyond the realm of our belief that we ourselves could ever be miracle workers.

Yet miracles come in all sizes. Anne Sullivan worked a miracle with Helen Keller. Mother Teresa works miracles among the poor and dying of Calcutta. Every time someone listens to the nudgings of God and acts in love, a miracle is possible. We negate the power of God within us when we rule out the possibility of our own participation in God's miracles.

Prayer: *God of Miracles, let me be open to your spirit working in me and those around me. Help me live in expectation of miracles rather than suspicion of anything that looks out of the ordinary. Thank you for your gift of miracles. Amen.*

Saturday, January 14   Read Isaiah 62:1-5.

For the people of Judah, the time of exile in Babylon had been a time of hopelessness and abandonment. Even after they had returned to Jerusalem, they were debilitated and despondent, all vestiges of former glory withered away. Isaiah the prophet spoke to them in their present state, reminding the downcast people that God was not through with them yet: "I will speak out to encourage Jerusalem; I will not be silent until she is saved, and her victory shines like a torch in the night" (TEV).

The prophet helps the people of Jerusalem look to their future, a future where their present situation is turned around:

No longer will you be called "Forsaken,"
Or your land be called "The Deserted Wife."
Your new name will be "God Is Pleased with Her."
Your land will be called "Happily Married" (TEV).

Isaiah had a long history of prophecy. Many times he called the people to accountability and faithfulness. Isaiah was called to speak the truth as he understood it from God.

It is easy to imagine some of the Old Testament prophets: those of inner strength and fiery speech. Yet Paul mentions that "the Spirit gives one person . . . the gift of speaking God's message" (1 Cor. 12:10, TEV). Most of us feel uncomfortable with the prophet role. Who are we to speak out for God?

If called to prophecy, we simply speak in our own situations. A family confronting an alcoholic parent may speak God's message of wholeness. A person working to pass a clean water act may be speaking God's message of stewardship for the earth. Open to God's Spirit working in us, we may clearly hear the message we are called to deliver.

Prayer: *God of all words, may all of our speech be spoken in the power of your love, in courage and in clarity. Amen.*

Sunday, January 15   Read 1 Corinthians 12:4-7.

The gifts of God come in all sizes and shapes and colors. Some gifts are readily apparent, others are available to us only when we are ready to ask for them. We receive physical gifts (food, shelter, clothing), emotional gifts (strength, peace of mind), intellectual gifts (discernment, knowledge, insight), and spiritual gifts (faith, healing, miracle-working, discrimination of true spiritual gifts, speaking God's message, speaking in tongues, and interpretation). We may be gifted with a double rainbow, a new idea, or a loving hug.

But all gifts ultimately come from God. And each of us in some way manifests God's gifts to others. As Paul writes, "The Spirit's presence is shown in some way in each person for the good of all" (TEV).

Take some time now and consider the following questions:

How is God's Spirit made known in your life?

In what ways are you fostering openness to the Spirit of God?

How do you live out your thanks for God's multitude of good gifts?

Prayer: *Generous God, for all that has been, thanks! And for all that is yet to come, yes! Amen.*

LEST WE FORGET THE POWER OF THE SPIRIT

January 16-22, 1989   **Cain Hope Felder†**
Monday, January 16   Read Nehemiah 8:1-4b.

The traditional revelry of New Year's Eve culminates often with the raucous singing of "Auld Lang Syne," beginning with "Should old acquaintance be forgot, and never brought to mind?" On this Monday, however, those lyrics seem so inappropriate as our hearts and minds turn to another holiday (holy day), namely the birthday of Martin Luther King, Jr., the modern-day American prophet and spokesman for civil/human rights, peace, and justice. As opposed to the opening lines of "Auld Lang Syne," today we read, sing, pray, and gather together to remember birthdays of significant "old acquaintances" who remind us that spiritual power proceeds only from God.

One such acquaintance was the scribe Ezra, who, four hundred years before Jesus Christ, brought the Torah-story, refined by the bondage of the Babylonian Captivity, to Jerusalem for a bold public reading. We discover that the Torah (our Pentateuch) was, in effect, being reintroduced as an old acquaintance that unfortunately had been forgotten! When the Jerusalemites began remembering the lost vision contained in this Law of God's steadfast love, they wept for joy. Ezra commemorated a birthday of the Torah-story; we today commemorate the birthday of Martin Luther King, Jr., who, by the power of God, helped us to see how the Spirit can still humanize us as worthy to be called the children of God.

Prayer: *O Lord, may we give reverent attention to your word and to all those through whom your word comes. We are grateful that you allow even us to be used by the power of your Spirit. Lest we forget! Amen.*

---

† Professor, New Testament Language and Literature; editor, *Journal of Religious Thought*, Howard University School of Divinity, Washington, D.C.

Tuesday, January 17   Read Nehemiah 8:5-6;
                                              Luke 4:14-18.

Most of us prefer to receive good news rather than bad. The wicked witch of the West in the colorful screenplay *The Wiz* epitomizes our human disposition at times when she warns, "Don't bring me no bad news!" Yet, life can seem to be a plague of bad news in our homes, communities, nation, and world. Many collectively groan for relief from the depressing, harsh realities of daily life. Indeed, the bad news of living in a world of competing self-interests and intolerance of others who are in some way different brings gloom and despair to our souls. For those who have the presence of mind to turn to God, there is always the reminder that the Good News is accessible so that we might be the bearers of God's Spirit for the benefit of others.

Lest we forget, consider again Luke's account of Jesus' inaugural sermon at Nazareth; the context is as important as the content of Jesus' words. Luke 4:14 begins with the report that "Jesus returned [from the wilderness] in the power of the Spirit." Many of us often overlook the fact that for Luke, Jesus could so enter Galilee because his faith in God and sense of commission by God (Luke 3:22) had been fully tested as he again and again resisted the devil in the wilderness of life. Jesus could thus easily identify with Isaiah 61:1 and proclaim that "the Spirit of the Lord" was truly upon him—not merely for his own personal benefit but for the benefit of bringing good news in tangible and direct ways to the poor, those imprisoned, the blind, and the oppressed, the victims of the world's bad news.

Prayer: *God of our mothers and fathers, teach me how to trust in you so that I might transform the bad news of the world through your good news! Amen.*

Wednesday, January 18   Read Psalm 19:7-10.

The so-called Songs of David, or the Psalms, are not all original compositions by David the king. Rather, cast in Hebrew poetic form, these are mostly ancient hymns expressing the sublime aspirations or posing the vexing questions of God's people. The Psalms represent compositions from different eras of ancient Israel; as such, they capture a wide range of moods visited upon persons who take spirituality seriously enough to praise as well as to interrogate God!

The reading for today is a selection from a post-exilic psalm that opens with a general praise of God as eternal creator and sustainer of nature. The greater part of Psalm 19, however, focuses on the marvelous nature of the law as God's particular gift that is perfect for "converting" (KJV) or, better, "reviving" (RSV) the soul. We are often uncomfortable with praises of the law as found here, preferring instead a pristine notion of a gospel that stands over against the law. Rather than insisting on any such dichotomy, the unity of the Bible sees law and gospel as correlative gifts embodied in Jesus of Nazareth. By the law (Torah-story), we are reminded of our accountability to God and one another in society. By the gospel, we are reminded that the law alone is insufficient as a motive for God to adopt us as heirs to the promise. We must want to be so adopted; ours must be a voluntary yearning to be joined to the Spirit. Lest we forget, that is the nature of grace!

Prayer: *Eternal God, use us to restore your creation's intended beauty. Stop us from destroying the goodness of your world, people, and law. Show us the grace-full use of our freedom. Amen.*

Thursday, January 19   Read Psalm 19:11-14.

The seventeenth century French comedy *Tartuffe,* written by Molière, was performed only for small private audiences for five years, although the king loved the play. The problem was that the church saw in *Tartuffe* a bitter parody on religious hypocrisy. One of the bourgeois characters, Dorine, comments on the lofty posturing of Monsieur Tartuffe: "If one believes him and his principles, everything that we do becomes a crime."* There are times when meditations on God's law lead one to ask as once did Jesus' first disciples, "Who then can be saved?" (Matt. 19:25) The "higher righteousness" seemingly demanded by law or gospel can appear to be too high for most and thus an "impossible ethic."

The psalmist no less than John Wesley knew that God's gift of law was pure, clean, and righteous. Both also knew that it was but an ideal standard by which one could embark upon a path of righteousness. Lest we forget, the path itself is a spiritual pilgrimage toward perfection because the Author and Finisher of the path is perfect! Each pilgrim, from the psalmist to Jesus in the wilderness and even us today, must petition God for strength and courage. There is available to each of us a distinct power of the Spirit to overcome possible hidden faults so that evil in its manifold guises will not have dominion over the seeker along the path. The "impossible ethic" becomes possible with every forward step, for along the way one discovers that she or he has done many good things in the power of the Spirit.

Prayer: *"Let the words of my mouth, and the meditation of my heart, be acceptable in thy sight, O Lord, my strength, and my redeemer" (KJV). Amen.*

---

* *Eight Plays by Molière,* Morris Bishop, trans. (New York: The Modern Library, 1957), p. 155.

Friday, January 20   Read Luke 4:19-21.

To his Jewish contemporaries Jesus must have seemed a brash young man indeed. Luke's account of Jesus' "Trial Sermon" in the synagogue of Nazareth reports that not only did Jesus claim to be anointed to speak and act on behalf of God (4:18) but that he proclaimed "the acceptable year of the Lord" as having now arrived. The audience was evidently stunned by Jesus' bold initiative to revitalize biblical texts that had been relegated to the status of inspirational relics with little relevance for daily life. It is noteworthy that Jesus begins his public ministry in the church of his day; and later, upon his arrival at Jerusalem toward the close of that ministry, Jesus again goes first to the temple to cleanse it for the dawning new order (see Luke 19:45-46). Lest the home folks forget, church is the place to rediscover the power of the Spirit.

The truly new element in Jesus' sermon is not the clever combination of Jubilee texts (Lev. 25:10; Isa. 58:6; 61:1-2) but Jesus' declaration that, at that very moment, he himself was inaugurating the ancient vision of loving care for all those who hurt or otherwise languish on the margins of society. Jesus' words call the church to rediscover the same power of the Spirit to challenge conventional values of selfish comfort and to become the people of God at a deeper level.

Prayer: *Lord God, we give thanks that "the signs of the church have always been the dove, the lamb, the lion, and the fish, but never the chameleon."* * *Amen.*

---

* Allan A. Boesak. *If This Is Treason, I Am Guilty* (Grand Rapids, MI: William B. Eerdmans Publishing Company, 1987), p. 47.

Saturday, January 21   Read 1 Corinthians 12:12-21.

As in Jesus' parable of the sower (Matt. 13:3-9), the Corinthian converts were but rocky ground with little depth of soil; they delighted in Paul's proclamation about the unity of the Christ-event, but once he had departed, the seedlings became scorched. We see the deterioration of the Corinthian church clearly in the first epistle Paul wrote to it; and chapter after chapter, we groan with Paul. Cliques had formed, egos competed, great moral lapses had occurred to make the church of Corinth a mere caricature of Paul's original vision about what the church, united in love and properly exercising the gifts of the Spirit (*charismata*) might be.

One of the greatest challenges to a church member is at a time of crisis to join Jesus in Gethsemane and say, "Not my will but thy will be done" (see Mark 14:36). Were members to focus on their particular "spiritual gift" and develop it properly in relation to the gifts of others, ruptured congregations in crises, petty and major, could be eliminated. Lest we forget, Paul reminds us that "by one Spirit we were all baptized into one body—Jews or Greeks, slaves or free—and all were made to drink of one Spirit" (1 Cor. 12:13). Professor James Cone offers a sobering reflection: "How can one speak about the church as the body of the crucified Jesus of Nazareth when church people are so healthy and well-fed and have no broken bones?"*

Prayer: *Lord God, let not our broken bones result from fighting within the church but from our unified witness as the church in a broken world. Amen.*

---

* James H. Cone, "What Is the Church?" in *Hammering Swords into Ploughshares: Essays in Honor of Archbishop Mpilo Desmond Tutu.* Buti Tlhagale and Itumeleng J. Mosala, eds. (Grand Rapids, MI: William B. Eerdmans Publishing Co., 1986), p. 143.

Sunday, January 22   Read 1 Corinthians 12:22-30.

Affluent nations like the United States very often have great difficulty identifying with the weak, the suffering, and the dispossessed beyond their borders and, sadly enough, even within their borders. The apostle Paul insists upon honoring the poor and the weak and entering into a helping solidarity of shared suffering with them. This honoring and solidarity seems out of place in modern societies, which do all they can to insulate themselves from the harsh realities of human suffering, homelessness, and despair. We tend to throw a few dollars at the problem, turn off the television, and go shopping! But a genuine empathy for others who suffer comes to us as Christians in a unique way, for it was our Lord Jesus who, even until his death, showed us by example the righteousness of precisely this path.

When Paul reminds the Corinthians about the dangers inherent in the abuse of their "spiritual gifts" in First Corinthians 12 (cf. Rom. 12:3-8), he attempts to stop that church in its downward spiral to narcissistic chaos. Paul would rather the strong help the weak, and from that experience find that the weak have helped them rediscover the power of the Spirit. For many of us, organized religion has accommodated itself to the commercial values of the world to such an extent that we abandon church buildings when the neighborhood changes or we bolt church doors so that the homeless vagrants might not soil the church property. Nevertheless, no Christian is thereby relieved from her or his obligation to discern and, against all odds, to use their spiritual gifts for the glory of what the church is supposed to be.

Prayer: *Lord, we pray that you keep us ever mindful that it is through the power of your Spirit that we may grow into the fullness of being Christian, not only as individuals but also as a church. Lest we forget, keep us ever mindful of why we are whose we are. Amen.*

WHEN GOD CALLS

January 23-29, 1989   **Richard Bowyer†**
Monday, January 23   Read Jeremiah 1:4-10.

People are inclined to take either too seriously or too lightly what they understand to be a call from God. All too often we use scripture to reinforce already-held notions. Approached with openness, however, scripture can clarify our experiences.

In his dialogue with God, Jeremiah seems to take the call too seriously. Jeremiah knew the task was too great for him. It was beyond his ability and experience.

But God's response makes it clear that Jeremiah took the matter too lightly. Inexperience and limited ability are incidental when God calls. It is clear from the calling of Moses, Isaiah, Amos, and Paul that whoever God calls, God equips. Gifts and graces are God's to give; God is engaged in equipping the saints.

God has called you to some particular task or broader vocation. Receive God's gifts and graces which alone make you equal to the task.

The challenge may appear ominous viewed from our perspective and measured against our limited resources. If the challenge is the focus of our attention, like Jeremiah, we may seem to take the matter too seriously. But if God is the focus, we may be assured that there is nothing to fear and that neither nations nor kingdoms are too great as obstacles.

Prayer: *Gracious God, may I focus on you who call me and not on the calling. Amen.*

---

†Campus Minister, Wesley Foundation, Fairmont State College, Fairmont, West Virginia.

Tuesday, January 24   Read Jeremiah 1:4-7.

Many of us respond to God's call in our youth. While young people offer God abundant opportunities for shaping and molding a ministry, there are hazards and difficulties with youth.

Some will respond like Jeremiah, as though their youthfulness is a liability or restriction on their ability to serve. For those conditioned in a culture which lauds strength and beauty, there are problems also. American society has conditioned many to respond with a sentence beginning, "Ah, Lord God! Behold, I am only ____."

Such a response is based on a perverted narcissism. Although focused on self, the respondent fails to sense her/his own beauty as a gift of the image of God. One cannot fulfill God's calling to love one's neighbor as one's self if the self is not also seen as God's gift and a recipient of God's love.

I recall a story which makes a similar point. A gifted Latin scholar in the middle ages loved to dress in old clothing and walk in the woods. On one occasion he wandered too far and, in the darkness, fell over a cliff. Those who found him unconscious took him to the doctor. Seeing his dress and condition, the doctor observed in finest Latin, "Since he is worthless, I will use this opportunity to experiment." The injured man rallied and replied, also in the finest Latin, "Would you call worthless one for whom Christ did not disdain to die?"

Prayer: *Dear God, help me remember that I am one for whom the Christ did not disdain to die. Amen.*

Wednesday, January 25   Read Luke 4:21-29.

Those who respond to God's calling as youths understand well the experience of Jesus. That first performance, job, or sermon back home tends to generate certain responses.

Some will say of the young person, "Hasn't he done well to be the son of Joseph the carpenter?" In its less subtle version, this "compliment" reads, "Can anything good come out of Nazareth?"

Patronizing is a common means of containing those whom we do not wish to take seriously. Youth, the elderly, persons with handicapping conditions, women, and minorities encounter it often. Hopefully they will not hear the false compliment as the real meaning of the response.

On the other hand, if God has touched the mouth of the called person and placed God's words there, the response may be to get the speaker out of town not by the road but over the cliff!

It is easy to discount those whom we know. We are conditioned to their voice, their lives, their messages. Persons who speak the word of truth are often discredited by their peers. Many are the scars of the discounted spokesperson for God. Some of those scars are deep.

The challenge of today's scripture in light of our theme, "When God Calls," is much the same as that of Jeremiah 1:4-10. The danger is that we who are called will have our attention diverted. Jeremiah's diversions were himself and/or the task. In Luke 4, the diversion is the audience and their response.

Prayer: *Gracious God, may I focus on the One who calls and equips me, that I may faithfully minister to those I am sent to serve. Amen.*

Thursday, January 26   Read Psalm 71:1-6.

All who respond to God's call are not young, for we may hear the call at any age. And those who responded in youth may hear God's call in a different way as they mature.

We need to read the remainder of the psalm (v. 18) to capture the anguish of this elderly person. "So even to old age and gray hairs, O God, do not forsake me." The American Standard Version describes it as a "Prayer of an Old Man for Deliverance."

The psalmist has neither of the limitations which Jeremiah claimed: inexperience and inability. Like the prophet he understands his link with God—beginning in his mother's womb. His experience provides for him a cause for hope no matter what the cause of his distress.

Even after a long life of service in the call of God, we may be tempted to turn our attention away from God. The problems and perplexities of life, the cruelty of people, injustice and wickedness make their claims. But it is not the task which overwhelms the psalmist. It is not the limitations which the writer feels personally. It is not the patronizing of the hearers.

The psalmist struggles to remain centered in God, to avoid the despair of hopelessness, to keep hold of his faith. His anguish is the struggle of one who knows in whom to trust. The experienced saint, faithful to the call, knows (but needs to be reminded) that his or her attention must be focused upon the One who calls. It is God who is a refuge, who delivers, saves, and sustains.

Prayer: *Dear God, when my hair is tinged with gray, may I still be able to exclaim, "Thou, O Lord, art my hope, my trust, O Lord, from my youth . . . . My praise is continually of thee." Amen.*

Friday, January 27   Read Jeremiah 1:7-9

It is common knowledge that talk is cheap. Western society is highly verbal. For all the growth in electronic communication, the volume of print media seems to keep pace. Words crowd our whole environment.

Popular and would-be popular preachers and evangelists talk endlessly about the "word of the Lord." Many in the broader Christian community refer frequently to "the word the Lord has laid upon my heart."

Jeremiah's assurance is not quite the same. "Then the Lord put forth his hand and touched my mouth; and the Lord said to me, 'Behold, I have put my words in your mouth.' "

Reflecting on diversions which may take our attention away from God who calls us, we dare not ignore the word itself. It is tempting to focus on the message rather than the One who provides it. We are inclined to focus on the words instead of the Word to whom they point.

When God called Jeremiah, direct dialogue occurred. Jeremiah's inability or hesitancy to speak was not a sufficient reason for God to call someone else instead. God gave the word to Jeremiah. The same sort of experience is reported of Isaiah and others. The effectiveness of the prophets was grounded in their faithfulness in proclaiming the word of the Lord. Their ability to do that depended upon their trust and confidence in God who called them.

Facing daily the challenge to keep before us the Word-Giver, the prayer of Paul in Ephesians 6:19 might be our own.

Prayer: *Dear Lord, may "utterance be given me in opening my mouth boldly to proclaim the mystery of the gospel." Amen.*

Saturday, January 28   Read 1 Corinthians 13:1-3.

Those who are called by God are given gifts of speaking, prophecy, and understanding. Such gifts are instruments to be used to serve God's purpose. Speaking in the tongues of both humans and angels is surely a gift. So, too, are prophetic powers and the ability to understand all mysteries and knowledge. The latter remind us of the gift of wisdom which God gave to Solomon. Paul also notes gifts of faith and great generosity or philanthropy and even martyrdom.

There is no attempt by Paul to downplay or discredit these gifts. His purpose is to put things in perspective. One of the great temptations confronting Christians is to take our gifts too seriously. We are frequently faced with opportunities to perceive such gifts as evidences of particular virtue or merit. Some even encourage the seeking of these gifts.

Paul insists that those who are called by God are called to a higher calling. They are called by Love to love. If the gifts become ends in themselves or goals to be sought, they have neither value nor usefulness. Gifts from God are meant to be used for God's glory and the service of others.

It is quite significant that Paul does not speak of love as an alternative to the other gifts. Love is what infuses our gifts with their value. Love empowers and enables us to use God's gifts for their intended purposes.

No matter what gifts we possess, without the gracious empowering love of God we are nothing and we have nothing to gain.

Prayer: *Gracious God, enable me to love. Amen.*

Sunday, January 29   Read Jeremiah 1:4-10;
                                          1 Corinthians 13:8-11.

There is no reason to doubt that Jeremiah was a young man at the time of God's call. There is a sense, spoken of by both Jesus and Paul, in which persons of any age may be children before God. Maturity in faith is an important factor for Christians.

In many ways, even as we hear God's call today, we have need for maturity. We are going on to perfection. Whatever resources we have, whatever gifts and graces, skills and abilities, they are limited by the reality of death. They will pass away. It is imperative that we know this. Otherwise, those things may take on too great a significance in our lives.

Another characteristic of immaturity is insecurity. Jeremiah expressed it in terms of lacking experience or ability. Others may do so by parading their gifts before others.

When God calls, one is likely to feel insecure and to sense his/her immaturity. Such is the moment of God's grace. In the face-to-face moment with God, the perfect may come. One knows and is known, one is filled full with the Spirit of God. It is the moment experienced by Job: "I had heard of thee by the hearing of the ear, but now my eye sees thee" (42:5). It is both humbling and exalting. It is the enabling, empowering moment.

Those who hear and respond to God's call must experience it anew from time to time. We need to be nurtured and to mature in our relationship with God. We need the assurance that God has both called and enabled us to do God's work.

Prayer: *O God, call me anew. Amen.*

GOD'S GLORY REVEALED

January 30–February 5, 1989 **Duane and JoAnn Watson†**
Monday, January 30 Read Psalm 99.

As the psalmist surveys God enthroned in glory, he exhorts us to praise God for God's justice and grace. He reveals that God forgave the great leaders of Israel "who called on his name."

Since God is a God of justice and grace, we can be assured that God will be forgiving to us when we call in faith today. God freely offers us forgiveness for our sins. Assurance of that forgiveness instills us with courage when our faith is shaken by our own trangressions.

The psalmist also reveals God to be a God of judgment. God judges our unjust and unrighteous ways and calls us to repentance. The psalmist tells us that the leaders of Israel responded to God's judgment and grace with obedience. We too are to turn from our sin and follow faithfully.

Although God's promises of love and forgiveness in Christ are freely offered to us, the judgment of God reminds us of our obligation to obey. Since Christ has taken God's judgment upon himself for us, we are called to offer ourselves back to God in loving obedience and praise. Truly then we can behold the glory of God with confidence and joy.

Prayer: *Help me to praise you, O God, and thank you for the gift of your Son, Jesus Christ. May I respond to your grace offered in Christ and confidently stand in your glorious presence. Amen.*

---

† Co-pastors, Tri-Church Parish of the United Methodist Church, North Western, New York.

Tuesday, January 31   Read Psalm 99:1-5.

The psalmist paints a magnificent portrait of God's holy splendor, power, and greatness. Awe and fear arise in us as we contemplate the majesty of God.

The psalm not only reveals God's glory but also God's character. We learn of God's love for justice. Justice finds its origin and most powerful and complete expression within the very nature of God.

Let the thought of God's justice take hold of your heart. Think about prejudice, oppression, poverty that you encounter in your own life or see in the lives of those around you. Hear the words of the prophet Micah: "What does the Lord require of you but to do justice, and to love kindness, and to walk humbly with your God?" (6:8)

We are to model our own character after the character of God. We can offer ourselves to God in reverence and trust. In an attitude of prayer we bow down with righteous intent to make God's love of justice a part of our character and our dealings with others. We will find joy and peace as we strive to manifest and exemplify God's holy presence and divine justice in the world.

We may not be able to make great strides in overcoming injustice. However, we can strive to treat everyone we meet with respect, avoid being a party to ridicule, and contribute our time and energy to charities which work to eliminate inequities. In these and many other ways, God's love of justice can find its expression in our lives.

Prayer: *Help me, O Lord, to work to bring about your justice in the world. Amen.*

Wednesday, February 1   Read Luke 9:28-36.

The disciples were privileged to witness the ministry of Jesus firsthand. For Peter, one of the highlights of his discipleship with Jesus was the time spent on the Mount of Transfiguration. Imagine looking upon Jesus, Moses, and Elijah engaged in conversation and surrounded by heavenly glory. The scene so overwhelmed Peter that he suggested to Jesus that shelters be built so that all three of them could continue to dwell there together. He wanted the moment to last so he could continue to bask in heavenly glory.

God, however, overshadowed the three and demanded obedience to Jesus, who was about to make his final trip to Jerusalem to face the cross. This event was crucial to the salvation of humankind. Jesus needed obedient disciples who would help him fulfill his mission.

There would be dark moments ahead when the glory of God would be hidden. To bask in the temporary glory on the mountain would be to mistakenly equate the glory of the preparation for the mission with the glory that would be the outcome of the mission.

Like Peter, we all experience moments in our spiritual lives when the glory of God seems so close and overwhelming that we would like nothing more than to bask in it. However, we must obey God's Son and help extend his mission in places and situations where the glory of God is not easily seen. To live only to recapture the few "mountaintop" experiences is not to obey Christ's command to further his mission.

Prayer: *Almighty God, help me to serve you even when your glory seems so far from my place of service. Amen.*

Thursday, February 2   Read Exodus 34:27-32;
Luke 9:28-36.

When we think of the glory of God, we often visualize what God looks like. In our mind's eye we behold God in splendor, sitting upon a great throne in heaven, surrounded by rays of bright light and the hosts of heaven.

However, in our scripture passages today, it is the ear that is aware of the glory of God. The ears of Moses hear God's commandments as he sits under God's private tutelage. The ears of the Israelites hear the commandments of God read by Moses as his face reflects the glory of God. As God speaks from the cloud, the ears of Peter, James, and John hear the command to obey God's Son.

In our time, God also speaks to us. We hear the voice of the Holy Spirit, the words of scripture, and sound preaching and teaching. Often, as in today's passages, God's glory is revealed to instruct the people and seek their obedience. God is also self-revealing to us, desiring our obedience to the commandments taught by the scriptures and the Son. It is with our ears that we need to behold God's glory as we listen intently for the divine voice of instruction and guidance.

Prayer: *Lord God, help me to open my ears to hear and obey your precepts so that I may behold your glory anew. Amen.*

Friday, February 3   Read 2 Corinthians 4:1-2.

Our passage today is part of Paul's defense of his Christian service. He says that he never lost heart in the great and difficult task of ministry God had given him. He reminds the Corinthians that he has been constant and steadfast in serving them and that he finds strength for his calling in the mercy of God.

Have you ever been asked to do something that was difficult for you and then when you did it you found the strength to accomplish it? Serving God in a world such as ours—a world torn by poverty, oppression, war, and suffering—is guaranteed to bring difficult moments. However, God meets our needs, giving us grace and strength. God enables us to live, love, and serve in the world when the task is not easy.

Like Paul, we are called to make a difference in the world for Christ. We, too, stand as witness to redeeming grace which brings God's power, love, and peace to a tattered and torn world. Being Christ's witnesses means being his disciples, following his example, and doing as he did. He ate with sinners, healed the sick, and forgave the tax collectors. He met the needs of those around him without prejudice.

As Christ's disciples we can give a word of encouragement, hope, and comfort to those who are hurting. We can help those that others are not willing to help; be it the elderly, our neighbors, or our colleagues at work. We have the example of Paul, and we can trust that God will empower us, whatever the task.

Devotional exercise: *Think about the work you have to do today. Does it lend an opportunity to witness to God's grace in Christ? Call upon the strength and power of God to take advantage of each opportunity.*

Saturday, February 4   Read 2 Corinthians 3:16–4:6.

The glory of God is not something our minds naturally perceive. In fact, it is not perceived at all by those who have yet to respond to the gospel. Paul makes it clear that it is the mind turned to the Lord, and thus enabled by the Holy Spirit, that perceives the glory of God. The veil of disinterest or stubborn refusal to attend to the claims of the gospel is lifted by the Spirit so that the mind can then behold the glory of God unhindered.

The glory of God perceived by the Christian receives its best representation in Christ himself, the likeness of God. The glory of God is reflected in the face of the Son.

This knowledge of the gospel and glory of God is a power that transforms our lives. The transformation is not complete with the initial moment when the veil is lifted from our eyes. It occurs slowly as we strive to be Christlike. This transformation becomes complete in the resurrection when we will be glorified as Christ is glorified.

To turn our minds to Christ, who is the likeness of God, is to be transformed into the likeness of Christ. Inversely, to turn our minds to the things of the world is to place the veil of ignorance and blindness over our eyes again and to deprive ourselves of the transforming power of God's glory.

Prayer: *O glorious God, help me to keep my unveiled eyes upon your glory as revealed in Christ my Lord. May I be transformed more and more into his likeness. Amen.*

Sunday, February 5
Read Exodus 34:29-35;
2 Corinthians 3:17-18.

This unique story centers on Moses who acts as the intermediary in the transmission of God's law from God to the Israelites. Moses' face reflects the glory of God's presence to the people. To reflect the glory of God is astounding and awesome. With Moses, the glory was so powerful that he had to put on a veil or mask to cover his face so as not to frighten the people.

God's glory is revealed in Jesus, God's Son. That glory is reflected in the lives of those who commit themselves to Jesus. Perhaps there are moments in your life when you have glimpsed the presence or glory of God in the face of a fellow Christian. Meditate on that for a moment.

God's glory is often revealed through Christians in unusual times, places, and ways. For example, a young woman was dying of cancer in the hospital. She recounted that she had been touched by Christ and felt his calming presence and love. As she told her story, her face lit up and reflected the peace and presence of God's glory in Christ.

God's glory is also revealed in the face of a missionary feeding a hungry child, of a volunteer helping an elderly woman, of a hospital chaplain extending love and care to patients, or of a mother nurturing a sick baby.

Like Moses, may we be so constant in the presence of God that our lives reveal God's glory to those whose lives we touch each day. May we abide in that presence until we are transformed into God's likeness and more perfectly mirror God's splendor.

Prayer: *Help me, O God, to reflect your glory and presence to everyone I meet this day. Amen.*

LISTENING TO GOD

February 6-12, 1989   **Timothy Kelly, O.S.B.**†
Monday, February 6   Read Deuteronomy 26:1-4.

In this reading from Deuteronomy, the voice speaking is conveying such confidence in the future that already plans are being made to acknowledge what God has done and to thank God for doing it. And it hasn't happened yet.

Life is like that. We cope with the day-to-day problems and worries—or we hope we cope! And once in a while we look back and dream of a time when responsibilities were not so grave . . . or maybe to a time when we had more responsibility. But if looking back does not inspire a forward look, it becomes only nostalgia and ends in death.

Life looks hopefully forward because it remembers the faithful presence of God. The word of God says: "When you come into the land which the Lord your God gives you. . . ." "When," not "if." What God promises God delivers.

Perhaps it is not always according to my design. But the meaning of trusting God is that it doesn't have to happen according to my design. It must happen according to God's design. The call is to the hope that is born of faith in God's faithfulness. God is faithful and draws us in mysterious but sure ways.

Prayer: *Loving God, teach us to trust you in all things so that secure in your embrace we may face the future in peace. Amen.*

---

† Monk of St. John's Abbey and lecturer in theology at St. John's University, Collegeville, Minnesota.

Tuesday, February 7   Read Deuteronomy 26:5-11.

Christians have always been a backward looking people! But that is so they can look forward. Joseph's brothers sold him into Egypt. This evil deed was used by God to save the chosen. Jacob thought he had lost his son forever. But the years of loss proved to be blessing.

Then the blessing turned into bad times. The people were enslaved, maltreated, oppressed. Was this God's plan too? The people cried out to the Lord, and God heard their cry.

That slavery took many years. A lot of crying out happened. If God was going to answer the cry anyway, why the long wait? Wouldn't it have been more compassionate to respond immediately? Or was there more at stake than just these people? Was there a broader plan that maybe we still do not comprehend?

Our lives are like that. Our tragedies, trials, and tribulations are terrible. To us their continuation is senseless and without meaning. How could the death of a child, or the loss of a spouse, or the termination of employment, or the storm-destroyed village possibly bring any good for us or for anyone?

But Jacob trusted God just as Joseph had, and as Abraham before him had. And Moses learned by looking back so that he could lead on into the future. Deuteronomy directs that the first fruits of the products of the soil are to be offered to God. This is hope. It is giving God the best; it is giving to God from the top with no assurance that there will be more to come. No assurance, that is, except the trust we have in God. Will God give second fruits? Not necessarily. But we do trust that God knows the plan that we don't know.

Prayer: *Just God, teach us to listen to you not only for ourselves but for generations yet unborn, that our faithful and hope-filled loving may bring future generations to know and love you. Amen.*

February 8 (Ash Wednesday)

Read Romans 10:8*b*-13.

Ash Wednesday is a day for rededication to listening to the Lord. The proclamation at the beginning of the holy season of Lent is this: "The word is near you, on your lips and in your heart." The program for the beginning of the holy season of Lent is: Listen to this word of faith.

What makes this difficult is that the word always challenges us. It challenges us in our selfishness. It announces to us the reign of God. No longer is there room for hatred, jealousy, competition, envy, lust, greed, vengeance, acquisitiveness, insecurity, loneliness, power-plays.

This is very interesting. It tests our faith and our hope. It makes demands on us we may not feel ready for. So we ritualize our response which keeps us from that "faith in the heart" which "leads to justification."

We have an invitation to look at God. Lots of sinners have been cured by looking at God, by listening to the word of God, by embracing the salvation so freely offered. But always it has been necessary to acknowledge sinfulness in order to embrace salvation. We don't want to see our own sinfulness, so we don't look at God.

And we will never acknowledge sinfulness unless we have faith in the one who is our hope; the one who "bestows his riches upon all who call upon him." But call we must.

Prayer: *Merciful God, give us the courage to face the reality of sin in our lives, that acknowledging our need we may allow your forgiveness to enter in. Amen.*

Thursday, February 9   Read Luke 4:1-4.

Had any good temptations lately? If so, it's because God is calling loud and clear. The louder God calls, the worse the struggle to answer. As gold is tried in the fire . . . Mighty struggles. Dark nights. Desolation. Weak hope. All these seem to be so un-Christian, so unworthy of the calling that is ours.

But who is it we have put our faith in? Is it in a God who provides for our every bodily need? for bread on the table? for shoes on the children and gas in the tank? We want a God who will do what we say!

But Jesus shows us another God. This is not the God who gives victory to our armies, drives out the enemies, and returns captured lands to the oppressed. This is a God who sacrifices a son and lets the awful reality of death play itself out to the very bitter end. This is a God who allows a son to fast for forty days and then allows him to be tempted by the devil.

But who is this Jesus who remains faithful to such a God through it all? He is the one who is hungry but will not initiate the reign of God at the bidding of the devil just for a piece of bread. He is the one who will starve rather than move in a direction other than the will of God. He is the one who knows that food and the other necessities of life are God-given, but who will not put necessities even above answering the call of God.

We are challenged by the single-heartedness of Jesus. Our affluent and hedonistic age needs the Jesus of the desert who prefers to lay down his life rather than do good things for evil purposes.

May our hunger for bread remind us to become more hungry for the word of God, and may we prefer nothing to it.

Prayer: *Purifying God, open our hearts to your word that we may prefer nothing whatever to you and your will. Amen.*

Friday, February 10   Read Luke 4:5-7.

Success is the goal. It comes in many forms. It looks good to us. It gives us security. It provides for our need to be esteemed. It satisfies our craving for power. It helps build ego. And it shows all those who never thought we would amount to much that they were wrong, very wrong.

Success is dictated by the values of the culture. That which gives the greatest security, esteem, and power is what is sought after. Why even argue the point?

But what about Jesus? The devil certainly knew the values of the culture when he attempted to sidetrack Jesus. But Jesus was not taken in. After forty days of prayer and fasting in the desert, Jesus was aware that his security was in God, his need to be esteemed was fully supplied by God's love for him, and all the power he needed he had at his command.

All this—because he had vision. He knew the context of creation and he knew the Creator. He knew pain and hunger and desire too; and he wrestled with all the things we wrestle with. But he knew God. Thus he could put in proper perspective all that was within him and outside of him.

We have no particular trouble seeing why Jesus would respond the way he did. But what about us? To be a discerning person or discerning people surely we have to recognize when our desire for security or esteem or power motivates our decisions.

But in fact our security is in God; we are highly esteemed by God; we live by the power of God's Spirit in us. Insofar as we are convinced of this are we able to listen to God because our hope is in God alone, not in riches or esteem or power.

Prayer: *Rich, loving, powerful God, show us the way to know you that we may overcome the desires of flesh and seek the things of your reign. Amen.*

Saturday, February 11   Read Luke 4:9-13.

It is one thing to trust God. It is another thing to put God to the test. Jesus trusted God. But he would not put God to the test.

Why shouldn't we trust God? Well, God doesn't always do our will. Trusting God cost Jesus his life. Why should we trust a God who allows that to happen?

All this is akin to another question: Why don't we love our neighbor? Because our neighbor might take advantage of us. That's true. But what are we protecting? To love, one must be vulnerable, which literally means woundable. To trust God we must also be woundable.

Trusting God is born of the virtue of hope. Hope is the knowledge, the heart-knowledge, that God will never abandon us. The God who created us embraces us and will take nothing less than all of us.

If we love God and trust God, we still might not become rich or avoid pneumonia or snake bite. In fact, if we love God and trust God we'll probably die just like those who don't love God or trust God. But if we put God to the test, if we test God to see if the love proclaimed is genuine, we'll die twice!

We are in a season of listening to the God who can be trusted even though we will not live unless we die with Christ. We follow Christ from the temptations in the desert, through his months of persecution, even to his suffering and death on the cross. Yes, the temptations in the desert didn't end his trials. "When the devil had finished all the tempting he left him, to await another opportunity." Evil continues to assail us as well. Jesus never put God to the test. Nor should we.

Prayer: *Forgiving God, empower us to be faithful and trusting, that remembering the suffering and death of Christ we may look forward to full victory with him in his resurrection. Amen.*

Sunday, February 12   Read Psalm 91:9-16.

Sometimes the light is so bright we can't see; or the music is so loud we can't distinguish the tones; or the smell is so pungent we can't appreciate its delicacy. If we sit too close to the screen we can't see the movie.

Sometimes we get so taken up in our own lives and problems that we become blind to the broader picture. We need to step back and get perspective. Some of life's tragedies have turned out to be blessings in disguise. Some haven't. Some can never be seen as blessings in terms of this life. Without becoming super-spiritual or unsympathetic to the real pain of real people, we need to step back from today's events, even this decade's or this century's events, and see the plan of God that includes us and does not exclude us.

No, we aren't suggesting an attitude of "pie-in-the sky." Quite the opposite. Because we have a wider view of reality we can give our lives for one another; we can promote justice and peace even though we may risk our own necks in the process.

Jesus Christ believed in the wider picture. He believed in God's protection of him and of others. But he knew also that a grain of wheat must fall into the ground in order to bear abundant fruit.

No one has found a way of living with God without trust. To trust God we need the wider vision, a vision that teaches us that no matter what the pain or disaster or tragedy we might be facing in life, God is faithful.

A living, loving, trusting hope expands our vision.

Prayer: *Most faithful God, teach us to trust you and to be faithful to you as you are lovingly faithful to us. Amen.*

LENT: THE PROMISE OF THE LAND

February 13-19, 1989   **Roberta Bondi†**
Monday, February 13   Read Genesis 15:1-8.

During this first full week of Lent, the readings remind us of God's mysterious choice of Israel to be God's people and of the gift of the land in which God's people are to dwell. This sense of mystery and wonder is deepened as we ponder how through the death and resurrection of Jesus we are incorporated into that people and look forward to entering the land of God's promises to us.

Abraham is an old man in this narrative. Trusting the promises of God that he will become a great nation, he has left the life he knew to immigrate to Canaan. But he is still childless. How can he have descendants without a child? In Genesis 15, God repeats the promises. We are told that Abraham believed God, yet we next see him expressing his continuing doubts and arguing with God. He reminds us of the centurion who has asked Jesus to heal his daughter and tells Jesus, "I believe; help my unbelief" (Mark 9:24).

God repeats the promises: a childless man will be the father of a whole nation in a new land. Wonderfully, we know that the promises were fulfilled and also passed along to us: through Abraham to David, through Mary to Jesus, through the Holy Spirit to us. We have become that nation and have inherited that land in the kingdom of God.

Prayer: *Loving God, your goodness to us is beyond our imagining. Help us to enter Lent with a hope in your promise of life, even if we are not always entirely able to trust that promise. Amen.*

---

† Associate Professor of Church History, Candler School of Theology, Emory University, Atlanta, Georgia.

Tuesday, February 14   Read Genesis 15:8-12, 17-18.

In this passage, God seals the promise of descendants and land to Abraham with a covenant, a contract. There are three primary covenants in the Old Testament: the first is between God and Abraham, the second the Israelites entered into along with Moses at Sinai following the Exodus, and the third was God's promise to David that he would always have descendants to rule from his throne.

As for the covenant with Abraham, notice that although God made promises to him, nothing is being required of Abraham. Obedience to God is important, but it is not a condition here. The covenant is the absolute gift of God's love and gracious goodness, not because of some particular righteousness of Abraham but because of God's mysterious generosity.

The New Testament writers found this language of covenant deeply significant for their faith in Jesus Christ, through whom we enter into a new covenant with God. Abraham's covenant was sealed with the shedding of the blood of the sacrificial animals. The new covenant was sealed not with animal blood but with the blood of Jesus Christ himself. It is this blood of the crucifixion that brings us in communion to share one common life with him and each other. This blood, the symbol of God's love for the world, cries out to us to care for and feed God's beloved world.

Prayer: *Dearest God, you have bound us to yourself in a covenant of life. Help us remember the greatness of your love for all life. Teach us to share your life, both materially and spiritually, with all who need it. Amen.*

Wednesday, February 15   Read Psalm 127.

The first half of this psalm picks up a major theme of the week's readings: whatever we may do, the success of all of our work depends first of all upon the work of God and not simply upon our own efforts. This is true of our life in the church, and it is also true of our individual Christian lives. There is no such thing as a "self-made Christian."

How easy this is to forget in a society like ours that values independence and self-reliance more than mutual care and dependence! We Christians know that all we have comes to us as gifts. We do not build our lives by ourselves. We receive God's gift of gracious help in the form of our own gifts of intelligence, insight, and skills; the presence of God in our prayers; the opportunities we are given to worship, work, and love; the love and care that comes to us from others; and the support and challenges of the community to which we belong.

The second half of the psalm reminds us again of the significance of children for the people of the Old Testament. The writers of the early church, who were made uneasy by the "concrete" idea of these children, understood them symbolically to be virtues which we cultivate for growth in the Christian life. Even so, the psalm reminds us again that we, like Abraham, receive everything we have as God's gift.

Prayer: *Generous God, we could do nothing without the gifts of your goodness. Help us to delight in these gifts. Amen.*

Thursday, February 16   Read Philippians 3:17–4:1.

In this passage we move to life in the New Covenant. While reading, it is important to remember that Paul did not regard himself as living in ordinary times: since the days of Jesus, he and the other Christians with him expected, as he says, the return of Jesus to transform "our lowly body to be like his glorious body." Out of a sense of urgency, Paul exhorts his audience not to get their priorities turned upside down. We see the same warning in his advice that Christians remain in whatever married state they were when they joined the community, whether single or married (1 Cor. 7). A change of condition offered simply too much opportunity for distraction in the light of the crisis at hand.

Notice that the homeland which on Monday we saw promised to Abraham has now become for us the kingdom of God itself and that we are to dwell in it, not as disembodied spirits but resurrected in the form of the body of Jesus Christ. Are we as Christians more willing than God to give up on a material world filled with flesh-and-blood bodies because of the hardship and pain associated with life in those bodies? Yet God's affirmation of what it means to be human beings of flesh and blood is what we get in the incarnation and death of Jesus Christ of Nazareth.

Prayer: *God of love, help us never to discount one another's mental or physical pain as insignificant, for you yourself chose to live among us and share our human life. Amen.*

Friday, February 17   Read Philippians 3:17–4:1.

What does it mean to speak of our homeland as heaven? Because of the suffering and brokenness of life "in the flesh," the Gnostic sect believed that ordinary life in our world is evil. Instead, they thought that we human beings were meant to be "spiritual," unconcerned with the physical world at all. Many of these Gnostics identified themselves as Christians; they believed in Jesus, but not a flesh-and-blood Jesus. On the contrary, they thought Jesus was like a ghost sent to give us the saving message of his father, who dwelt outside creation to draw us to a spiritual world beyond.

The early church fought hard against such a dualism which denied the goodness of God's creation as well as the reality of the incarnation. Instead, our Christian ancestors affirmed that God never intended our world to be broken. In Romans, Paul insists that creation itself is groaning in a kind of bondage connected with human sin. At the end of time, when we receive our resurrection bodies, he says, the physical world will also be restored to God's original and loving intent. This restored earth is our homeland (see Rom. 8:18-25).

What form this restoration will take and its timing is not for us to know, however, and speculation on it can sidetrack us from the real job of Christian loving and living. Nevertheless, we need to be reminded of God's love and care for this very world we live in.

Prayer: *God of all creation, teach us to know your world as you intended it to be, and help us love it and live in it as your gift. Amen.*

Saturday, February 18   Read Luke 13:31-33.

Throughout the Gospels, the Pharisees have an ambiguous relationship to Jesus: they oppose him continually, yet Jesus often receives their hospitality at meals. In this passage, they warn Jesus that Herod plans to kill him. Jesus replies that he is a prophet; he must die in Jerusalem where the prophets die. Meanwhile, he will continue to cure the sick and announce good news to the captives, a message which Herod can only understand in political terms.

The mention of Jerusalem brings us back to the readings from the beginning of the week. Jerusalem is the capital of the land promised Abraham. In Genesis 15, Abraham tried to believe God's promises that a nation would descend from him to live in the land God would give them. Yet how could this be while Abraham remained childless in his old age? But compared to Abraham's promises, the promises of God which Jesus gave his followers would at the crucifixion seem even more implausible: Jesus was not only childless but about to die as well.

In this season of Lent, we ponder as the people of God the meaning of God's promises in the face of our own despair. We need to remember that the very pattern of God's life with us, begun in Abraham and shown forth in the death and resurrection of Jesus, is to bring life out of death in ways we cannot even imagine.

Prayer: *God of all hope and life, in our pain and loss remind us that as you have shared in grief, loss, and death with us, you will bring us also into your life. Amen.*

61

Sunday, February 19   Read Luke 13:34-35.

In this passage from Luke we see Jesus accepting that God's people, for whom he is prepared to die, do not want him. He is expecting his death, perhaps at their hands. Yet instead of responding in anger against Jerusalem, he speaks over that city words full of tenderness: "How often would I have gathered your children together as a hen gathers her brood under her wings. . . !" Through this image which picks up so many images of God from the psalms we encounter God's mothering, yearning love. We see God, and God within Jesus, who would surround us with the warmth and life of a bird protecting and caring for her young.

Sometimes it is hard for us who have a strong sense of the righteousness and judgment of God to take the gentleness of God's love for us seriously. Somehow, we can't really believe in it in the light of our own inadequacies. Surely God only loves us when we are good. But if we can't believe in a love that will stay by us even in our terrible imperfections, what can we make of the crucifixion? Meditating on this image of God who longs for us like a mother bird for her little ones can bring the gentle God close. We can begin to feel the healing touch of Jesus as we prepare ourselves for the crucifixion and resurrection that is coming.

Prayer: *Gentle God, although we reject you and often can't see your love for us, feed us, cover us with your wings, and bring us to our full growth in you. Amen.*

DOES GOD HAVE YOUR ATTENTION?

February 20-26, 1989 **Earl H. Lassen, Jr.**†
Monday, February 20 Read Exodus 3:1-6;
John 10:14-18.

Moses gets up expecting a very ordinary, routine day. What else would an eighty-year-old shepherd expect? After forty years of shepherding in the desert, what would be different?

Moses had lived a routine life. And at this point, he is very close to being forgotten in the eyes of other people—but not in the eyes of God.

Little does Moses realize that this day will be the turning point in his life. God will get his attention through a burning—but not consumed—bush. God can use anything to get our attention, including unusual circumstances. We tend to wait to be presented with something sensational or some great opportunity.

More often, however, God uses the everyday events and experiences going on in our lives. For instance, God may speak through a hurting friend, a child, a sour relationship, a frustrating job, a sense of failure, a worship service, or an illness. The truth is that God is communicating with us most of the time. Whatever way God chooses to get our attention, however, our problem is that we tend not to be listening. We seldom seem ready to respond to what God has to say.

We must learn to keep close to God, take sufficient time daily to be alone and strengthened by God, and train ourselves to listen for God's voice each day of our lives.

Suggestion for meditation: *God met Moses while Moses was working; God met Isaiah while Isaiah was praying; God met Paul while Paul was traveling. And you?*

---

† Executive Secretary, Middle East Baptist Conference, Canfield, Ohio.

Tuesday, February 21   Read Exodus 3:7-15.

The lessons contained in this short passage are many. Let's look at three of them. First, the Lord says, "I have seen the misery of my people. . . . I have heard them crying. . . . I am well aware of their sufferings" (NJB). How encouraging to know in times of stress that we have a God who knows and is concerned about what we are going through.

In this passage, we are next told that God cares so much about the plight of the Israelite people that he acts: "I have come down to rescue them from the clutches of the Egyptians and bring them up out of that country, to a country rich and broad, to a country flowing with milk and honey" (NJB). Then God says to Moses, "After you have [notice the assumption] led the people out of Egypt . . ." God is going to fulfill his promise. We have a God who knows, cares for, and has the power to help us. When Mary was troubled, the angel reminded her that nothing is impossible with God. We need to remember that. That means God can meet any need in your life right now!

Lastly, when God calls Moses, God does not provide a full, detailed plan of all that God is going to do. God simply tells Moses the next step and then promises, "I will be with you." That's how God usually does it—one step at a time. That is what we can handle, and that is God's way of also building our faith. Can you live with that?

Suggestion for prayer: *We usually tell God where we would like to go and what we would like to do. For the rest of this week don't* tell *God anything. Instead, ask what God would like for you to do and where.*

Wednesday, February 22   Read Psalm 103:1-7;
                                                 Philippians 4:4-7.

This is a psalm that can be read every day. It gives us an unshakable confidence in God.

We need the reminder to praise the Lord. We live in a very negative period of time. Whether people are talking about life, work, politics, family, friends, or fellow workers, almost everything said these days is negative. Think about the conversations you have heard or shared in during the last few days. Were they positive, or were they cynical and negative? Most of what I hear is quite negative. Very few people have a life that is characterized by a spirit of thanksgiving and praise.

The psalmist wanted everything within each of us to praise the Lord—to do what we need to get rid of the clutter that is within each of us. Therefore, self-examination is good for us. Ask yourself some basic questions. Are you glorifying Christ in your life right now? Is there unconfessed sin in your life? Is there someone who needs your forgiveness? Is there a lack of compassion, self-control, or humility in your life? Is there anger, bitterness, or judgmentalism? Is there a relationship that needs to be surrendered to the Lord's wisdom and guidance? Whatever the need in your life, talk with God about it and deal with it. Then you will want to praise God, too.

Notice that this passage says our Lord "forgives . . . heals . . . redeems . . . satisfies." He also "crowns (surrounds) you with love and mercy . . . works vindication and justice." This is a God who is willing to help us and desires only what is best for those who call on him.

Suggestion for meditation: *Ask yourself today not just what you have given up for Christ but what positive qualities you have taken on because of Christ.*

Thursday, February 23
Read Psalm 103:8-13;
1 John 1:8-10.

Many people would say confession is the most difficult thing a Christian must do. It is pure agony to go before a perfect, holy God and admit, "I blew it!"

It is difficult to confess a deed that demonstrated poor judgment, pride in action, a deliberate lie, or any other sin. And what frustration when we have to admit, "I did it again!" Consequently, we don't take sufficient time for confession and, without realizing it, we miss the healing, peace, strength, and joy that comes from this important discipline.

Have you ever thought about the results of confession? It does several important things for us. First of all, it is the means God has advanced and ordained so that we can maintain a close relationship with him. Secondly, it is only through confession that God can deal with our sin. Third, confession brings growth and development. Our actions and attitudes gradually change, feelings are reversed, affections and loyalties are changed. We get better at distinguishing between truth and error, between sin and obedience. Fourth, confession brings peace. Simply put, confession is good and necessary for each of us.

Is there sin in your life? Confess it. Name the sin and admit that you willfully sinned against God. Admit that you did it on your own accord. Don't blame your past, your circumstances, or someone else. Admit that you were disobedient or that your goals and priorities got out of focus. When you do, God will gladly forgive you. Our scripture passage says, "As far as the east is from the west, so far does he remove our transgressions from us."

Suggestion for prayer: *Take time to confess your sin today. Then, also take the time to be quiet and feel God's loving forgiveness.*

Friday, February 24   Read Luke 13:1-9.

We have two kinds of calamity brought to our attention in verses 1-5. First, there is the deliberate brutality inflicted by a cruel military power. Second, there is the accidental disaster of the tower of Siloam.

Both events raise a question which men and women never tire of asking in the face of suffering—why? And then there is a second question that is often raised: Were these disasters brought about as punishment for sin? Christ cuts through all that both times with, "I tell you, no." It is always dangerous to attribute human suffering to human sin. Christ goes on to warn us that the calamaties and hurts of life ought to impress on us the fact that life is brief and often uncertain, and spiritual death is certain unless we are reconciled to God. The message is strong and direct: Repent or perish.

The parable in verses 6-9 compliments the teaching of Christ in the previous verses. A fig tree normally takes three years to reach maturity. If it doesn't bear fruit by that time, it probably never will. This fig tree is given a second chance. How like our Lord! Peter, Mark, Paul, and many others could also say they were given a second chance. God is infinitely kind to the person who falls but rises again. However, notice that the parable also makes it clear that if we presume on God's grace and mercy, if we reject God's appeals again and again, we may eventually shut God out of our lives. What a tragic mistake that would be!

Prayer: *Thank you, Lord, for your forgiveness, your patience with me, and your unending love for me. Amen.*

Saturday, February 25   Read 1 Corinthians 9:24-27;
                                       10:1-5.

Is there any complacency in your spiritual life right now? As you live out your life, would you say that obedience, faithfulness, and discipline are evident characteristics? When temptation confronts you, does your loyalty to God come through? The apostle Paul wrote that he really is tough on himself to be sure that he doesn't fall away or become disqualified. He wanted his life to count for God and to be a blessing to others.

The children of Israel were highly favored. They had seen firsthand the work of God in very special ways. Think of it—they were miraculously guided by the pillar of cloud, they had been brought through the Red Sea, and they had been fed manna from heaven and water from the rock. You would think these marvelous experiences would ensure that they would be obedient and faithful. Yet they fell away and most (all but two) of them died in the desert. Would you decide right now that you are going to follow after God throughout your earthly journey—there will be no turning back? Some decisions need to be made in advance.

Notice how many times the word *all* is repeated in these few verses. All of them—the strong, feeble, weak, young, old, and others—experienced the wonderful guidance and protection of God. All of them were sustained day after day by the supernatural power of God. At times, you may feel weak, inadequate, ineffective, poor, or useless, but be assured you too are known to God and all of us are under God's guiding hand.

Suggestion for meditation: *List all the ways God cares for you. Then, thank God.*

Sunday, February 26   Read 1 Corinthians 10:1-13.

In today's passage we are given three reasons why God was not pleased with the Israelites. Then we are commanded not to follow in their footsteps. Let's take a look at why God was frustrated with them:

1) *Idolatry.* Verse 7 is a reference to their worship of the golden calf in Exodus 32. When they took the sacrifice out of their religion and it became comfortable and easy, it led to sin. Don't get too comfortable!

2) *Sexual immorality.* Verse 8 refers to illicit relationships the Israelites were involved in (see Numbers 25). Sexual immorality abounds today. It takes a passionate love for purity to keep from impurity.

3) *Unbelief.* Verses 9-10 refer to the time when the people began to get impatient with God's ways and provisions (see Numbers 21). They began to grumble about their lot and wondered if God could do what God had promised. We need to learn to check ourselves when the temptation comes to complain about what we have or don't have in life. We need to work at being thankful.

Paul insists on vigilance on the part of the Christian and then shares the good news about temptation.

1) Our temptation is common—we are not alone.

2) God is faithful and will protect us.

3) God will provide a way out of every temptation.

Are you facing temptation? Run for your life! Where? Into the arms of Jesus Christ.

Suggestion for meditation: *Is more discipline needed in your life? Determine what you need and then ask God to help you carry it out.*

RETURNING HOME

February 27–March 5, 1989
Monday, February 27

Julie D. Hammonds†
Read Luke 15:1-3.

Sitting in the shadows of the candlelit room, you are mesmerized by the quiet voice of the Teacher who reclines at the table. Though the hour is late, the guests linger, entranced by the soft-spoken power evident in the Teacher's every word.

Many factions are present in the room tonight, from tax collectors to teachers of the law. Tension has built, and at last the mutterings of one of the Pharisees become clearly audible. "This man welcomes sinners and eats with them," he growls. (NIV)

Looking up quickly, the Teacher captures the Pharisee's gaze with his piercing eyes. Instead of trading insult for insult, he begins quietly to tell one story, and then another, followed by another. The tales speak of loss and recovery, of estrangement and reconciliation. When at last the Teacher falls silent, not an eye in the room is free of tears.

You recognize the fact that the Teacher's words present a directive to the Pharisee, a directive that urges the man not to resent the healing work occurring in the room this night. Though your mind understands this, in your deepest heart you feel as if the stories had been spoken directly to you. You find yourself longing for the kind of relationship that existed between the father and his son in the Teacher's final story.

Suggestion for meditation: *Imagine your favorite parable being told you by Jesus himself. What added power does it have in this setting?*

---

† Christian writer; active in the college and career group of People's Church (affiliated with Assemblies of God), Fresno, California.

Tuesday, February 28   Read Luke 15:11-16.

The power of this familiar parable rests in our instantaneous recognition of its common occurrence in daily life. Perhaps our neighbor's son drives recklessly and awakens the community with ear-splitting music; perhaps our own daughter comes in late on a Friday night, sullenly avoiding our questions. We recognize the lost son of the parable in friends, in relatives, and even in memories of our own youth.

Yet it is the mirror of our spiritual lives that reflects the image of the lost son most clearly. Each of us is the son or daughter of an eternal Father, a Father whose gifts to us have been most generous. Simply to be given life is to receive beyond hope of repayment. Yet all that we need, all that we ask for, and all that we require is given us freely.

The tragedy of our lives is that, in some way, every one of us has "set off for a distant country and there squandered his wealth in wild living" (NIV). The gifts of life and of character and of purpose, gifts which our Father gave so freely, have been exhausted on a world which greedily absorbs such treasures and constantly thirsts for more. Finally, we have reached the point at which we have no more to give. Yet in our moment of deepest need, the world has turned a deaf ear to our cries.

Who will see our tears in this hour of exhaustion and anguish?

Suggestion for meditation: *Remember for a moment the last time you knelt before the Lord, hidden in the darkness by a sin which kept you from his presence. At that moment, you shared the feelings of the lost son of the parable. What action did you take?*

Wednesday, March 1   Read Luke 15:17-20.

Who can forget that moment in which, exhausted by the world's demands, no longer able to provide for even the simplest of our own needs, we turn our thoughts at last to the Lord?

The moment is laden with guilt, not only the guilt of the sins we have committed but also the guilt of our own tardiness in looking to the Lord for help. We sense that the Lord could justly resent us for coming to him only after his gifts have been wasted and all other means of rescue have been tried. Yet Jesus says that the lost son "came to his senses" in this moment. It is not the logical pursuit of all other courses of action that the Lord calls sane, but the moment of turning, the moment in which the lost son acknowledges his own weakness and looks to his father's strength. The Lord does not resent our recognition of personal need and divine power. Instead, he meets us on the dusty road, arms open wide.

In turning at last toward God, we feel rightly compelled to confess our guilt. We prepare a speech for the Lord's benefit; at least, we imagine it is for his benefit. We almost believe that our Father is unaware of our activities in that "distant country," and we fear that once he knows of them, we will be turned away as unworthy of forgiveness. When the Lord runs to greet us, as the father rushed to greet his son, we accept the strong embrace with fear. At last, we fall to our knees in the dust of the road, ready to confess our sins. We fully expect to be punished once our Father hears "the whole story."

His response will surprise us.

Suggestion for meditation: *Consider the range of emotions which the father must have experienced when he greeted his son. Which ones did he emphasize? Why?*

Thursday, March 2 Read Luke 15:21-24.

In the poignant vision of a son kneeling in the dust at his father's feet, pouring out his sins and his regret, we see a reflection of our own tears, and we hear an echo of our own confessions. The image may be repeated a thousand times over in the course of our spiritual lives. Yet the Lord's response never changes. In the moment of our confession, the Father's forgiveness, sure and complete, flows over us like healing water.

Like the lost son, we simply do not deserve the forgiveness that comes. Accustomed as we are to earning our rewards and deserving our punishments, we frown at the unfairness of receiving a gift that cannot be repaid. Indeed, this gift of forgiveness that the Lord freely gives us is beyond price. It can never be reciprocated! It must simply be accepted, as freely as it is given.

We understand more clearly the motives of the Lord as we look to the words of the father in this passage. "For this son of mine was dead and is alive; he was lost and is found" (NIV). No mention here of squandered wealth and wasted opportunity. Instead, the father empathizes with his son's experience. He shares the anguish of separation and the pain of relationships broken by sin. Because of his wise understanding, the father's relief at his son's return is total, and his forgiveness is complete.

Forgiveness paves the path of reconciliation between father and child.

Suggestion for meditation: *The Lord meets us on the road of forgiveness whenever we decide to return home to his arms. We depend on his presence there, yet how often do we thank him for that assurance?*

Friday, March 3 Read Psalm 34:1-8.

In these verses, the psalmist could easily be writing from the perspective of the lost son reacting to the forgiveness and acceptance which his father so lovingly poured over him. The intensity of joy and thanksgiving which the son must have felt are sounded here in a ringing melody of gratefulness to God, a melody which we share each time we experience the Lord's forgiveness in our lives.

We find four elements intermingled in these verses: history, truth, promise, and invitation. In verses four and six, the writer recounts past experiences and remembers the active role the Lord played in their outcome. "I sought the Lord, and he answered me," he writes, adding later, "This poor man called, and the Lord heard him" (NIV). From his experiences, the writer has learned several truths, which he shares in verses five and seven. "The angel of the Lord encamps around those who fear him," the writer attests, "and he delivers them" (NIV). His personal reactions to the Lord's faithfulness are recorded in the promises of verses one and two. "I will extol the Lord at all times; his praise will always be on my lips. My soul will boast in the Lord" (NIV). The writer's greatest desire is to share news of the Lord's faithfulness with his community. He invites everyone to the banquet in verses three and eight, writing, "Taste and see that the Lord is good . . ." (NIV).

We cannot ignore this call to reconciliation.

Suggestion for meditation: *Think about the elements of history, truth, promise, and invitation in your own recent experiences with the Lord's forgiveness. How well do your memories fit the psalmist's model?*

Saturday, March 4   Read 2 Corinthians 5:18-21.

These verses formally introduce us to the concept of reconciliation, an event we have seen modeled in Luke 15 and Psalm 34. The reconciliation message is profound in its simplicity. When Christ gave his life at Calvary, he took upon himself the burden of sin that lay upon the world, enduring a punishment that rightfully belonged to all humanity. His death and resurrection bridge the gulf that once existed between an imperfect people and their perfect Lord. Our only task is to cross the bridge for which Christ gave his life and accept the gracious forgiveness which the Lord extends to us. This reconciliation message is the very essence of the gospel.

As Paul presents it in this passage, however, the message of reconciliation is inextricably bound to another message, one which Paul directs to all who will read his letter. He presents the message in verse 18, in 19, and again in verse 20, always linking it to the message of reconciliation itself. This second message is the call to ministry, an appeal directed by Paul to all who share in the divine reconciliation. He asks that we consider ourselves Christ's ambassadors, "as though God were making his appeal through us" (NIV).

Our status as ambassadors is both a privilege and an obligation. We who have crossed the bridge of forgiveness bear a responsibility to those still separated from the Lord. This obligation becomes a privilege, however, as we recognize that in our ministry of reconciliation, we serve the Lord.

Suggestion for meditation: *Consider the many communities in which you serve as Christ's ambassador. What is one positive step you can take to spread the message of reconciliation today?*

Sunday, March 5   Read 2 Corinthians 5:16-18.

As disciples of Christ, we occupy a special post in the kingdom of God. We are Christ's ambassadors, serving in the ministry of reconciliation. Because we ourselves have been reconciled to God, we long to share the message of forgiveness with all the members of our community. On what basis can we reach out to others with our message?

We look to Paul for answers. "If anyone is in Christ," he tells us, "he is a new creation" (NIV). The sacrifice of Christ has reconciled us to God, healing the relationship that once lay broken between us. Indeed, we are new creatures: "The old has gone, the new has come!" (NIV) In every relationship, our perspective is now radically altered. We have ceased to see Christ as a mere wise man or healer; instead, he has become our brother, friend, teacher, and guide. Next, we cease to see ourselves as slaves to habits and sins beyond our control. Christ's power frees us from bondage, and we learn that even those aspects of our personality which we once thought useless can be used for God's glory! Finally, we cease to envy the achievements of others, to proclaim their faults, or to covet their positions. Because we ourselves are new creations, we see the limitless potential of Christ within every person.

As we reach out to our world community with the message of reconciliation, this is our perspective and our purpose for ministry.

Prayer: *Gracious Lord, we accept our calling as ministers, filled with the humility of our own unearned forgiveness and prepared to announce the message of reconciliation to a world that longs to know the peace of a healed relationship with you. May we serve you faithfully to the end of our days. Amen.*

March 6-12, 1989   **Bruce C. Birch†**
Monday, March 6   Read Isaiah 43:16-17.

The image is of Exodus. These verses speak of Israel's great salvation story. When they were slaves in Egypt, the Lord delivered them. The climactic moment came at the sea where the way was blocked before them and Pharaoh's army was closing in behind them. Death seemed about to speak the final word. Yet, through the gift of God's saving grace a further word of life was still to be spoken. A way was opened through the sea, and the children of Israel passed through to new life while the waters closed over the chariots of those who had oppressed and enslaved them.

The image is of Exodus, but the time is of exile. These verses are not reporting but remembering. These are the words of an anonymous prophet speaking to the community of Judeans carried away into Babylonian exile almost seven centuries later than that Exodus story of deliverance out of bondage. The prophet is speaking to a people in the midst of a crisis where they too fear that death and despair have spoken the final words. They cannot "sing the Lord's song" in this strange land (Ps. 137:4).

The prophet calls on them in the midst of their overwhelming present to remember what God has done before, and as an Exodus people to believe that God can bring new life yet again—even in exile.

Prayer: *O delivering God, kindle in our hearts the hope of new life and new paths into the future through the gift of thy saving grace in the midst of our crises of despair and death. Amen.*

---

† Professor of Old Testament, Wesley Theological Seminary, Washington, D.C.

Tuesday, March 7   Read Isaiah 43:18-19.

The setting of these verses is once again the despair and hopelessness of the exiles in Babylon, and the prophet declares to them, "Remember not the former things, nor consider the things of old." This is strange advice since the prophet has just himself reminded the exiles of the mighty deeds of their God in bringing Israel out of bondage in Egypt.

While the prophet sought to remind those in crisis of what God's salvation had done in the past, it was important that memory not become an end in itself. The people could simply become locked in a nostalgic wish for the past.

What is important about remembering is that it empowers our vision for God's future. God who has delivered can bring new life yet again if we will look with fresh eyes to the future as well as the past. "Behold, I am doing a new thing; now it springs forth, do you not perceive it?" The prophet knows that remembering God's activity of grace does no good if the people cannot see that same divine activity in their own present circumstances.

We must seek to look ahead as well as back. What we know of what God has done must enable us to see what God is still doing in our world. We must scan the horizon—in our own lives and in the wider world—seeking to find God's "new thing" emerging and join our efforts with God's. Remembering must be coupled with vision, and it is this coupling that enables our mission as the church.

Prayer: *O God of new beginnings, help us to discern thy faithful work of life and grace in our world. Take away our fear of new things, and give us courage to undertake the mission of thy grace to a broken world wherever that mission might lead. Amen.*

Wednesday, March 8   Read John 12:1-3.

Jesus is visiting his friends Mary, Martha, and Lazarus in Bethany. During the meal Mary anoints Jesus' feet with a costly ointment and wipes his feet with her hair. Judas objects that this money could have better been used for the poor. In Matthew and Luke it is the disciples who object to such costly attention, apparently out of sincere belief that the lavishing of such costly ointment on Jesus was poor stewardship.

Let's face it. Our instincts are to agree with the disciples. We are used to serving on church committees where our responsibility is to watch out for unnecessary expenditures and to make our programs cost effective. We still have a hard time regarding Mary's actions as anything but unnecessarily extravagant.

Extravagance for its own sake is poor stewardship, but the focus of Mary's action is on Jesus. And it is filled with special meaning. Jesus has just raised Lazarus, her brother, from the dead, but in so doing has aroused the anger of Caiaphas and others. "So from that day on they took counsel how to put him to death" (John 11:53). Anointing with ointment is the last rite in preparation for burial. Mary knows that no matter how costly the ointment, it is small in comparison to the price Jesus is to pay for the pouring out of his life in behalf of the poor, the outcast, and the suffering. In their tending of budgets, Judas and the disciples have lost sight of the cost of discipleship.

The vision of discipleship to which we are called will not always fit easily into budget years, and the pursuit of our mission as the church will not always be cost effective. The true measure of our activities comes in asking if we are daring to travel with Jesus the way of the cross.

Prayer: *Blessed Savior, help us to measure our gifts by the shape of the cross rather than the size of our budgets. Amen.*

Thursday, March 9   Read John 12:4-8.

"The poor you always have with you, but you do not always have me." Some have used this statement by Jesus to justify a lack of attention to material needs in a world where many still lack food, are homeless on the streets of our cities, and are denied adequate health and education programs. They would have us believe that Jesus directs our attention only to spiritual needs and away from the material needs of a broken world.

Such a reading of this story and its final statement shows little knowledge of Jesus' ministry. He was constantly identified with the poor, the sick, and the outcast, and he called for those who would follow him to do the same (see Matt. 25:31-46).

Jesus is not giving us an either-or choice between tending spiritual needs and material needs. He is, first of all, reminding Judas and the disciples of their covenant obligation and quoting to them from Deuteronomy 15:7-11, "For the poor will always be in the land; therefore, I command you, open wide your hand to your neighbor, to the needy and to the poor." On the other hand, Jesus reminds them of his coming death, as does Mary's act of anointing. Jesus calls the disciples to faithfulness in the present by calling them to *remember* who they are as covenant people but to look ahead to the *vision* of cross and resurrection.

Like the disciples, we are called in reading this story not to measure our activities as the church in terms of immediate budget planning concerns alone. We must ask if those activities serve to remind us of our calling and point us to God's future, even through the cross.

Prayer: *Gracious God, we give thanks for the gift of thy Son who showed us the costly way of true discipleship. Remind us of our calling to be the covenant community, and empower us to claim thy future through the cross which leads to life. Amen.*

Friday, March 10   Read Philippians 3:4-14.

Paul is writing to the church at Philippi in Macedonia. At the time of his writing he is in prison (1:7, 13), yet the quality of his whole letter is one of joy and gratitude in his faith. What enables such faithfulness even in the face of adversity?

In this reading Paul lists some of the qualities and earlier accomplishments in his life. But Paul had learned that righteousness is not a matter of what one does but is instead a matter of what one receives—the free gift of God's grace in Jesus Christ. Righteousness cannot be one's own but is from God.

Here is the clue to Paul's joy and hope even in prison. If these qualities were rooted in our own accomplishments, then every setback in life becomes a collapse of what we thought we were building for ourselves. But if our joy and hope is rooted in the activity of God, shown in the resurrection of Jesus Christ, then we know that even setbacks in our own efforts are not hindrances to God's grace. Paul knew where true hope lay—not in his own work but in the work of God in Christ.

This has always been a hard lesson for the church to learn. We are so prone to think our own efforts are building the kingdom and earning righteousness for ourselves. And in the earnestness—and sometimes conflict—of church meetings and denominational issues, there is so seldom any expression of joy and thanksgiving for the righteousness which comes only from God. The absence of joy, hope, gratitude, trust, and humility should warn us that we may be focusing too greatly on our own efforts and failing to open ourselves to the work of God's grace. It is from God that true righteousness comes.

Prayer: *O God, the source of all true righteousness, in the midst of our activities in the service of thy church grant us the humility which allows us to reject self-importance and opens us to the gift of thy grace. Amen.*

Saturday, March 11   Read Psalm 126.

This psalm shows the movement from what God has done to trust in what God can do, which is at the heart of our faith.

The psalm summons the worshipers in a time of crisis to remember what God has done in the past (vv. 1-3), and to trust in God's power to enable new life in the future (vv. 4-6). God had restored Jerusalem (Zion) in previous times of danger, and the psalm gives thanks for God's mercy. Only then does the present danger receive attention in petition to "restore our fortunes, O Lord." But even this momentary view of the present gives way to confidence and hope. "He that goes forth weeping . . . *shall* come home with shouts of joy."

So often we are overwhelmed by the challenge of present difficulty, whether as individuals or as congregations. We act as if our moment of crisis were both the beginning and the end of our experience with God. An early Methodist circuit rider wrote in his journal of despair over the death of his horse, stranding him awkwardly in some forested wilderness. He cried out, "Where is my God?" only to realize as he cried out that he had come safely through a flood, an encounter with outlaws, and a serious illness within the last few months. In those moments he had had a strong sense of God's presence. Why should he not assume God was present now and had some further grace-filled future yet ahead for him? Like the psalmist and the circuit rider, it is knowledge of God's past grace and trust in God's future that frees us from the tyranny of our present crises, whatever their form.

Prayer: *We remember with thanksgiving, O God, thy abundant mercies in our lives and the lives of those who went before us. We trust that our future will be filled with thy grace. Enable us now to face present challenges with confidence. Amen.*

Sunday, March 12   Read Isaiah 43:20-21.

"The wild beasts will honor me, the jackals and the ostriches."
This is a disturbing word. We want tame and manageable evidences of God's "new thing." Couldn't we have eagles and stallions? Could God possibly be at work in the violent and complex struggle for freedom in South Africa? Why was I surprised that in volunteering time in a ministry for the homeless I found myself ministered to? Is it really that kid we had so much trouble with in junior high that is going into the ministry?

"I will make a way in the wilderness and rivers in the desert."
Most of us would like God's salvation to deliver us straight into the promised land, but all of us will know some wilderness times. The prophet promises a "way" in the wilderness, but it will not always be the expected or hoped for way. People of faith do not always get what they wish for, but they are promised that where there seems to be no way God will make one possible; where there seem no possibilities all things are possible in God. What could be more unexpected than "rivers in the desert"? Can it be that facing that controversial issue head-on in our congregation actually helped build community when we tackled it in love? Can the crisis that seemed like the end of my life have really become a time of renewal with the support of the church?

Earlier this year I found myself in a large southern city having lunch in a restaurant and discussing a project with four colleagues: two black, one Hispanic, and one white. With a shock of recognition I realized I had been there before, on the outside; in a picket line; looking at large "Whites Only" signs and a determined owner at the door with a shotgun. I realized that even in the wilderness of racism which stretches on before us yet, there have been rivers to sustain us on our desert journey.

Prayer: *In the wilderness of our lives, lead us on, O God of fire and cloud. Amen.*

GOD'S PENETRATING WORD

March 13-19, 1989   **Judith Craig**†
Monday, March 13   Read Luke 19:28-40.

The story of Jesus in Jerusalem is one of triumph reached through amazing twists and turns. Underlying all that happens, from the joyous to the agonizing, is an inescapable truth: The penetrating word of God will be heard even if only the stones shout it.

Built into the created order is the word of God. It will not be stifled. No matter how extended the distance between what is now and the intention of God in creation, the word of God is built in and will not be silenced. That is what Jesus meant when he said to those ordering him to quiet the celebrating crowd, " . . . if these were silent, the very stones would cry out."

There is much in the world attempting to silence the word of God—greed, anger, suspicion, pride, threats of destruction. But the word of God is built in, and that word will speak. With that confidence Jesus approached the passionate days of the Jerusalem encounter. He invites us to carry the same confidence into the encounters of our every day.

Prayer: *Thanks be to you, O God, for your word which cries out even when we are, or believe you are, silent. Amen.*

---

† Bishop, Michigan Area, The United Methodist Church, Detroit, Michigan.

Tuesday, March 14   Read Isaiah 50:4-9*a*.

God's penetrating word is given to the tongues of the faithful. Morning by morning God's penetrating word is put into the ears of those who carry it in their being (incarnate it). What a powerful image of how God's word enters human knowing.

In the thought of the biblical writer, the ear is the entry into the inner being of a person. It is entry to the mind, the thought out of which a person lives. It is also entry to the heart, the source of will which directs life. God's penetrating word comes with the return of each dawn. Morning by morning, steadfastly God whispers into our ear that penetrating word for the day. It goes through our hearing, onto our tongue, and is for us life-forming instruction.

In some cases it is a fortress against all those who would threaten, assail, attack, ridicule, disagree. The word of God on one's tongue gives strength sufficient to endure whatever the reaction of those who hear it spoken. The intimate, penetrating whisper in the ear offers strength greater than that of those who would challenge in any way. It is as sturdy as flint and so wise as not to be confused.

Every day God seeks to equip us with that whisper in the ear. Just as we ought to start a day with praise of God on our lips, so, too, should we start with a moment of listening silence.

Prayer: *I will be silent, God. Penetrate my silence with your word for this day. Amen.*

Wednesday, March 15   Read Psalm 31:9-16.

God's penetrating word is always present. That is a confession of faith. But hearing that word, being able to speak it, is sometimes something else! Life experience may make us deaf to God's word in our ear. Our tongues may become mute, unable to carry God's word. Then our tendency is to retreat into painful silence.

The biblical writers from whom we learn about prayer did something quite different. If they felt troubled, burdened, persecuted, abandoned, they told God about it in no uncertain terms! While we tend to sanitize prayer and form pretty words of thanks and careful words of request, the biblical writers "let it all hang out" in their prayer life.

"Lament," the name given that form of communication with God, is the full expression of the darkest moods and experiences of the faithful one. It is a way of saying, "Hey, God . . . do you see what is going on here? Do you see how miserable I am, how awful things have become?"

If God's penetrating word seemed dulled, lament was the way of searching for it again. What is there in your experience today that seems to be blunting God's penetrating word of hope or healing or justice? Try crying out to God about it. Try lamenting.

Suggestion for prayer: *Speak (out loud if you can) to God about where you feel the divine word is not penetrating.*

Thursday, March 16   Read Psalm 31:9-16.

Lament is a form of prayer that is very honest. It speaks to God about the reality of one's immediate experience. Lament also is a means of pushing against a sense of the absence of God. It is a way to rediscover the penetrating word of God.

In every true lament there is a change of mood. That change is often signaled by a little word, like the words *but . . . yet*. Psalm 31 recounts feelings of terror and abandonment. But—*but*—a memory creeps in. It hasn't always been this way. *But*—even in the midst of all this, I still trust you, God.

One of the great powers of lament is the rediscovery of the penetrating word of God. Listing the woes and ills of the day often calls up a time when they were not the foremost reality. Our complaint to God acknowledges that God still is, and in that acknowledgement is the jogging of memory. There were times when we sensed God was very present, when the word penetrated clearly with engaging power. I remember. To that memory I will cling.

So the mind works when lament runs free. It is a tutor of memory. The psalms are full of the rhythm of complaint and confidence. *It is really bad, but I remember when. I am sinking fast, yet in the past God was able to hold me.* So the litany instructs the mind of one who laments. God's surprising gifts keep taking blessed turns. The power of lament to evoke memory is one of them.

Prayer: *Thank you, God, for penetrating my complaints with memories of your faithfulness. Amen.*

Friday, March 17   Read Luke 20:41.

Jesus knew how to lament. In another version of this story of the entry into Jerusalem we hear him say, "O Jerusalem, Jerusalem, killing the prophets and stoning those who are sent to you! How often would I have gathered your children together as a hen gathers her brood under her wings, and you would not!" (Matt. 23:37) In Jesus' lament we catch something of the sensitivity to reality which he carried, painful though it was.

Lament sensitizes memory where we tend to forget. We need to be newly sensitive to all the ways we are impeding God's purposes, wounding and destroying God's good creation, violating the image of God in human beings and degrading the things of God in the universe. Lament energizes us to become agents of reconciliation and healing. Allowing ourselves to speak to God about the ugly pain of life as we see it opens us to see even more. Lament unlocks the hard places in our heart, making entryway for the gentle Spirit of Christ. Lament reopens ears to hear the penetrating word, causes tongues to speak it, and forms lives to make it visible in the world.

Lament not only reconnects us with the penetrating word of God, it molds us to be agents of that penetrating word by keeping us sensitive to the pain toward which the word surges with compassionate promise of wholeness.

Prayer: *O God, move us to cry out the pain of the world that we may never lose our sense of that pain and thus be emboldened to join you in relieving it. Amen.*

Saturday, March 18   Read Psalm 118:19-29.

Lamenters know how to praise and give thanks. The early verses of Psalm 118 are a recitation of despair—lament! But rising after it is a great note of confidence and celebration.

The psalm is one of the songs used in public worship as the people approached the holy places of the Temple. All the imagery of gates and building stones and a day of rejoicing speak of the gathering of God's people to celebrate the activity of the penetrating word in their midst. Here is where all the memory is gathered up, all the confidence restated, all the goodness of God recounted in spite of the list of difficulties which preceded and surrounded that moment of exhilaration and praise.

That we pair it with the story of the entry of Jesus into Jerusalem is no mistake. Circumstances surrounding that procession were certainly not such as to evoke great confidence and hope. The storm clouds of confrontation loomed on the horizon. Here was a moment of promise and hope about which to shout. Never mind what is to come in the next few hours. Let us enjoy the great moment that is ours now. "O give thanks to the Lord . . . for his steadfast love endures forever." That is the final word of faith that penetrates all the words of despair and fear, past and future. It sustains us both when we discern and when we cannot find the penetrating word of God.

Devotional exercise: *Carry verse 29 with you through the day, and say it several times aloud.*

March 19 (Palm Sunday)
Read Luke 19:28-40.

Here we go again! Palm Sunday—also called Passion Sunday—is the doorway to Holy Week with all its recitation of familiar events. We know the stories so well that we will tend to run ahead and get to the ending before we have read the whole beginning, much less lived the middle scenes.

The story cannot be fully comprehended without living through all its moods. This would not be a week of happy memories for Jesus and the disciples. It would be a week of passion and compassion. It would be a week in which there would be much to lament before they would break into the startling invitation to unequaled celebration.

We live from high moments of praise to deep depressions void of even the memory of praise. The Christ of the Jerusalem Road says the very stones shout though we are silent. The universe contains the penetrating word though we are deaf and blind to it and unable to speak it.

As we move through the week's lessons we will meet Jesus in the Garden of Gethsemane, lamenting. It is the same Jesus who rode into town triumphantly. The lamenting Jesus is the trusting Jesus, the Jesus who, in saying "Nevertheless . . . ," recovers the power of the penetrating word of God with him. So it is in all seasons of our lives. The penetrating word is our companion in the highs and lows of the roads of our lives.

Prayer: *Thank you, God, for the penetrating word always with us as guide and giver of power, crying out to us and speaking for us in our silence. Amen.*

| March 20-26, 1989 | **Elizabeth Canham, Obl. OHC†** |
| **Monday, March 20** | Read Isaiah 52:13–53:12. |

The Holy Week scriptures generate resistance because they invite us to pay attention to some of the more painful dimensions of human experience. If we choose to follow Christ through these last days of his life on earth, we have to confront a number of fear-filled questions about injustice, mortality, human frailty, and divine inaction. We resist this because it not only leads us back to the actual story of Christ but expresses our own fear.

The Suffering Servant songs of Isaiah plunge us into the ambiguity of human life. These poems, sometimes seen as expressing the grief of Israel collectively and sometimes as the experience of a single individual, were soon embraced by the Christian church. The Christ, whom God exalted and lifted up, was despised, rejected, bruised, chastised, oppressed, and led like a lamb to the slaughter. Jesus, the Suffering Servant, did not escape the indignity, injustice, and evil present in the world he came to redeem, and God did not "rescue" him.

Jesus consented to a risk-filled living out of God's will. His daily yes to vulnerability and obedience opened up the possibility of new levels of trust for those who followed. The suffering of God's Servant became the means of freeing others from evil and establishing righteousness. It did not answer all the painful questions but made it possible to live them with integrity.

Prayer: *Creator God, give me courage to live the difficult questions and to risk the future with hope. Amen.*

---

† Episcopal priest; author and workshop/retreat leader in spiritual direction; program director, Holy Savior Priory, Pineville, South Carolina.

Tuesday, March 21   Read Hebrews 5:7-9.

The Gospel writers give us glimpses of Jesus at prayer. From them we learn that he wept, groaned in spirit, and struggled with temptation. The author of Hebrews is even more bold in describing the "loud cries and tears" which sometimes accompanied the prayers of Jesus and the obedience he learned through suffering. The picture which emerges reveals him deeply engaged with life at all levels and courageously responsive to his vocation.

The transitoriness and frailty of human life is emphasized by the reference to "the days of his flesh," and undoubtedly the agony in Gethsemane was in the writer's mind. In the garden Jesus offered up, in a representative and sacrificial way, the anguish of all people at times of extreme need. He confronted the fear of death, asking God to remove the cup, but finally consented to the divine will. In this terrible struggle the human Jesus learned obedience to God's will through the suffering he endured.

Maturity or "perfection" in human character is not static but develops through the responses we make to life's constantly changing circumstances. We are told in Luke 2:52 that "Jesus increased in wisdom and in stature" through obedience to earthly parents and God. The wholehearted embracing of life's ambiguities and responsibilities, along with the relinquishing of self-interest, made it possible to speak of his "being made perfect." Living each day attentive to God's voice is the means by which we identify our fear, pray our anguish, and grow to full stature as those created in the divine image.

Devotional exercise: *Consider areas in which God is calling you to growth through obedience.*

Wednesday, March 22   Read Hebrews 4:14-16.

The compassion of Jesus, our great high priest, gives nerve to us as we face life's vicissitudes. In Christ, God shares our human weakness, experiences the frailty of our resolves, and receives the full impact of evil and pain. His vigorous, realistic response to human experience gives hope to our endeavors because he literally suffered-with us. The temptations of Jesus spanned the full range common to all people, and his sinless dealing with them enables us to envision God's way. Like us, he struggled with the desire to give willful consent to sin and the willingness to remain steadfastly obedient to God.

However, while the compassionate Christ reveals the possibility of living in harmony with God's purposes, his obedience throws into sharp relief our sinfulness. That could lead to despair if we did not also have the promise of mercy and grace held out to us. We are invited to approach God confidently, not because we have attained perfection but because grace draws us. Mercy is God's free gift for our failure, sin, and disobedience. The future is assured too. Not only does the penitent find forgiveness but "grace to help in time of (future) need."

As Holy Week progressed, the intensity of suffering increased. Jesus confronted the Establishment by a deliberate, provocative act on Palm Sunday and a violent attack on consumerism in the temple. He worried his disciples, challenged the people, upset social structures, and caused fear in political authorities. And in Gethsemane, aware of the consequences of his actions, he said, "Your will be done!"

Prayer: *Living God, help me to discern your will and to say yes to life. Amen.*

March 23 (Maundy Thursday)

Read John 18.

The author of the fourth Gospel portrays the cross as the throne from which Christ reigns and, in so doing, plays down some of the more humiliating aspects of the Passion. He does not record the agony in Gethsemane or the cry of dereliction from the cross. Instead, he offers us a series of vivid character sketches which reveal a variety of human responses to Christ. These portraits are painted in such a way that we are caught up in the drama and compelled to ask ourselves where we stand.

Judas, the betrayer, puts us in touch with one of the most devastating human emotions. We can only guess at his motives, but we can certainly know what Jesus felt as the trusted friend switched allegiance to collude with evil. Simon Peter, first impetuously defending but soon denying Jesus, added to the sense of loneliness and pain. The non-comprehending Annas and Caiaphas made clear the distance between the message of Jesus and religious orthodoxy. Pilate, vacillating, asks, "What is truth?" and then sentences to death the Truth standing before him. It is all too easy to see ourselves on the side of Jesus as we read the story, but more honest to search our hearts for evidence of betrayal, denial, obtuseness, and vacillation.

The conversation between Pilate and Jesus focuses on the nature of kingship, and it is clear from the narrative that a role reversal has taken place. Pilate is on trial, and Jesus remains free from the shackles of fear and compliance with evil. The question being asked, then and now, is, What kind of authority does Christ exercise in your life?

Devotional exercise: *In imagination, become the characters in the story and look at Jesus from their perspective. Do you find any connections with them in your own experience?*

March 24 (Good Friday)

Read John 19.

After several attempts to escape responsibility for the death of Jesus, Pilate handed him over to be crucified. The designation "King of the Jews" angered those who cried out for his death for they wanted no part in kinship with him. From the cross, Jesus drew into a relationship of mutual love and support his mother and the beloved disciple. Earlier he had called into being a community based on love to continue his work in the world (John 13–17). The new commandment to love one another as he had loved them was sealed by the final outpouring of his love in death.

The humanity of Jesus is expressed in the words "I thirst." But more than human mortality is implied by his final words. "It is finished" is a cry of triumph, consummation, and fulfillment, not a despairing groan that death had won. All that he came to accomplish in his earthly life was now complete. Lifted up, exalted on the cross, he would now draw all people to himself. Eternal life, a quality of life described as abundant, was now available to all, for "As Moses lifted up the serpent in the wilderness, so must the Son of man be lifted up, that whoever believes in him may have eternal life" (John 3:14-15).

Two more portraits are offered. Joseph of Arimathea, a member of the Sanhedrin and a secret disciple, risked himself by asking for the body of Jesus. Nicodemus, the Pharisee who first came to Jesus by night, brought embalming spices. Together they dignified Jesus' body, burying him according to custom. It all seemed quite final.

Suggestion for prayer: *Remember in prayer those who are suffering the loss of a loved one and all for whom hope of resurrection is not a reality. Pray for all who take the gospel where it is not usually heard.*

Saturday, March 25   Read Psalm 22;
                                          Isaiah 65:17-25.

Holy Saturday marks a period of waiting when time is suspended between the anguish of the crucifixion and the triumphant joy of Easter morning. This day reminds us that we live in a tension between pain and pleasure, loss and fulfillment, death and life. Consent to live the tension and to resist escape into premature celebration is an important part of growth.

Psalm 22 expresses the sense of abandonment which God's people experience both collectively and individually. The absence of any sense of divine presence is excruciatingly difficult to endure, and the temptation to pretend things are different is strong. The psalmist tells it like it is and asks a question, "My God, my God, why hast thou forsaken me?" These words came readily to the lips of Jesus in his agony on the cross. He spoke the truth of his experience and was honest in his prayer. The psalms encourage us to be real. They encourage us to sing of hope and joy and to express to our Creator the feelings of fear, rage, and disappointment that are an inevitable part of being human. Frequently the outpouring of pain leads to new perceptions of reality. In the course of genuine expression of feeling, healing takes place.

The new heavens and new earth described by Isaiah point to the future hope that belongs to God's people. Harmony, peace, and plenty are the birthright of the called-out community. Keeping the vision before us enables us to live authentically in the "not yet" time.

Suggestion for prayer: *Write your own psalm expressing the feelings that are real for you at this time.*

Sunday, March 26 (Easter)
Read John 20:1-18.

One of the motifs running through the post-resurrection stories is initial non-recognition of Jesus. It is as though a refocusing needs to take place before old ways of looking give way to the vision of faith. After Mary Magdalene discovered the empty tomb and told the disciples, she remained in the garden, consumed by grief. When Jesus first spoke, asking the reason for her tears, there was no sign of recognition. Only when he spoke her name did she experience his living presence.

It is all too easy to miss the reality of resurrection because we see only what we expect to see. The disciples' despairing gaze backwards had to be redirected to the future with all its hopes and obligations. A new possibility of relationship was opened up by the death and resurrection of Jesus—a relationship rooted in faith. The personal word of Christ transformed Mary's grief into inexpressible joy, but she had to learn not to cling to her preconceived notions of relationship. Letting go of the past so that there was room for Christ in the present meant new life for her.

On this day of celebration the risen Christ comes to take away our blindness so that we can see and know and share his risen life. Thomas, who moved beyond the honest expression of doubt as the Christ of faith exploded into his consciousness, offers us a model. As we allow the Mystery of a God who lives in and through us to take hold of our beings, all we can do is fall at the feet of the living, loving, compassionate one crying, "My Lord and my God!"

Prayer: *Risen Lord, open my eyes to see your presence in the world you made. Help me to share your risen life with all I meet, that together we may celebrate the joy and hope of believing. Amen.*

OBEYING GOD

March 27–April 2, 1989   **Avery Brooke†**
Monday, March 27   Read Psalm 2:10-12.

We are still caught up in the joy of Easter, and it is hard, but suitable, to turn our minds to a subject such as obeying God. Christ has obeyed his Father. How may we obey Christ?

In many ways, each of our lives is a mirror of the biblical story of God's people. Like Adam and Eve, we too were once innocent and cared for. In our personal gardens of Eden we were babies and knew nothing of obedience or disobedience. We cooed and gurgled and were fed and held and loved. But as toddlers, we had to begin to learn to obey. It was simple as long as we did obey, but there came a time when we were tempted to disobey, and we did. And then, like Adam and Eve, we were ashamed and hid and tried to pretend it was all right. But it wasn't.

One of the ways that the people of the Old Testament tried to obey God was to remind themselves of the wrath of God if they disobeyed. As Christians we know that we are forgiven, yet it is good for us to be reminded of God's righteous anger. At the very least it brings us up short and pulls us out of our little worlds, our drifting into not caring and thinking it doesn't matter. It is like being awakened by a loud noise. Reading of the wrath of the Almighty reminds us that obeying God does matter.

Even in the joy of Easter, we remember that obeying God matters so much that Christ died for us.

Prayer: *Help us, Lord, to always remember what you have done for us, so that in remembering we may love you, and in loving you, we may obey you. Amen.*

---

† Author, teacher, and spiritual director, Norton, Connecticut.

Tuesday, March 28   Read John 20:24-30.

When we are conscious of God's presence, faith is strong, and we feel that we can do all things through him who strengthens us (see Phil. 4:13). But often, for hours, days, weeks, even years, God seems distant and faith is weak. It is not as easy then to obey God.

What do we do when faith is weak? It helps to realize that far from being cast out for his lack of faith, Thomas remained one of the twelve close followers of Jesus. Jesus may have wished that Thomas had more faith, but he also helped him to believe.

"Blessed are those who have not seen and yet believe," says Jesus in today's reading. Weak as our faith may be, we are blessed by what little we have. It is good to remember this. To scold ourselves for our weak faith makes matters worse, not better.

What matters is not the amount of our faith but how we use it. Do we hide our light—little as it may be—under a bushel basket, or do we use it to light the way? Faith that is unused grows dim. For every touch of faith granted to us, for every grace from God, for every perception shown by the Spirit, for every forgiveness given by Christ, we should, in some way, no matter how inadequate, respond. The kingdom of God, Christ had said, is like a mustard seed, a very tiny seed that grew into a large tree (Mark 4:30-32). But we have to plant that seed, to respond to the faith we have been given.

Prayer: *Lord Jesus, you know our weakness and our little faith. Help us to use what you have given us and to so increase in faith and love that in our gratitude obedience becomes joyful. Amen.*

Wednesday, March 29 Read John 20:19-21.

"As the Father has sent me," said Jesus, "even so I send you."

Jesus was speaking to the disciples, and the disciples went into the world as they had been asked. They preached and healed and taught and loved. Through the disciples, others came to know Jesus, and they brought the good news to yet more. And finally it came to us.

We, too, are sent. For most of us the mission on which we are sent is not as clear-cut as it was with the first disciples. We often feel awkward about preaching and teaching. Very few of us have been instruments of miraculous healing, and we are never as loving as we know we should be. On the other hand, simply by living as Christians we all have some experience of being sent. We all witness and teach something of Christianity to family, friends, and neighbors; and we pray for their healing when they are sick.

It is usually in loving that we have the greatest opportunity of being sent, and when we lose ourselves in love and in sharing someone else's joys and sorrows, we often discover that we have become stronger than we thought we could be. Love empowers. We find ourselves doing things—good things—that we would find too hard to do for ourselves alone. It is suddenly easier to pray, easier to love God, easier to be obedient. And we know that we gain strength both from Jesus who sent us and from those to whom we have been sent.

Prayer: *Lord Jesus, help us to remember that you have sent us into the world to do your work. Help us to forget ourselves in loving and serving you and our neighbors. Amen.*

Thursday, March 30   Read Acts 5:27-29.

Our ideas of how we should behave come to us from many sources: from our parents and those who bring us up, from teachers in school and church, from childhood friends and adult friends. We learn how we should behave as we read the Bible and hear it preached and taught. We learn from the example of other Christians, both known and read about.

Usually the only inner conflict we have about what we have been taught is between our desire to obey and our temptation to disobey. But sometimes two aspects of what we have been taught is good pull us in two different directions. So it was when Jesus healed people on the Sabbath. This was not considered "good" by the leading religious teachers of the time. So it was when the early Christians were told to call Caesar God. So it was also when, in today's reading, the apostles were told by the high priest to stop teaching people about Jesus. "We must," said Peter, "obey God rather than men."

In less dramatic ways, we face these choices every day. When we know that something is not loving, do we do it because all our friends do? When we are told to hate our enemies, do we hate them or do we pray for them and try to find out why they are acting as they do? When we are with a group of people who are not Christians and they propose actions we think God would disapprove of, do we speak up?

Prayer: *God, grant us the courage to obey you when everyone else seems to be telling us that it is better to obey them. Amen.*

Friday, March 31   Read Acts 6:30-32.

In today's reading, Peter says that the Holy Spirit is given to those who obey God. Those words, coming as they do at the very end of Peter's speech, are easy to overlook. They are slightly puzzling, and so our minds are apt to take them simply as Peter's "amen" to what has gone before. Peter has stated that they were witnesses to Jesus' death "to give repentance" and "forgiveness of sins" and that the Holy Spirit was also a witness and so, in a sense, it is the Holy Spirit's "amen" rather than Peter's. But then, almost as an afterthought, Peter adds that the Holy Spirit is given to those who obey God.

What do those words mean? Surely, we need the aid of the Holy Spirit *before* we obey God, not after.

It helps to think back to earlier in Acts (Acts 1:4-14). Here Jesus, about to go to his Father, told his disciples to stay in Jerusalem and wait for the Holy Spirit. And the disciples obeyed, going to the upper room and devoting themselves to prayer.

There are times in our lives when the Spirit makes clear to us what we should do and empowers us to do it. There are other times when we may only wait and pray in obedience to some of Jesus' last instructions to his disciples, trusting that in God's own time the Spirit will come also to us.

Prayer: *Lord, grant us the strength to do what we know we should do, the patience to wait for the Spirit's guidance, and the power to do those things that will in due time be made clear to us. In Jesus' name we ask. Amen.*

Saturday, April 1   Read Revelation 1:4-5.

The words I wish us to concentrate on are simply: "Jesus Christ, the faithful witness." Our focus has shifted from our own obedience to Christ's obedience.

To be faithful is to be perfectly obedient. But what of the word *witness*? The disciples were witnesses to the life, death, and resurrection of Jesus. But to what did Jesus witness? And one can only answer, "To his Father."

We know only one story of Jesus' childhood. It was when his parents thought he was lost, but he was in the temple with the teachers. "Did you not know," he said to his parents, "that I must be in my Father's house?" (Luke 2:49) For all of his life, he was in his Father's house, "about his Father's business" (see KJV). In temptation, in prayer, in preaching, teaching, and healing, Jesus was "about his Father's business." He commissioned the disciples to also be about their Father's business. Before his death, he prayed, "My Father, if it be possible let this cup pass from me . . ." (Matt. 26:39). But it was not possible, and he submitted to his Father's will and was crucified.

Jesus' life is the supreme example of how a Christian's life should be lived in "faithful witness." But we are overwhelmed. It is too much. It is light years beyond us. We do not even know when, where, or how to begin.

Perhaps we should begin at the beginning. Although it is the Easter season, remember the infant Jesus lying in the manger while angels sing. But remember, too, all that lies before this baby who was to be a faithful witness. With the shepherds and kings we can fall on our knees and simply love him.

Prayer: *Father, help us to love your Son and in loving him learn to love you and our neighbor. Amen.*

Sunday, April 2　　　　　　　　　Read Revelation 1:5*b*-8.

In a number of places in the Gospels, Jesus warns us to be ready. The end, judgment, death, the Lord will come like a thief in the night—when we least expect it. But today's passage rings with immediate expectation: "Behold, he is coming!" And, in essence, the same verse goes on to say: "Everyone will see him, and those who hurt him will see him, and all the peoples of the earth will wail. Even so" (AP).

There is a tremendous difference between today's reading and the psalm we read on Monday. No one is warned of the coming wrath of God; instead everyone will simply see Christ. We will see Christ and we will see ourselves in the light of Christ. All of our sins, big and little, our selfishness, self-centeredness, everything that we have made excuses for or hidden or denied will be clear and seen in the light of Christ.

I have always loved the next to the last verse in the Bible as rendered in the King James Version: "Even so, come, Lord Jesus" (Rev. 22:20). In shorter form it is in today's reading: "Even so." Even though I shrink at the thought of seeing my unloving and self-centered nature in the clear light of Christ, to receive his love and forgiveness I must will his coming. These words are the last call to obedience: "Even so, come, Lord Jesus."

Prayer: *Help us to be ready for your coming, Lord. But if we are not ready, even so, come Lord Jesus. Amen.*

FOLLOW ME

April 3-9, 1989   **Phyllis R. Pleasants†**
Monday, April 3   Read Acts 9:1-9.

Jesus calls the most unlikely people to follow him. A proud, self-sufficient, zealous, devout Saul decides he knows how to deal with the Christian heresy and receives authority to carry out his plan. But blind, helpless, and stunned, Saul is at the mercy of others to lead him into the city he planned to take by storm.

In the midst of Saul's proud certainty, Jesus dramatically intervened. If we would only listen, would we hear the risen Lord saying to us, "Why are you persecuting me? Why are you persecuting me with your strategies, power plays, programs, doctrines, and meetings? Why are you persecuting me?"

Sometimes, devotion to our own plans to protect God leaves us blind, helpless, stunned, and utterly at the mercy of others. If we would listen, we, too, would hear the risen Lord say, "You will be told what you have to do. I will tell you what to do. It is my will that is to be done, not yours."

Jesus calls the most unlikely people. Perhaps those who seem most devout are the most unlikely of all. As we allow our lives to become centered in Christ instead of ourselves, even the most unlikely people can respond to Jesus' call.

Suggestion for meditation: *In silence listen for Jesus' call to you today. In the midst of your service for God, is Jesus calling you to listen to be told what to do?*

---

† Ph.D. candidate, Southern Baptist Theological Seminary, Louisville, Kentucky.

Tuesday, April 4   Read Acts 9:10-20.

Jesus not only calls the most unlikely people to follow him, but he calls people to the most unlikely tasks.

Ananias couldn't believe what he was hearing. He must have had a very special relationship with the Lord to feel free to remind the Lord who Saul of Tarsus really was!

Think about the task Ananias was called to do. What would be our response if the Lord told us to go and be the vehicle for God's grace, healing, and instruction to the person who had come to persecute us? What would be our response if we were told the person we had doubted could ever be a follower was the Lord's own chosen instrument to spread the word throughout the world? Would we willingly embrace being a footnote in the history of someone else's life?

Ananias went quietly, obediently, and immediately to do what the Lord had called him to do. He recognized that Saul was not the only chosen instrument of the Lord in this situation. He did not question the Lord's choices but faithfully followed.

Verse 20 records that Saul was soon "proclaiming Jesus publicly in the synagogues. . . . [and] all who heard were astounded"(NEB). How many more Sauls would there be to proclaim Jesus as Lord if we would be willingly, joyfully obedient to the unlikely tasks to which Jesus calls us. Truly all would be astounded.

Prayer: *Enable us by your grace, O God, to be centered in you so that we may be vehicles of your grace, healing, and instruction instead of satisfying our own egos and calling it ministry in your name. Through Jesus Christ our Lord we pray. Amen.*

Wednesday, April 5   Read Psalm 30:4-12.

Our confidence in our ability to provide for ourselves will be our undoing. When self-sufficiency, a necessary finite virtue, becomes an ultimate value for us, we turn away from God.

"I was so carefree I thought I could never be shaken!" (AP) How human that is. We become so self-confident we take life for granted; blessings are no longer accepted as gifts, but expected as entitlements. We become so smug when things are going our way we assume life owes us a healthy return on what we see as our investment. According to the psalmist, God turns away in order to shock us into recognition of our dependence upon God.

Undergirding the lament of God's absence in this psalm is the certitude of God's providence. While viewing God as the author of troubled circumstances, the psalmist testifies to God's overwhelming care to stay in relationship with God's creation. "Tears may linger at nightfall but joy comes in the morning" (NEB). God is personally involved in all our circumstances offering us the opportunity for deep communion.

This psalm, sung in the corporate worship of both the Hebrew nation and the early church, issues a clarion call to our corporate context also. Whether as a prayer group, local church, or denomination, our pride in our self-sufficiency, especially when it is self-sufficiency disguised as humility, is the beginning of our demise.

Only when we confess God as our God can we experience the assurance of God's care even in the midst of chastening experiences. Only when we are willing for God to be God instead of self being God can we begin to follow.

Suggestion for meditation: *Listen in the silence of this time for where in either your individual or corporate context God is trying to lead you to stop depending on yourself and begin trusting God.*

Thursday, April 6   Read John 21:1-14.

In the bewilderment following the crucifixion and resurrection, Peter and some of the other disciples go back to Galilee. One day Peter announces he is going fishing, and the others join him. In the midst of their labors, the Lord, unrecognized at first, calls to them from the shore.

How like the first-century disciples are the twentieth-century disciples! Life is confusing. There are spiritual highs and incredibly mundane lows. The kingdom just isn't working out the way we thought it would. While we wait for God to show up and straighten things out, we return to whatever it was we were doing before the last encounter. For the first-century disciples it was fishing. For us it may be committee meetings, education, administration, visitation, career advancement, or anything to take our mind off our bewilderment that things just aren't turning out the way we thought they would.

We toil all night, so to speak. We labor and labor, spin our wheels going nowhere on a treadmill we call life. Into the midst of our labor, usually unrecognized, comes the Lord calling to us to follow his directions. "Cast your net on the other side, turn around, head in a different direction, follow me." In the following suddenly we recognize the Lord, and he greets us as we come to him with sustenance often found in the breaking of bread.

Once again the realization seeps in that we have been following our selves, depending on our own strength and vision, and we need to be redirected. Following is a constant process of being called to from the shore and being redirected.

Prayer: *You come into the void of our lives, O God, and fill it with your presence if we have the eyes of faith to see and the ears of faith to listen. Redirect us to you. Through Christ our Lord we pray. Amen.*

Friday, April 7   Read John 21:15-17.

Can't you see Peter now? He is too busy trying to make this fishing venture work to recognize who is telling him to pitch the net to the other side of the boat. He is doing everything he can to try not to lose the fish they have suddenly netted when the beloved disciple says, "Peter, it's the Lord." Impulsive Peter drops everything, throws on his clothes, jumps in, and madly splashes to shore ahead of everyone else. He wants to be with Jesus more than anything.

In spite of Peter's dramatic response, Jesus begins questioning Peter's devotion. Three times—"Peter, do you love me?" Can't you see Peter now? All the self-sufficiency gone. He couldn't even catch fish on his own! Now his Lord is questioning his love. He can't even love on his own! "Peter, do you love me?" No bravado now. Just the desperate plea, "Lord, you know everything; you know I love you."

We are the Peters of today, charging ahead, doing what we think is an extravagant show of devotion, splashing madly to be first to Jesus. But in the midst of what we think is our obvious love comes the haunting question, "Do you love me? If you do love me, then I have a task for you to do. Stop trying to be first. Feed my sheep. Take care of others, nurture them, tend to them as I would, if you love me."

How extravagant is God's grace! Although we repeatedly let God down, God, who loves us enough to die for us, trusts us with a task, calling us once again to follow. "Do you love me? Then feed my sheep."

Suggestion for meditation: *Reflect on how you can love Jesus today in others.*

Saturday, April 8   Read John 21:18-19.

"He said this to indicate the manner of death by which Peter was to glorify God. Then he added, 'Follow me' " (NEB). Death glorifying God? That is the ultimate "follow me," isn't it? We think, especially during times of devotion, "Yes, Lord, we will follow you even unto death." We mean it fervently at the time. However, we will not do it; we will not even recognize the need to do it unless we are willing to die to self first. The call to follow is always accompanied by predictions of death—the death of our false self in order for us to be the self God created us to be. Only as we stop living for self will we become centered on God and detached enough to be able to discern a situation that requires being faithful even unto death.

Death of self comes when we no longer fear for our lives, jobs, property, or sacred honor. Death of self comes when we learn to live as if opposition no longer exists because it no longer defines us. Death of self is a process of growing detachment from ego and increasing involvement in the ultimate reality of God. Death of self is a process of letting go of our ability to strategize, formulate, determine the outcome. It is trusting God while working as hard as we can for truth as best as we can discern it.

If our false self has already died, we will not fear physical death. We will face death not with our own courage or our own strength but with God's. We will be centered in God, willing to follow no matter what the call. Such is the death which glorifies God.

Prayer: *Dear God, we so thoughtlessly cry, "Yes, we are able!" Forgive us for our cheap discipleship that entails no cost. By your grace break us, and shape us again after your will. Through Christ our Lord we pray. Amen.*

Sunday, April 9   Read Revelation 5:11-14.

Praise is at the heart of our worship, our communion with almighty God. In our passage for today there is a crescendo of praise starting in verse 9 that begins with the elders and ends with all of creation praising God. The Lamb is proclaimed worthy as God's chosen vehicle for revealing God's self. It is the Lamb that will reveal to us the future.

What does the Lamb reveal? The future is in God. The one who calls the most unlikely people to the most unlikely tasks holds the future. The God who turns away in order to allow us to turn to God is the future. The one who comes to us in the midst of our vain toiling and redirects our labor is directing the future. The one who leads us through the excruciating pain of dying to self is the one who created us for eternal praise. The Book of Revelation testifies to the faith that the future is God.

To our eyes, raw, unmitigated power appears to be in charge as creation is ravished and destroyed. The eyes of faith can see that God is at work bringing the world to God's future. Raucous voices use and abuse people in order to be noticed, to be powerful, worshiped and adored. The mouth of faith praises God even when God appears to be absent from the horizon. The ears of faith hear the "myriads upon myriads" (NEB) in the presence of God praising God, also. The One who calls us to follow even unto death is not revealing to us a cosmic joke at our expense. Rather, the Lamb reveals through his own death and resurrection that all creation is being directed to praise God. The future is directed by God, within God; the future *is* God.

Suggestion for meditation: *Spend at least five minutes in uninterrupted praise of God through whatever vehicle you choose—prayer, song, writing, sketching. Listen. In the silence do you hear the "myriads upon myriads" praising God, also?*

THE LORD IS MY SHEPHERD

April 10-16, 1989   **Carroll Gunkel†**
Monday, April 10   Read Psalm 23.

Of the many images in scripture, that of the shepherd has become the most obscure for twentieth-century people. Fewer and fewer people live in rural areas, and even for those who live on farms the day of the solitary shepherd has passed.

State of the art fencing has made it possible for the farmer to safely confine the sheep. Modern transportation enables the shepherd to get to the flocks quickly. Rather than the slingshot, the shepherd may carry a high-powered rifle as a defense against predators. The biblical image of the shepherd has been vastly altered by twentieth-century reality.

But has the image really been lost? Just because we do not regularly encounter shepherds does not mean the picture fostered by the word *shepherd* has changed.

Shepherd causes us to think of one who cares.

Shepherd conjures a vision of faithfulness.

Shepherd affirms dependability.

Shepherd is synonymous with willingness to sacrifice.

I have come to the previously noted conclusions about the nature of a shepherd from reading the Shepherd's Psalm. Further, I believe I have seen the quintessential shepherd in Jesus of Nazareth. When I say, "The Lord is my shepherd," it is the face of Jesus that shines through the words.

Prayer: *For gentle leading into green pastures of blessing where every want is assuaged, for cool water that fills and invigorates the soul, for the shepherd's directing staff that both chastens and comforts, for your holy name, the very sound of which is a call to righteousness: Good Shepherd, thank you. Amen.*

---

† Senior pastor, Bethesda United Methodist Church, Bethesda, Maryland.

Tuesday, April 11   Read John 10:22-26.

Jesus was frequently placed on the defensive by his critics. Such was the case in today's lesson; however, as was also frequently the case, he deftly rebutted his detractors.

For what reasons did the religious establishment refuse to accept Jesus? Perhaps it was because he didn't meet their expectations of what the Messiah should be. Jealousy about his great ministry may have been another reason for their spiritual myopia. Intellectual or spiritual arrogance may have led them to question his ministry.

Whatever the cause, confusion reigned. His enemies, for that is what they perceived themselves to be, did not know what to do with him . . . nor do we. Jesus' detractors remind me of a young woman who plaintively said to me, "I don't know what to do with Jesus. I don't understand him." My response—perhaps a simplistic one—was, "Don't try to understand him; just love him." My answer was merely an echo of our Lord's observations in today's reading. Jesus was sure he knew why so many of the religious leaders of his day challenged him: they were not his sheep. If they had been his sheep, they would have believed him and followed him, for sheep are able to discern the voice of their shepherd and respond.

How are we doing with Jesus? Do we know him as sheep know their shepherd? What do we believe *about* him? Do we believe *in* him? Are we willing to *follow* him? And perhaps, most importantly, does Jesus know *us* as one of his sheep?

Prayer: *O God, amid the confusion of our world and time, help us to hear always the voice of the shepherd. And hearing, may we believe; and believing, may we follow him in whose name we pray, even Jesus Christ our Lord. Amen.*

Wednesday, April 12　　　　Read Revelation 7:1-12.

Are you saved?

This question has become idiomatic in contemporary Protestantism, evoking memories of evangelical Christianity's penchant for "saving souls" through the preached word.

Are you saved?

This question recalls images of tent meetings on hot summer evenings, a camp organ rasping out evangelistic hymns as persons are invited to walk the proverbial sawdust trail.

Are you saved?

For most mainline churches, the question is either an anachronism of a bygone era or an irrelevant theoretical issue to be carefully pondered by theologians.

Are you saved?

For John the Evangelist, the question was neither anachronistic nor theoretical; it was simply and significantly asking who would be saved. The Revelation indicates that 144,000 persons would be saved. Subsequent verses indicate that in addition to the 144,000 there will be an *unnumbered* multitude of saved souls arrayed before the throne of God.

Are you saved?

Those multitudes *were* saved. They were saved through the blood of the Lamb, a sacrificial offering for the sins of all earth's people.

Are *you* saved? Some may answer no. Others may not be sure. John has helped us all answer yes. We are saved. We are saved as Christians have been saved for two thousand years, by the Lamb of God, Jesus Christ.

Prayer: *Blessing and glory and wisdom, thanksgiving and honor and power and might, be to our God forever and ever. Amen.*

Thursday, April 13   Read Revelation 7:13-17.

If you were to travel in the north of England and do your own driving, you would need to remember two things. The first thing to remember, of course, is that you must drive on the left side of the road. The second is that you will undoubtedly encounter many sheep in the dales and across the moors, and by law the sheep have the right-of-way. Should you strike a sheep, you are liable to be fined, you must pay any damages to the car, and you must reimburse the owner of the sheep.

The driver quickly discovers that not only do sheep have the right-of-way, but they seem to know it. They amble across the road or walk leisurely in the center; they whimsically change direction; although usually slow-moving, they can periodically bolt into a run. Road shoulders are favorite resting places.

It can be argued that such behavior merely reinforces the reality that sheep aren't very smart. It may be asserted that such behavior is the result of great trust, for whether this is an inherent trait or a learned characteristic, we cannot deny that sheep are trusting animals.

We who are God's sheep are called to be just as trusting. After all, hasn't it been said of God's Son, the Good Shepherd Jesus, that "he shall wipe away every tear from our eyes and death shall be no more"? Isn't this but another way of saying that we are protected, just as the sheep of England's northern lands are protected? There is one difference, however. The sheep are protected by law, and we are protected by love.

Prayer: *Fearful and fretful though we may be, we ask you, O Lord God, to remind us of your unfailing care in life and in death, to the end that such a reminder will enable us to trust you in all seasons and in all circumstances. Through the same Jesus Christ who trusted you on the cross, and in Joseph's garden, and throughout eternity. Amen.*

Friday, April 14
Read Psalm 127:1-2;
Matthew 6:25-33.

Sheep are vulnerable creatures, perhaps as defenseless as any beings in nature. Their vulnerability is heightened during the dark hours of night when predators can strike with impunity. Only the diligence of the shepherd protects the flock.

We, like sheep, are also vulnerable, never more so than when we sleep. Sleep renders us oblivious to our immediate surroundings and makes us defenseless, as defenseless as sheep. Circumstances that are seemingly controllable during daylight threaten us and our loved ones.

In reality, we are not defenseless. As the ever-alert shepherd guards the flock through the darkness of the night, so does God guard us through darkness. The uncertainty fostered by the night becomes certainty under the control of God, to whom light and darkness are alike. It is true that sleep makes us incapable of controlling our lives, but how can we be so foolish as to believe that the mere presence of physical sunlight makes it possible for us to exercise control? We need the shepherd's care as much in the day as in the night; it's just that the darkness of night heightens our awareness of the need, while the light of day, coupled with human pride, fosters delusion.

Darkness is a blessing, and the blessing will become a miracle when it leads us to recognize our need for God's shepherding, night or day. Dawn, like the night, is a blessing, for each new dawn evokes the memory of the Shepherd's care.

Prayer: *Light of Light, cast out the darkness of night and darkness of sin so that we may walk in your reflected glory and so that your glory may be reflected in us. Amen.*

Saturday, April 15   Read Psalm 23.

What a marvelous picture is painted in the closing lines of the Twenty-third Psalm, "my cup runs over," thus affirming that not only does the Divine Shepherd provide for basic needs, but that same Shepherd has provided *more* than we need.

It has been said that once we have food, clothing, and shelter, everything else is an "I want." Most of us have probably reached the "I want" plateau, but more than that, we have probably reached the "cup running over" stage.

Physically, our bodies are miracles of both design and execution. Our hearts begin beating six months before we are born and, on the average, function well for more than the allotted three score and ten years. We are born with the organs and limbs that will serve us for the rest of our lives. Our minds are marvels of creativity. Physically and intellectually we have the ability to grow. Our cups overflow!

Materially, most of us are very well off. Beyond the essentials, we have enough money to buy luxury items. We engage in self-gratification and then rationalize our actions by noting that we give to charities. Our cups *do* run over, and we share the excess.

There is yet another way in which our cups overflow—they overflow with grace. God has seen to that. The psalmist has sung that mercy (grace), like goodness, shall follow us all of our days. Our cups run over with the grace of forgiveness through the Good Shepherd who gives us what we need and then gives us more than we need.

Prayer: *Creating and sustaining God, we acknowledge with joy that you fill our cups, indeed, fill them to overflowing. Thank you for caring about our physical and spiritual needs. In Jesus' name. Amen.*

Sunday, April 16   Read John 10:14-16, 27-30.

Unity is an elusive but essential quality. Coaches for athletic teams stress the need for unity. Political candidates call for unity in their election campaigns and pledge unity to their opponents should the latter prevail in the election. Parents know the importance of presenting a united front when facing difficult child-rearing decisions.

Jesus dealt with the ultimate in unity—unity between God and humankind. He said, "I and my Father are one." If anyone else but Jesus had made such an assertion, we would be appalled by the arrogance. But for Jesus it was just the natural result of the unique relationship he had with God.

He and his Father *were* one!

Throughout his life Jesus regularly sought God's will and then in total submission united his will with that of his Father.

He and his Father were *one*!

Who else could make such a claim? The majority of us truly desire to be one with God, but we allow personal considerations to intrude so that the oneness eludes us.

All is not lost however, for the same text that celebrates the unity of Jesus with God implies our unity with God. If Jesus and God are one, then it follows that we who are brothers and sisters of Christ are thereby united with God.

Jesus has built the bridge that has spanned the chasm between human and divine. That bridge was the cross, and it has established our unity with the Divine One. We must maintain that unity by doing as Jesus did, by saying to our Father, "Not my will but yours be done" . . . and meaning it.

Prayer: *O Divine One, as broken people in a broken world, we ask humbly for the blessing of being united to you through your Son who is one with you, to the end that as individuals and as a world, we may be made whole. Amen.*

THE PROMISE IN GOD'S LOVE

April 17-23, 1989   **Judith Freeman Clark†**
Monday, April 17   Read Psalm 145:13b-16.

It is comforting to believe that God keeps promises. Perhaps the most significant one is the promise never to leave us or desert us. In early childhood, we are taught that God is omnipotent and that God loves us unconditionally. It is that faithful love to which we turn as adults when we are confused, grieving, or troubled.

Imagine having a nurturing friend who gives us strength and encouragement, who soothes, comforts, and waits patiently day in and day out. This is the type of friendship that God extends.

The promise to love us *always*, to be unchanging and unwavering, is an eternal commitment. Nowhere but with God can we find a love like that. God can fill our empty places in our spirits, the void that remains despite frantic efforts to fill our days with work, play, and companionship.

"In all his promises the Lord keeps faith" (NEB). We know we can trust God, who is with us no matter what we say or do. We know God will never let us down.

These assurances are more than simple reminders of divine presence in our lives. God is kind, infinitely patient, and active in providing for our needs. God upholds us with an open and generous hand. God loves us vigorously, without reservation. And most important, God never breaks a promise.

Prayer: *God, we cannot comprehend the infinite quality of your love. Remind us to seek your comfort, strength, and quiet presence whenever we feel friendless, weary, or frightened. Amen.*

---

†Professional writer; member of St. John's Episcopal Church, Northampton, Massachusetts.

Tuesday, April 18   Read Psalm 145:17-21.

We usually envision God as a merciful figure who accepts us under any circumstances. This image is strengthened by New Testament teachings on which many of our twentieth-century Christian beliefs are based. That's why it is confusing to read Old Testament passages in which God is described as a vengeful, punishing entity.

Because of this conflicting imagery, some psalms can be misleading. "He fulfils their desire if only they fear him" and "The Lord watches over all who love him but sends the wicked to their doom" (NEB) are passages suggesting that God will destroy us if we displease God. How can we believe God cares *only* for converts or "good children"? If we trust this biased line of thinking, we are even more confused by New Testament descriptions of a loving Creator.

Old Testament verses of praise, as well as those which admonish, were written to describe more fully a God *who was yet to be revealed*. Through psalms, people voiced joy, fear, woe, thanks, wonder—all the emotions and feelings known to humanity. Psalm 145 depicts God the way ordinary people saw each other—with human capabilities and frailties. For modern times, the power of such an expression as this psalm rests in the spirit in which it was written. Like the ancients, we can know God without fully understanding God's nature. We can be grateful to God without being completely aware of God's intentions. Like so many expressions of trust and praise, this psalm is an enduring affirmation of God's splendid love.

Prayer: *God, as we lift our hopes to you, remind us that we owe all our bounty and our dearest joys to your gracious and merciful love. Amen.*

Wednesday, April 19   Read Acts 14:8-11.

When Paul looked at the lame man, he saw one thing—faith. And through that faith, the man was cured. This narrative is difficult to accept, maybe because the story is so simple. We deal with the bewildering complexities of modern life, but we fear an unquestioning faith in God's power to heal.

It *would* be miraculous if a lame person actually stood up and walked as described in Acts 14. But many of us would be uncomfortable with such a cure. Today, we minimize the role of faith in making people whole. If someone is healed and credits only faith, we demand scientific documentation based on medical expertise. Without such proof, we are suspicious and inclined to dismiss the healing incident as a hoax rather than a miracle.

But faith *does* play a central part in healing. Disease is controlled or eradicated via wonder drugs and complex treatment. The faith of thousands of researchers is responsible for these miracle cures. We rely on technology to make hospitals, nursing homes, and doctors' offices operate efficiently. These developments, born of faith in human ability, are proof of God's healing power.

There were no drugs, no special medical treatments, available to the lame man; there was only faith. But that was enough. And like the man who was healed, if we accept the possibility of being made whole by faith, it will be sufficient to our needs.

Prayer: *God, help us remember that you are always willing to make us whole, to heal us and to give us strength to walk unaided. Give us the faith we need to be healed each day. In Jesus' name. Amen.*

Thursday, April 20　　　　　　　Read Acts 14:12-18.

The depth of God's love often exceeds human comprehension. When Paul and Barnabas tried to explain this all-encompassing love, the people of Lystra did their best to understand, but it is easy to see why they remained uncertain. How often we are like those confused and wondering crowds who saw a lame man walk! Even when shown a sign as miraculous as healing, or when reminded of God's kindness in the form of rain and plentiful crops, the Lystrans were reluctant to believe. And although we try hard to be faithful, we often remain unconvinced of God's infinite power.

Swept along by the ruthlessness of contemporary life, it is difficult for us to maintain a simple belief in God's love. Like the people of ancient Lystra, we ignore signs of God's infinite caring. We continually forget that we owe all we have to the graciousness of a merciful God.

Over and over again, we are asked to rely on God's willingness to heal our weaknesses. As God gave the lame man ambulatory powers, God gives each of us physical strength, or intellectual capacity, or patience, or compassion. Each day our needs are met, in thousands of ways, by the love of God. We need only to believe in that love, without faltering, to turn "to the living God, who made heaven and earth and sea and everything in them" (NEB) and God will provide.

Prayer: *God, we know that, through you, all of our many needs are provided for. We are thankful and ask that you remind us daily of your unending love. Amen.*

Friday, April 21   Read John 13:31-35.

When Jesus met with his disciples for the last time, he tried to prepare them for his death. He asked that they show love to the entire world as proof of God's love for all humanity. He wanted their promise to continue his work when he no longer dwelt among them.

But, troubled by Jesus' words and manner, the disciples were afraid. They wanted assurances that he would not leave them. In their fear, they were deaf to his words, "I give you a new commandment: love one another; as I have loved you, so you are to love one another" (NEB).

If they had been able to listen, they would have understood that God's promise was being fulfilled. Jesus explained to his friends that if they found God's love in each other, they would not be bereft of his presence. He knew they could serve God best through love.

Sometimes we are like the disciples. Fear prevents us from hearing what others say, and we cannot take comfort in the love others show us because we are afraid. Most tragically, fear robs us of our ability to love others—or to love God.

Jesus offered God's healing love to his disciples *and* offers it to us. We can accept the message of that love as long as we are not afraid. Loving each other fulfills God's promise and reassures us that we have nothing to fear.

Prayer: *God, make us unafraid to reveal your promise to others, and help us find your promise revealed in our own lives. Amen.*

Saturday, April 22   Read John 13:31-35.

It was troubling for the disciples to hear Jesus say, "Where I am going, you cannot come" (NEB). Until then, Jesus had encouraged his friends to follow and had urged these friends to gather many other followers. Now, the situation was different. Soon, Jesus would leave them behind and he let his disciples know he depended on them to carry God's message into the world.

We are messengers no less than those who gathered during Jesus' farewell discourse. Like the disciples, we are called to love one another and to spread God's love in everything we do.

Jesus said, "As I have loved you, so you are to love one another" (NEB). This is not a simple task. But we are each called by God to follow this commandment despite our reluctance or lack of enthusiasm.

We have Jesus' life as a model of how to put God's love into practice: by caring for the least attractive and least powerful of those among us; by attending to people around us who may, in silence, ask for our help; by seeking opportunities to serve where others may refuse through ignorance, hostility, or selfishness.

Sometimes in the simplest act of listening we carry out God's will and show God's love, just as Jesus listened to the desires, hopes, and fears of his disciples. We have only to look to Jesus' example as a guide for how to show God's love.

Prayer: *Dear God, help us to find new avenues of service and prayer as we travel the roads of our lives fulfilling Jesus' commandments. Amen.*

Sunday, April 23   Read Revelation 21:1-6.

In Revelation, God's promise to create an ideal world is revealed: "The old order has passed away. . . . Behold! I am making all things new!" (NEB) God says that in this ideal dwelling place there will be no evil and suggests that there will be a time when people will have no problems.

To most of us, this utopian vision is a distant, unattainable dream. We know that millions of people have no permanent shelter and millions go to bed hungry at night. Reports of crime, misery, death, disaster, war and greed are constant reminders that we do little to make the world a more perfect place.

Reality aside, we all yearn for perfection, for lives filled with infinite joy and enduring peace. By telling us that "there shall be an end to death" (NEB), God is promising to crack the cycle of good and bad in life. God vows to replace this cycle with perfection—and although it is difficult imagery to grasp, God asks us to believe that it will be so.

In God's loving vision there is an ironclad guarantee. We are assured that our longing for perfection will be satisfied, our desire for harmony will be fulfilled. We are asked to believe this promise for humanity and to rejoice in the perfection of God's transforming love—for God's love makes all things new.

Devotional exercise: *God invites us to envision a perfect world. Today, take the first step toward making that vision a reality by treating those around you with love.*

AN AWESOME AND GRACIOUS GOD

April 24-30, 1989   **Roy I. Sano†**
Monday, April 24   Read Revelation 21:10, 22-27.

The Book of Revelation culminates in the vision of "a new heaven and a new earth." The vision depicts the fulfillment of God's creative and redemptive work. Descriptions of the "new Jerusalem" in Revelation 21:10, 22-27 must therefore be read within the contexts of the fuller picture (21:1–22:5) and seen within the sweep of salvation history which leads up to it in the Book of Revelation. The additional readings for the week fill out the vision.

In Revelation, we come face to face with a God who is holy and loving. Today, we consider the holiness of God in relation to nature and nations. Revelation describes creation under the sway of powers less than God. Because they are less than God, they cannot deliver the life and love, truth and peace, which only God can provide.

This God takes offense at the resulting sin and evil dominating creation. Through Christ and his saints, God goes on the offensive to recreate and reclaim the cosmos. Evil offers resistance. Despite setbacks and much suffering in the ensuing rounds of apparently unresolved conflict (chapters 6-19), God finally overturns the reign of sin and evil and thus rectifies what has gone awry (chapter 20-22, especially 21:27). Nations shall thus walk in accord with the radiance of God's holiness permeating the landscape (21:22-24) of the "holy city" (21:2). Hallelujah!

Prayer: *O God, I bow in reverence before your awesome acts. Despite all the sufferings in our day, I trust you as One who is rectifying all that is wrong in the world. Amen.*

---

†Bishop, Denver Area, The United Methodist Church, Denver, Colorado.

Tuesday, April 25   Read Revelation 21:10, 22-27.

The God we see in the climactic moment of the divine work is not only awesome but gracious. The God we meet is not only holy but loving. Thus we turn to God's gracious love toward nature and the nations which we can so easily neglect in the picture of the new Jerusalem (21:1–22:5).

Although the nations and their leaders will be cleansed of "abominations and falsehood" (21:27), this purging does not do away with their distinct gifts. While the glory of God will radiate a light in the new Jerusalem, there is also the glow of the nations and their leaders. The gates of the holy city will never be closed to the glory and honor which the nations and their leaders will bring into it (21:24-26). Thanks be to this gracious God! This openness embraces the Children of Israel (Jews) as well as the Gentiles whom the Apostles represent (21:12-14 and 7:1-12).

In order to insure life in its abundance for the diverse peoples, God's care reaches beyond the people to nature. God overcomes the "cussedness of creation" (22:3), the stage on which the nations build their cities and act out their history. The polluted waters which induce sickness and kill children, women, and men will bring forth life; the once-barren plants will bear fruit and nourish the people (22:1-5).

When we celebrate and welcome the distinct contributions of people and their nations, we therefore bear witness to the gracious openness of a loving God. As we purge creation of its pollution and renew its sustaining and healing powers, we thereby join the caring God in recreating the earth.

Prayer: *Hallowed be thy name, awesome yet gracious God! Thy kingdom come, thy will be done, on earth as it is in heaven. Amen.*

Wednesday, April 26   Read Acts 15:1-2, 22-29.

What we have seen of God's actions in nature and the nations applies to individuals. Today, we focus on the gracious outreach of a loving God toward those who are outside the fold. The writer of the Acts of the Apostles highlights this particular point as it applies to those who are different from the Jewish male adults who were the leaders of their people.

When the Holy Spirit descended upon the disciples at Pentecost, Peter proclaimed that "all flesh" would experience salvation. Barriers of race and gender, age and class, would be transcended (2:17-18).

This did not mean that differences would be obliterated. It is true that Paul said "There is neither Jew nor Greek, . . . neither slave nor free, . . . neither male nor female; for you are all one in Christ Jesus" (Gal. 3:28). We should be careful to read this as an affirmation of the unity we genuinely experience in Christ. But as we say, unity does not require uniformity. We do not all have to become the same at all points for us to be "one in Christ."

This becomes most evident in the early church's decision concerning circumcision. This was no easy decision, as is evident from the letters of Paul where the issue arises again and again. We can understand why. God, after all, commanded circumcision for the covenant people (Gen. 17). It had become a witness for those who had become people of God.

In Acts 15, we read of the joint decision that Gentiles were not required to bear the marks of the Jewish people of God. They could be Gentiles, without circumcision, and yet be God's people in the new covenant community.

Prayer: *Thanks be to you, gracious God, for your inclusive embrace which takes in our distinct identities regardless of race and gender, age and class. Amen.*

128

Thursday, April 27　　　　　Read Acts 15:1-2, 22-29.

The lectionary passages listed for any given week act like oases in the desert. We can draw from their springs and pools. Spread underneath the surface, however, is a reservoir fed by waters flowing from a nearby canyon or a distant mountain range, and fed from a cloudburst or a snowfall long since past.

Any full picture seen in a scripture passage must take into account the flow of the narrative within which it appears in the immediate context, as well as the wider sweep of God's creative and saving activities. Without the total picture we can draw unbalanced messages from the oasis of a given selection.

The acceptance of Gentiles with their distinct identities, therefore, cannot be read in isolation. That is to say, while God's gracious outreach and inclusive embrace welcome the distinct contributions of diverse peoples, the people involved nevertheless undergo changes. God is not only loving but holy.

When Peter argued against circumcising the Gentiles, he said to the gathering at Jerusalem, "[God] made no distinction between us and them, but cleansed their hearts by faith" (15:9). In the incident with Cornelius which made the point evident to him (Acts 10:1–11:18), Peter observed that repentance was involved when the Gentiles were "saved through the grace of the Lord Jesus" (Acts 15:11). Thus, while God works in and through our distinctive identities, we are cleansed of our sins when we turn to God (15:19) and trust in the grace of the Lord Jesus which saves us.

Prayer: *Even now, gracious yet holy God, I turn to you and entrust myself into your hands. Cleanse me by the grace of the Lord Jesus which saves me, even me. Amen.*

Friday, April 28   Read Acts 15:1-2, 22-29.

A lot more was involved than the issue of circumcision when the early church received Gentiles into the fold. That one issue was symbolic of much else in the Mosaic law. Peter said at the Jerusalem council, "Why do you make trial of God by putting a yoke upon the neck of the [Gentile] disciples which neither our fathers nor we have been able to bear?" (Acts 15:10)

Paul agreed (15:12). He wrote elsewhere that "Christ is the end of the law" (Rom. 10:4). But this can be misread. When Paul said, "We are discharged from the law, dead to that which held us captive" (Rom. 7:6), he went on to speak of a "law of the Spirit of life in Christ Jesus" (Rom. 8:2). In Paul's letters we are therefore not surprised that sections which proclaim the salvation in Jesus Christ are followed by sections calling Christians to service and ethical living.

While the Gentiles were not expected to live by certain standards which were not applicable to them in the Mosaic law, the apostles urged them to give witness to the healing and hallowing consequences of the Holy Spirit at work in their lives. Those who have studied these counsels notice reminiscences of the Mosaic law, as found particularly in Leviticus 17–18.

The early church departed from some ancient obligations as crucial as circumcision and the Sabbath, and yet, second, they drew upon the wisdom of their Jewish forebears. While affirming the unique contributions of the Gentiles and hence introducing changes, the early church also affirmed the enduring contributions in the spiritual heritage from the Jews. Thus as the holiness of God cleanses what is wrong in us all, the same God of love embraces all our unique gifts.

Prayer: *Just as you guided the early church in clarifying how you move among us, holy and gracious God, guide us in this day. Amen.*

Saturday, April 29   Read John 14:23-29.

Disciples are invited to bear witness to "the upward call of God in Christ Jesus" (Phil. 3:14), to the God who is bringing to pass "a new heaven and a new earth." Determining how this holy and gracious God is moving today, and how we are to follow, prompts much discussion and debate in the Body of Christ.

It is important that we bear in mind three foci in John 14:23-29; namely, love, the Holy Spirit, and peace. Because the quest will create tension within us and among us, we need love for each other. But the love emphasized here is interestingly our love of Christ and the Father. The point is well taken because knowledge of God and God's ways involves more than the head. It involves the heart and one's whole being. Without love of others, we cannot know their thoughts. So, too, with God. Hence, Jesus urges that we love him if we are to keep his word.

But more than an obligation is involved. He offers a promise. Jesus says the Holy Spirit "will teach you all things, and bring to your remembrance all that I have said to you." We can find encouragement in this Counselor who will guide us in the difficult task of making appropriate changes while continuing what is sound in our heritage, of keeping the gates open to the Gentiles while securing a place for Jewish contributions.

And thus, our hearts need not be troubled (14:27). The peace which comes from God is born of love. It is that perfect love which casts out our fear of conflict or of losing an argument.

Our discussions and debates about the will of God for Christians today are less likely to tear us up or dismember the Body of Christ if we love Jesus enough to hear his words, if we allow the Holy Spirit to teach us all things, and if we allow God's peace and composure to pervade our lives.

Prayer: *Teach us, Holy Spirit, to love you and to work for your peace. Amen.*

131

Sunday, April 30   Read Psalm 67.

We began the week by looking at the vision of God's climactic work in creating "a new heaven and a new earth." We saw the promise of God's holiness cleansing all peoples and embracing their distinct contributions (Rev. 21:10, 22-27).

Through the week, we have seen how God is creating signs of this ultimate promise. The community of faith will include a diversity of people bridging differences of race and gender, age and class, who have experienced the cleansing and healing of God's grace.

The precise details of what will be cleansed and thus removed, and what is continued and thus unchanged, is left open. The scriptural examples provided only the broad outlines (Acts 15:1-2, 22- 29).

But God is gracious to us and has blessed us. God's face has shone upon us. Our love for Jesus creates a readiness to hear his words. The Holy Spirit will counsel us in remembering what Jesus taught us. The peace God gives will create a composure within us so we can learn new truths (John 14:23-29). The knowledge we gain is not for possession by an inner circle. We are invited to make known on the earth God's saving power among all nations!

Prayer:

> *The righteous and true God has blessed us;*
> *Let all the ends of the earth fear this awesome God!*
> *The loving God, our God, has blessed us;*
> *Let all the peoples praise this gracious God! Amen.*

Triumphs Of Faith

May 1-7, 1989   **Talbert O. Shaw†**
Monday, May 1   Read Acts 16:16-34.

Obedient faith at times initially frustrates human designs and wishes. Indeed, our well-laid plans, even in response to divine call, may lead us into life-threatening situations. At such times faith may waver or even lead us to question why; or like Paul we may sing songs of faith in the night of our trials.

Paul made plans to preach in Asia, but he was forbidden by the Holy Ghost. His plans to preach in Bithynia were also changed by the Spirit. Although his intentions were motivated by obedient faith, they were still contrary to God's plan for his ministry at that time. Good intentions do not automatically represent God's will at crucial times in our pilgrimage. Obedient following involves responsive listening.

Paul responded to God's call to witness in Macedonia where severe trials awaited him and Silas, although they were sure that "the Lord had called us for to preach the gospel unto them" (KJV). Yes, "severe trials," even though they did all the right things: they kept the Sabbath holy by worship and prayer and even made disciples of Macedonians.

But Paul and Silas landed in jail after they were severely beaten. In apparent defeat, Paul could have asked, "Why are we suffering for our obedient response to God's call? God, where are you?" But Paul and Silas sang songs of praise in that Philippian jail. Then the prison gates were opened. Obedient faith will indeed triumph over trials.

Prayer: *Father God, teach us how to listen and learn your will and how to follow your call in spite of ourselves. Amen.*

---

† President, Shaw University, Raleigh, North Carolina.

Tuesday, May 2   Read Acts 16:16-34.

Christians are called to discipleship, that is, to personal salvation as well as to evangelical witnessing. Equally important to our efforts to achieve deep, personal relationships with God is the divine mandate to make disciples of others. But it is important that our witnessing be in keeping with God's plan. For no human effort without divine benediction will achieve lasting results.

Paul had some evangelistic plans for Asia. But on his way there, God disrupted his plans. Perhaps people in that country were not ready for the gospel. Paul himself might not have been ready for what awaited him in Asia. Whatever the reason(s), God said no to Paul's well-developed evangelistic plans.

Did Paul recoil in counterproductive self-pity? Did he nurture debilitating doubt regarding his call to discipleship? Isn't it natural to feel let down when we no longer experience accustomed successes? At such times faith confronts its trials, and the substance of belief is tested.

Although Paul did not know God's immediate plan for his ministry, he did not engage in self-pity. Rather, from Phrygia he went down to Mysia, only to be instructed not to go into Bithynia.

Remaining receptive to divine leadership, Paul heard the Macedonian call, a call which led him through great suffering. But his faith did not only release him honorably from jail; it brought about the conversion of the Philippian jailer and his family. Never again would Philippi be the same. Paul's trials of faith glorified God's name and expanded God's cause. Faith triumphs always.

Prayer: *Lord, help us to follow where we cannot see and believe when we do not understand. Amen.*

Wednesday, May 3   Read Psalm 97.

Few passages of scripture expand on the triumphs of faith like Psalm 97. Within glaring contrasts of power, darkness, light, righteousness, fear, and destruction, the delightfully refreshing, confidence-building, promise declares, "He preserveth the souls of his saints."

God's sovereignty provides the overarching theme of this psalm. It is a theme providing grounds for which the people are to be glad because they are not subject, ultimately, to the pride, greed, and the power-hunger of earthly potentates. Further, although "clouds and darkness are round about him" (KJV) suggesting God's incomprehensibleness to human understanding, we can be assured that righteousness or justice forms the foundation of God's reign. Although awesome indeed is God's presence, an awesomeness that causes the earth to tremble and the hills to disappear, God deals righteously with the inhabitants of earth.

For the heavens declare not only destruction of evil by the Lord; they also declare righteousness or justice, as well as glory. Indeed, one aspect of God's glory is righteous judgment. The psalmist writes, "Zion heard, and was glad; and the daughters of Judah rejoiced because of thy judgments, O Lord" (KJV).

Surely, the haters of evil and worshipers of the true God will be delivered from the enemy. It is reassuring to know that a loving God is continually present with us in a world of hate and evil. In addition to divine protection, the path of truth is made plain, for "light is sown for the righteous," and hope springs continually in the hearts of the faithful. Surely, a life of faith is a life of triumph.

Prayer: *God of all creation, reign within my heart; for your kingdom is everlasting, and your judgments are righteous. Amen.*

Thursday, May 4   Read Revelation 22:12-14.

Our text today identifies at least four characteristics of a life of faith which leads to Paradise: urgency, divine leadership, obedience, and entitlement. Verse 12 says that God intends to finish his work in the world quickly. "Behold," says God, "I come quickly" (KJV). Our text says we should live with eschatological urgency and expectation. Thus, a focus on our Christian vocation should take preeminence. It is time to eliminate distractions and engage in activities that will gain heaven's approval.

In the second place, a journey of faith proceeds with crucial confidence that the "Alpha and Omega," the God of all times, is taking that journey with us. Without this sense of divine presence, life's trials would most certainly overwhelm us. As the Alpha and Omega speaks, boldness and resolve surge through our souls.

Third, a life of faith is one of obedience. God's will, not ours, is both chart and compass for the Christian journey. "Blessed (happy) are they that do his commandments, that they may have right to the tree of life" (KJV). Yes, God's commandments, God's word, the holy scripture, contain what God expects of us. "Not every one who says to me, 'Lord, Lord,' shall enter the kingdom of heaven, but he who does the will of my Father who is in heaven" (Matt. 7:21).

Fourth, no one enters God's kingdom without the "right" to do so. Obedience to God's command gives us "a right to the tree of life" (KJV), a right exemplified by entrance through the City gates. When one has a "right," one is entitled, authorized to be there. Thus one uses the official port of entry. Other means of entry fall outside of God's plan and lead to destruction.

Prayer: *Teach us, dear God, the importance of keeping your commandments. And endow us with ability to know them and the capacity to obey them. Amen.*

Friday, May 5   Read Revelation 22:16-17.

Faith is predicated on belief, and belief generates hope. Although belief exists without total evidence, it does not exist without some evidence. Scripture declares, "The heavens declare the glory of God; and the firmament showeth his handywork" (Ps. 19:1, KJV).

Believers must, by necessity, live in a world that provides endless circumstances that severely try their faith. Often we are tempted to question, "Lord, why me?" At such times, doubt tends to cloud our faith. Therefore, it helps to know that under all circumstances, through light and shadows, God, the Alpha and Omega, is with us.

Accordingly, Revelation 22:16-17 informs us that the Author and Finisher of our faith declares that his promises are true; it is true that obedience to God's will assures entrance into Paradise; it is true that disobedience excludes one from the kingdom. The message of Revelation bears divine authenticity because its messenger is sent by the offspring of David, the "bright and morning star." David is an historical figure whose kingdom is a prototype of God's everlasting kingdom; Jesus is also historic and of the "root and the offspring of David" (KJV).

With these assurances, one can stand faithful when faith encounters sundry trials and temptations. One need not faint in life's darkness as long as we hold the hands of the "bright and morning star" (KJV).

The call to discipleship is universal. The Spirit, the church, believers—all are commissioned to invite souls to become citizens of God's kingdom. The call is for "whosoever will."

Prayer: *Heavenly Father, help me to recognize that your biddings are your enablings. Your invitation to life eternal contains empowerment of will and sustaining grace. Amen.*

Saturday, May 6   Read John 17:20-26.

The text for today calls our attention to numerous provisions designed by God to insure abiding trust in our Creator during the days of our pilgrimage. These provisions and promises appear in that magnificent prayer of Jesus for his disciples and believers just before his betrayal, trial, and crucifixion.

What could be more faith-building than the following supplication made by Jesus on behalf of believers:

1. In the first place, the fact that he took time to pray for each of us suggests that divinity sees faces in the crowd. We are not just cases in God's sight; we are individuals whose needs are individually addressed.

2. In the second place, he prayed for Christian unity, "that they all may be one." This is a call for unity of purpose, action, and expectations among fellow believers.

3. Third, Jesus prayed that Christian unity may be reinforced by the unity he has with his Father. "That they may be one in us" raises the level of Christian solidarity to its ultimate possibility.

4. Fourth, this three-fold unity involving the believer, other believers, and heaven helps convince the world that Jesus is indeed Lord; that his mission originated in heaven; that the church is an authentic divine instrument to convey a saving message to a dying world.

5. Finally, Jesus prayed that his followers will be with him, "where I am." His genuine love seeks us to walk with him among those in need in our land—in the jails or in the city streets. And when we follow we find that he leads us to an eternal home as well, where we will dwell together with him.

Prayer: *Dear God, I believe. Help my unbelief. Make me one with you in comfort as well as in service. Amen.*

Sunday, May 7   Read Revelation 22:20.

Faith, like physical life, thrives on movement. A faith that doesn't move from promise to fruition, that doesn't reach beyond the mundane to the celestial, that doesn't live for or anxiously await the triumphant hour when "the kingdoms of this world are become the kingdoms of our Lord, and of his Christ" is doomed to decay (KJV).

Christian pilgrimage covers the journey from Paradise lost to Paradise restored. Ever since sin destroyed the harmony between God and Creation, humanity has longed for restoration of peace, for absence of pain and sorrow, for harmony between God and humankind, for a life without anxiety and the threat of evil.

Christians are assured of such a kingdom of bliss and peace. In fact, the entire 22nd chapter of Revelation is devoted to reminding believers that in God's kingdom there will be no fear, pain, death, hate, unmet need, or mutual distrust, for the throne of God will reside there. The "tree of life" for "the healing of the nations" will be there. The healing of the nations means universal peace will be restored.

For such an Eden-like existence the soul longs and often cries, "O Lord, how long?" To meet this anguished cry of the human spirit, the Book of Revelation gives two assurances. First, all of these promises are true (Rev. 22:6). Also, their fulfillment will be soon, "for Behold, I come quickly," says the Lord. Soon, very soon, trials of faith will be replaced by triumphs of faith.

Prayer: *Lead me, dear Lord, step by step, through defeat and victory, laughter and sorrow, success and failure. For soon, very soon, you will declare, "Well done, good and faithful servant. . . . Enter into the joy of your Master." Amen.*

The Age of the Spirit

May 8-14, 1989
Monday, May 8

J. Stephen Lang†
Read Romans 8:14-17.

New status before God

The Acts of the Apostles could be called the "Acts of the Holy Spirit." Luke, author of Acts, emphasizes again and again the role of the Spirit in the young church. While the apostles play important roles in the gospel's spread, the Spirit is given the final credit for the establishing of Christ's church.

Because the Spirit is moving, new things happen. A new age, the age of the Holy Spirit, has arrived. *Newness* is, in fact, a recurring theme in this week's scripture passages.

In Romans 8:14-17, Paul tells believers that something new has happened because of the work of the Spirit: We can now be sons and daughters of God. This is not because of anything we have done—indeed, unregenerate persons could never on their own come into fellowship with a holy God. But the Spirit changes that, for we are adopted into the family of God. We can refer to God as "Abba," the endearing term for "Father" that Jesus himself used.

It is easy for us to miss the impact of this, for we commonly refer to God in familiar terms. But Paul was writing something shocking: The God of the universe has, through the working of the Spirit, enabled us to be his dear children. We are heirs to glory.

Prayer: *Lord God, thank you for your Spirit, who makes us heirs to your kingdom. Remind us daily that we live in the age of the Spirit, the age when you have mighty wonders to show us. Amen.*

---

†Author and editor, Tyndale House, Wheaton, Illinois.

Tuesday, May 9   Read Acts 2:14-21;
                                                   John 14:8-14.

A new people

"In the last days, God says, I will pour out my Spirit on all people" (NIV). Peter was quoting from the prophet Joel, who, like most faithful Jews, looked forward to "the last days," a time when God would dramatically intervene in the world. Peter's audience had certainly heard many times before about these "last days." But Peter added a new twist to Joel's words: He claimed that the amazing display of tongues was exactly what Joel had predicted. The last days were here already! The age of the Spirit had come!

This must have been shocking to some of the listeners. The idea of the Spirit being poured out on all believers, not just a select group, was contained in Joel's words. But no one expected to see it in operation. Yet here were Galileans speaking in other tongues. God was acting as prophesied. The Spirit was being poured out.

Jesus had already told the disciples to expect this. In today's reading from John he tells the disciples that they will do great things to bring glory to God. The Spirit will not act upon a tiny group of prophets or kings but upon all the faithful. All who honor God can accomplish wondrous things through the Spirit.

The Spirit is a great eqaulizer. White-collar and blue-collar, slave and free, educated and uneducated—nothing matters to the Spirit except that we be open to divine leading. We are living in the age of the Spirit, the last days, and we can all expect great things from God and attempt great things for God.

Prayer: *Lord, in this time spoken of by your prophets, empower us as we go forth into the world to do great things for you. Guide us and teach us with your Spirit as we proclaim that all who call upon you may be saved. Amen.*

Wednesday, May 10   Read Genesis 11:1-9; Acts 2:1-12.

New language

The "tongues" mentioned in Acts 2 are a sign that the human divisions begun at the tower of Babel have been undone. While Christians may disagree about whether the tongues at Pentecost were ecstatic utterances or proclamations in languages previously unknown to the speakers, the message is clear: The curse of Babel has been reversed. What was split apart by humanity's sin at Babel has been united by the Spirit.

The "roll call of the nations" in verses 9-11 shows the Spirit was doing a marvelous work, for people from across the known world were understanding each other. Jerusalem at the busy Pentecost time would have resounded with God's praises in many tongues. At Babel the people were scattered, divided. In Jerusalem, with the Spirit acting, people were united.

American poet Vachel Lindsay spoke fondly of missionaries, referring to them in one poem as "An endless line of splendor, These troops with heaven for home."* He admired the zeal of these people willing to spread the gospel in other languages and other cultures. We can still admire those hardy souls who translate the scriptures into other tongues and make God's praises known across the globe. The church today, as at Pentecost, speaks in other tongues, and if it is not with the miraculous power as it was then, the message is still the same: The age of the Spirit has come, and we may all be united as children of God.

Prayer: *Merciful God, thank you for enabling us to sing your praise in every tongue and in every land. Thank you for your Spirit, who since Pentecost works in humankind to heal division. Amen.*

---

*"Foreign Missions in Battle Array," *Selected Poems of Vachel Lindsay*, edited by Mark Harris (New York: The MacMillan Company, 1963), p. 91.

Thursday, May 11   Read Acts 2:5-15.

A new wine

I have an artist friend who does stunning calligraphic illustrations of the scriptures. One of my favorites is his rendering of Joshua 22:5: "Love the Lord your God . . . serve him with all your heart and all your soul" (NIV). *The Living Bible* paraphrases the last part of this verse by using the words "serve him enthusiastically." Looking at this art piece, I sense my friend's own enthusiasm in serving the Lord. The picture suggests a kind of holy intoxication that the words alone do not convey.

The Pentecost phenomenon—the Galilean believers declaring the wonders of God in different tongues—was so remarkable that some onlookers couldn't believe God was behind it all. Some were perplexed, and some scoffed: "They have had too much wine" (NIV). Peter corrected them: It was nine in the morning; too early for tippling, but not too early for the Spirit to be at work.

My charismatic friends puzzle me at times, yet I applaud their emphasis on *feeling* the wonder and power of God. They know, and I know, that the Christian life can be orthodox, proper—and dead. But so inspired were the believers in Jerusalem that some who were present accused them of drunkenness.

American colonial preacher Jonathan Edwards, a prime mover in the Great Awakening, spoke boldly against a rational religion that left no room for the power and spontaneity of the Spirit. Edwards recognized that calm, tidy religion can fail to confront and transform sinners. But the Spirit, the new wine in the new age, can truly change hearts.

Prayer: *Almighty God, teach us to abandon ourselves to your Spirit. Make your church so bold and so joyful that the world will know that something new, the age of the Spirit, has arrived. Amen.*

Friday, May 12　　　　　　　Read John 14:15-17, 25-27.

A new Counselor

Could anyone who had walked with Jesus ever forget his teaching? Time and time again the disciples had proven themselves to be a hardheaded lot. In his last discourse before the crucifixion, Jesus assured his followers that there would come a Counselor who would teach them the meaning of what they had seen. "The Holy Spirit, whom the Father will send in my name, will teach you all things and will remind you of everything I have said to you" (NIV). The church has this promise that the Holy Spirit, at work in every believer, will keep us in the truth. The world, materialistic as it is, cannot understand this. Yet we have Christ's word that the Spirit is with us, comforting us, teaching us, completing the revelation of Christ by showing us daily the full meaning of it.

Christian psychiatrist M. Scott Peck explains the phenomenon in this way: "God knows it is not enough for us thick-headed humans to give us his wisdom in history; he must continue to give it to us in the present moment, minute by minute by minute."* Wonderful as the revelation in Christ was, we still need something more: the Spirit, God dwelling in us, guiding us. In the new age, the age of the Spirit, all believers may take comfort in this.

Prayer: *"Blow, wind of God! With wisdom blow*
　　　　Until our minds are free
　　　　From mists of error, clouds of doubt,
　　　　*Which blind our eyes to thee!"** Amen.*

---

*M. Scott Peck, *What Return Can I Make?* (New York: Simon and Schuster, 1985), p. 123.
**Henry H. Tweedy, "O Spirit of the Living God."

Saturday, May 13   Read Psalm 104:24-34.

A new creation

As an undergraduate theology student I spent little time studying the doctrine of the Holy Spirit. Most books of theology have little to say about the Spirit. This is as it should be, for the Spirit is to be experienced, not written about in logical prose. The best writings on the Spirit are not theological works but, rather, hymns and poetry, for the workings of the Spirit in believers provoke mental music that can be hinted at—but perhaps never truly captured—in poetry.

Today's reading is a poem singing the glory of creation. The author was writing in a pre-Christian era, so the poem does not reflect the fuller understanding of the Spirit that came with the New Testament period. Still, the psalm is exciting to read, for we see the Old Testament understanding of the mystery and power of the Spirit. The psalmist understood that creation is ongoing. God energizes creation, and the Spirit causes creation and renewal.

Reading this hymn to the God of nature, we can appreciate Paul's words in Romans 8:20, where he speaks of all creation being renewed by the redemptive work of Christ. The psalm reminds us that the same Spirit that energizes the universe is also the author of the new creation, the renewed heaven and earth that began when the Spirit came upon the believers at Pentecost. In the new age of the Spirit, all creation can experience renewal.

Prayer: *"Author of the new creation,*
Come with unction and with power.
Make our hearts thy habitation;
On our soul thy graces shower." * Amen.

---

*Paul Gerhardt, "Holy Ghost, Dispel Our Sadness."

Sunday, May 14 (Pentecost)
Read Acts 2:1-4; Jeremiah 31:33.

New Pentecost, new law

The birthday of the church—that is how Christians perceive Pentecost. We forget that Pentecost was already a much-revered Jewish festival before the events in Acts 2. Pentecost was a thanksgiving day. Jews expressed thanks for the harvest and the giving of the Law at Sinai, God's best gift to Israel.

The Jews in Jerusalem on this particular Pentecost had come to the city to celebrate the Law. Then they encountered God's Spirit at work. The old Pentecost was a feast for God's Law for Israel. The new Pentecost became a feast for God's new law for all nations, a law of the heart, predicted by the prophet Jeremiah. The new age had come. The age of the Spirit had arrived!

The Pentecost parallels are intriguing. Moses ascended a fiery, thundering mountain and came down with the Law. Christ ascended to heaven and sent down the fire of the Spirit, the new law. The fire on Sinai was perceived by the corporate body, Israel. The fire of the Upper Room rested on each individual believer, fulfilling Jeremiah's prophecy.

Pentecost celebrates the giving of this new law, the Spirit working in ech believer, the Spirit which Christ had promised. If the Jews of the apostolic age were grateful for the Law, Christians should be even more grateful for the new law, written in our hearts. Pentecost is still a day of thanksgiving, a day to praise the Triune God for the Spirit moving within us.

Prayer: *"Spirit of Holiness, Let all thy saints adore*
Thy sacred energy, and bless Thine heart-renewing power." *

---

*Charles Wesley, "Father, in Whom We Live."

SEEING THE FACES OF GOD

May 15-21, 1989 **Cheryl Hammock†**
Monday, May 15 Read Proverbs 8:1-11.

I stood beside the woman's bed. I wondered how she could speak with such clarity and affirmation. She was dying. There was no hope of remission. She was only 54 years old—too young for Medicare. She had no wealth, not even insurance. Her English was broken and so was her body, but her spirit was not.

Her children and grandchildren flowed through the tiny stucco house like water cycling from earth to sky to earth again. Her husband stood nearby, bearing his own kind of pain.

She focused clearly through her morphine veil: "I am not afraid. We believe that God loves us like a parent. A parent would not leave children alone when they are tired or hurt or lonely. The Bible tells us this. The Bible is very clear. God is with us, and when death comes, we will be with God."

One Sunday afternoon, when friends and relatives came to what would be their last supper, she ate well and laughed long and even got up and danced across the room.

In the weeks that stretched out ahead of her like the long road from Pilate's palace to the Skull Place, she repeated the familiar refrain: "God loves us; God is with us." I could not doubt her truth. She had chosen Wisdom over silver and gold and jewels.

Then when all seemed blackest, she turned her face toward the high December morning sun, smiled not quite with surprise, and said, "Oh, look! There's Poppa!" And she danced away.

Prayer: *Help us, O God, to see your face in the faces of those who seek your truth. Help us hear and repeat the ageless refrain of Wisdom, that from beginning to end and beginning again, you are with us. Amen.*

---

†Ordained minister, Christian Church (Disciples of Christ), chaplain and interim pastor, DeLand, Florida.

Tuesday, May 16   Read Proverbs 8:22-31.

It was a Sunday afternoon baptismal service for our new little church. We were so small that we had to borrow the facilities of a neighboring church because we had no baptismal pool of our own. Still, it was a joyful day.

The candidates were excited and nervous. All of us were proud and a little tearful. We greeted one another and sang a hymn and then watched in quiet celebration as one by one these youths made this important commitment. It struck me as awesome that they were not only delightful but delighted with themselves and what they were doing. One of the boys waded out into the center of the baptistry and instead of following the instruction to look straight ahead to the other side of the waters, he turned and looked full-faced at his parents and friends—and he gave them a big broad grin. How appropriately inappropriate, I thought.

When it was finished, some of us stayed. Suddenly, the hush of the hour was broken by the laughter of a dozen or so children. They were perched on choir chairs, peeking over the baptistry glass to see what there was to see.

My startled awareness softened to joyful affirmation. This is the way it should be. These children are as comfortable in the presence of the Holy as the Holy is comfortable and takes pleasure in them. This is the best of what God created life to be—creatures at home in the creation, life and laughter multiplying in the simple humanness of children's curiosity and youth's freshness. And I understood why a little child shall lead them.

Prayer: *O God, help us to see your face in the delight of every child's exploration of what you called good, and what you call redeemed. And help us to create anew a world where children (even those in old bodies) can run free and without fear into the open fields, into the nooks and crannies of your dwelling place, even our own hearts. Amen.*

Wednesday, May 17   Read John 16:4-15.

The wedding ceremony was over. The guests were celebrating this poignant concoction of the bitter and the sweet. The bride wore white and an almost natural wig to cover what was left of her hair after chemotherapy. The groom swallowed hard as they danced "The Anniversary Waltz." Something in their resilient spirit said that making this commitment was "the right thing to do." They knew the future was both unknown and certain. In the eye of the swirling storm, they found a quiet space.

Then the wedding party gathered arm in arm for the video photographer. Sensing that movement was essential to memory, he coached, "Wave!" So they lifted their arms and the corners of their lips and hailed the future. I glanced up at the drama. The bride's face and hand and motion jumped off the flat page of the too-soon coming future and into the foreground of the moment.

She's not waving at the camera or the celebrants, I thought, and she's not waving "Hello" from Now. She's waving "Good-bye," and she's looking from Tomorrow. She's giving her bequest. She knows they can't hear the wisdom she could share about life's brevity—and eternality. So she silently gives them herself. And she looks at them with longing and comfort and promise and peace.

Was it like this for Jesus and his disciples in their last celebration? Could he speak of Comfort coming into their midst despite the indescribable pain and loss just before them? Was the essence of it the same as for the bride and groom—that in the face of the worst that life brings, the commitment not to abandon is God's way of claiming us, now and always?

Prayer: *God of the Now and the Then and the Always, help us to see your face in the faces of all who stand like the bride on the edge of time and eternity. Give us again the gift of your eternal seeing, that you may claim us and that we may claim one another for love's sake. Amen.*

149

Thursday, May 18 Read Psalm 8.

Truffles, the chocolate poodle. What is she, really? Just a dog? Not quite! A baby in our all-adult household? Sometimes! A creature made for joy? Indeed!

In the morning, she bounds into the house, barely stopping to note my presence, as nobility nods to the doorkeeper. And she's off like a shot to the bedroom, nudging my husband into the day. Then off to get the morning paper!

She's such a wonder. Ever since she discovered squirrels we've had a daily ritual. We sneak into the backyard and look for gray fluffs. At the slightest ground movement, we whisper, "Squirrel, Truffles, squirrel!" And the centuries-old retriever instincts take over.

But sometimes, late at night when she is very tired or disoriented or goes to her sleeping box, her own private den, she will not tolerate handling—the result of kennel abuse. Once, without warning, she ripped across the knuckles of my right hand before either of us realized what was happening. Remorse was instant and instinctive. I held her on my lap and intoned, "Poor Poodle," while holding ice against my cuts.

In those moments, I think I know a little of God's heart. To take such joy in this tiny life, the antics, the impulse toward communion, and yet to feel the snarling snap that breaks the skin—and the heart. And it is not clear whether the creature or the Creator hurts more.

Prayer: *Creator God, help us to see your face in the face of all your creation. Help us to love your creatures one and all, large and small, pitiful and prideful, joyful and lost in tiredness, disorientation, or remembered abuse. Put your heart in our hearts—even at the risk of being broken. Amen.*

Friday, May 19   Read Romans 5:1-5.

"God will heal me," she said. "I prayed to the Lord, and I know God will heal me," she said in words punctuated by shallow breaths. I turned to the nurse for confirmation. She did not respond. It was clear that the woman's condition was deteriorating, not improving. But we did not argue with her. Comfort, understanding, a releasing touch on the knotted hand—that was all we could do. We could not declare her hope null and void.

The days moved on, and the time came when life was measured in hours and then in minutes. The family drew close around her bed. They prayed. They held her. And they softly sang hymns to her like lullabies.

Something about the loss of this matriarch made them long distance runners, clustering together at the head of the race. They told stories of their life with her. It had been filled with struggle, often with no sense of where life would take them, except for her sense of survival that moved them from day to new day. And they had become what she was—love, poured out and overflowing, touching everything around them.

Now they were with her at the finish line. In the midst of the last gasping strides, a calm breath of air settled over them all. And the spirit came and went. And, indeed, God did heal her. God healed her of all that life had done to make her sick and tired, all that had slowed her steps but not her heart, all that had used up her energy but not her hope. God gave her the gift of the final healing.

Prayer: *God of our living and our dying, help us to see your face in the faces of all who cling to hope. You have made us your friends. You have loved us through everything we have been a part of. You have led us in the race of endurance and have blessed us with a hope that will never disappoint us. Help us, by your Spirit, to give your love to one another with the endurance that turns death into healing. Amen.*

Saturday, May 20   Read Genesis 32:1-32;
Romans 5:6-11.

Yesterday I felt like old Jacob—as tired as if I had wrestled all night with God. I limped into the office with a wounded spirit, exhausted by bickering in the ranks.

Then my best friend—the agnostic among us and my only real confessor—came to warn me she had given away confidences in the crunch of office politics. I listened in smoldering silence and choked back the anger that wanted to drive her or me or both of us or all of them into oblivion.

Decisions about alliances and programs demanded immediate resolution. Any way it went, someone was going to lose. But the worst, the very worst, was the broken trust. *I can never forgive this,* I thought. *This is the end of the relationship.* But even as I concluded this finality, she risked reconciliation—or rejection. She spoke with an uncertainty of speech but a clarity of heart: "I can live with whatever choice you make about this program—but I don't want to lose this friendship."

I looked at the benediction that hung on my wall. "You were God's enemies," it said, "but Jesus has made you God's friends." *She's more like Jesus than I am,* I thought.

I was being redeemed. Being redeemed—from my hurt, my anger, my isolation. Being redeemed—from the grinding machinery of systems that barely function under the weight of awesome commitments. Being redeemed—from all that is not love. I looked at her Innocent-in-World face, and I knew I had seen—behind the mask of unbelief—the face of God.

Prayer: *Help us, O God, to look into the faces of all your children, whether they know they are yours or not, and to see the love that you have given freely to all the world. Help us to befriend the enemies in one another and in ourselves, because you have made us your very own heart-treasured friends. Amen.*

Sunday, May 21   Read Acts 7:54-60;
                                          9:1-9, 17-20.

It's never been easy to see the face of God. We keep looking: in testimonies of true believers; in ceremonies that mark our comings and goings in life; in the wonder of creation and creatures; in hope that is unexplainable, unconfirmable, unfailing; in the efforts at relationships and trust that cannot go unbroken simply because we are human. And all the while, God is close enough for touching, for hearing, for wrestling, and for reconciling.

Then when we do acknowledge the certainty of seeing God, we find—like Stephen—that the stakes go up! No longer are we seeking a personal blessing or a last miracle. No longer are we seeking to justify our ways or document our heritage. When we see God—in the faces of those God loves and calls us to love— we risk the stone-throwing anger of the ones who refuse to see.

And maybe, when we are being booted out of the faith of our fathers and mothers, when we are being run out of town on a rail, when we are being martyred at the hands of the powerful and the pitiful—just maybe the heavens are getting ready to open up to an onlooker holding cloaks but reaching for hope. Just maybe when the final blow is struck, the power of love gives sight again to those blinded by hatred and self-righteousness. Then even murderous Saul becomes Paul, and each of us becomes God's new-born child.

Prayer: *God our Creator, Redeemer, Sustainer, give us the vision to see all your faces—as we work, as we play, as we rejoice in your world, as we weep for what is lost, as we hope for what is promised, as we bear the blows of those who are so angered by your inclusion and grace. Help us to breathe the breath of forgiveness that opens heaven's windows and hardened hearts in the dazzling light of your love. Amen.*

THE ESSENTIAL FOUNDATION

May 22-28, 1989   **Martin Pike†**
Monday, May 22   Read Psalm 92:1-4.

"It is good to give thanks to the Lord." The psalmist had no doubt about that. Over and over again this theme is repeated throughout the scriptures. When a person gives thanks, the act bears witness to an ingredient without which life becomes dull and meaningless.

I wonder what prompted the psalmist to write these words. Certainly it is not because life is without trial. The psalmist is confronted by the wicked who sprout up like grass, the evildoers and the enemies of the Lord. He knows the frustration of living in an imperfect world and still feels the need to "give thanks to the Lord."

We often give words a secondary place. Is not talk woefully cheap? Deeds are the object of our esteem. Yet at times a word alone can be redemptive.

Our Lord knew the importance of words of gratitude. To the disciples he said, "When you pray, say: " 'Father, hallowed be thy name' " (Luke 11:2). The apostle Paul knew the vocabulary of thanksgiving, too. "Thanks be to God, who gives us the victory through our Lord Jesus Christ" is how he put it on one occasion (1 Cor. 15:57). The heart may be near to bursting with words, but if the lips are silent, who will know our gratitude?

It may be that God appreciates most those times when we find it in our heart to thank a friend, a neighbor, a stranger, or even an enemy.

Prayer: *O God let my life be marked by gratitude. Each day let me thank you and all others who enrich my life. Amen.*

---

† Minister, Christian Church (Disciples of Christ), retired, Kingsville, Texas.

Tuesday, May 23   Read Psalm 92:12-15;
                                       Isaiah 55:10-13.

Psalm 92 suggests, "The righteous flourish like the palm tree. . . . They still bring forth fruit in old age, they are ever full of sap and green." That is an accurate description of my 90-year-old friend who has a sparkle in her eye and a spring in her step. She carries her years as if each one weighs no more than a feather. Occasionally a complaint slips out. "I just don't have the stamina I used to have," she will say. But having said that, she flails her well-worn hoe at a weed that has had the audacity to spring up in her lawn.

The porch and backyard are full of growing things that bear witness to a green thumb. She shows a bit of partiality to the many varieties of cacti that adorn her garden, varieties that can take the heat and accept the hard-baked soil of her present place of residence. She remembers when she lived in a more hospitable climate, where the soil was richer and rain more abundant, but she does not grieve overmuch. She has made a point of growing what will grow where she is.

Jesus was distressed by people who refused to enjoy life. To him they seemed like little children in the marketplace who would not dance even if someone played the pipe for them. My friend knows the true source of joy in life. She chose long ago to hunger and thirst after the righteousness of God's kingdom, and her spirit has flourished like the palm tree.

Prayer: *O God, teach me how to hunger and thirst after righteousness. Amen.*

Wednesday, May 24   Read 1 Corinthians 15:51-58.

Through the years, people who came to the church in search of help were, for the most part, not burdened by terrible sins. Rather, they were overwhelmed by great discouragements. They longed for reconciliation with those from whom they were estranged, but the power of pride discouraged them. They longed for peace in their hearts, but they were afflicted, as was the apostle Paul, with a war in their members. They longed to see some labor bear fruit, some effort rewarded, but they were confronted by defeat. It was not that they had done something wrong so much as it was that their best efforts had gone unrewarded.

The very nature of God is such that God not only forgives sinners but also renews the strength of those who are discouraged. God labors with the meek who have not yet inherited the earth and reaches out to those who mourn and have not been comforted. God has a place for those who have hungered and thirsted after righteousness without being filled.

Often we have experienced frustration not because of lust or greed or covetousness but because we were overwhelmed by discouragement. The bright hopes to which we had committed ourselves, the goals we had envisioned, the dreams we had for our families, our church, our community were swallowed up by the negatives that enveloped our minds. Paul's advice is worth remembering: "Therefore, my beloved brethren, be steadfast, immovable, always abounding in the work of the Lord, knowing that in the Lord your labor is not in vain."

Prayer: *Dear God, keep bright my best hopes, that I may continue steadfast in your work. Amen.*

Thursday, May 25   Read Luke 6:39-41.

Most of us like to read "the inside story." A genre of news-papers and magazines has sprung into existence to keep us informed about what is happening in the lives of the rich and famous that no one is supposed to know about. So hungry is the public for titillating scandal that some writers can make the most prosaic event seem wicked and wanton. There is a certain satis-faction derived from discovering that saintly people are a bit devilish, that honest people are not above lying, that rich people are a bit stingy. The higher the esteem in which someone is held, the more enthusiastic the search.

There is nothing new about this. When the disciples of old chewed a few grains of ripening wheat as they passed through a field on the Sabbath, it was public knowledge before the sun had set. Their reputations were besmirched accordingly. Jesus, par-taking of a bit of food and drink with friends, found himself labeled a glutton and a winebibber, an agent of Beelzebul.

The trouble with overly enjoying the "inside story" of some-one else's feet of clay is that if we are honest, we are deeply grateful that the author did not choose us as a target. What is amiss in our lives is no secret. The psalmist reminds us of this truth: "Thou knowest when I sit down and when I rise up; thou discernest my thoughts from afar" (Ps. 139:2). "Why," said Jesus, "do you see the speck that is in your brother's eye, but do not notice the log that is in your own eye?"

Prayer: *O God, help me to love my neighbor and to refrain from criticism. Amen.*

Friday, May 26   Read Luke 6:42-44.

In the late seventeenth century, Brother Lawrence said that just as the stone is set before the carver so that it may be transformed into a statue, so did he place himself before God. Brother Lawrence's desire was that the chisel of God's grace and mercy might transform him into the very image of the Creator.

Often I contemplate the need for change not in my own life but in the life of others. I long for them to be transformed. I want to see the hard edges of their anger softened. I long for their devotion and faithfulness to be deepened. I want them to reflect kindness, compassion, forgiveness, and love. Yes, I am always wanting someone else transformed by the hand of the One who fashioned us in the beginning of time.

If there is the possibility that I can get others to change their ways, there is the possibility that I can continue on my own course without inconvenience. If they can be maneuvered into accepting my selfish desires, my little idiosyncracies, then I need suffer no troublesome disruption of my lifestyle.

But as I think about this I know it will not do. It is I who must submit to God's transforming power. It is I who must be re-shaped by God's redemptive chisel. Reluctantly I remember my God who calls me out of the darkness of my own making with the words, "You hypocrite, first take the log out of your own eye, and then you will see clearly to take out the speck that is in your brother's eye."

Prayer: *O God, make me a new creature after your own image. Amen.*

Saturday, May 27   Read Luke 6:45.

"The good man out of the good treasure of his heart produces good." There is nothing particularly unusual about this observation which Jesus made. Even so, those who listened needed this advice even as I need it.

In the course of making the normal rounds that were mine as a minister, I often found myself marveling at the courage, compassion, and faith that prevailed in the hearts of many parishioners. In the face of painful illness, sorrow, and loss they were able to rejoice and reflect gratitude in spite of the trials that enveloped their lives. A man who had lost his job was not bitter or depressed but confident that life was good and that the future was an open door characterized by hope. A terminally ill cancer patient's plight did not keep her from remembering that each pain-filled day was yet another opportunity for loving her family and friends. These and others were radiant with gratitude for what had been and were not without hope for what was yet to be. They were able to believe that somehow God was at work in the world, eager to labor together with them to the end that they might know the fullness of God's love.

They manifested a spirit of generosity and good will. Even when they were the recipients of others' sympathy and concern, they perceived themselves as fortunate souls whose cup of blessing overflowed. From whence came these good treasures? They came from hearts leavened by years of loving God with all their strength and their neighbors as themselves.

Prayer: *O God, fill my heart with the kind of treasures that will produce faith, hope, and love. Amen.*

Sunday, May 28   Read Luke 6:46-49.

Life has a way of putting us to the test. Storms do come, often from an unexpected quarter. Jesus knew how important it was for us to understand as much. Life, he cautioned, ought to be built upon the foundations that can withstand the worst of tempests.

Surely the most devastating threats to the Christian life come from within. Temptations to be less than our best assail even the faithful. Patience wears thin. We become apathetic about loving an enemy or about turning the other cheek. The command to walk the second mile becomes a hateful imposition. The speck in our neighbor's eye blots out the log in our own. Insensitive to the needs of others, we insist on having our own way. These are the storms that beat against the foundations of our faith.

Who among us does not identify with the apostle Paul's observation: "I do not understand my own actions. For I do not do what I want, but I do the very thing I hate" (Rom. 7:15). Thus it was that our Lord encouraged his followers to build their faith on strong foundations, foundations that would not crumble when the flood of human weakness swept over them.

"Make every effort to supplement your faith with virtue, and virtue with knowledge, and knowledge with self-control, and self-control with steadfastness, and steadfastness with godliness and godliness with brotherly affection, and brotherly affection with love" (2 Pet. 1:5-7). Peter, having seen his own faith threatened, knew something about foundations. To follow his advice is to be ready for both the worst and the best that life may offer.

Prayer: *O God, when storms do come, let me be prepared. Amen.*

GOD'S GREATNESS: OUR WORLD VIEW

May 29–June 4, 1989   **Cecile A. Beam†**
Monday, May 29   Read 1 Kings 8:22-23.

The anticipated event was happening: the Temple was completed, and the priests were putting the Ark of the Covenant and other sacred vessels in their proper place. The cloud which had preceded the Israelites throughout their exodus and had been a daily symbol of God's presence now filled the Temple. All the people had assembled. King Solomon blessed the people and then praised the God they worshiped: second to none, a keeper of the Covenant, kind and just.

Solomon's speech was a timely reminder of the Covenant: God would be their God if they would be God's people. The theme was mutual faithfulness. God's promise would be kept as long as the people walked "wholeheartedly in [God's] way" (JB).

What does walking wholeheartedly in God's way mean for you today?

What do you allow to compete with God for your attention and devotion?

How do you describe God's greatness?

How does your description of God's greatness influence the way you live your life today?

Suggestion for prayer: *Read Psalm 100. Bathe yourself in the awareness of God's greatness. Ask God to show you the ways and places in which you can proclaim God's greatness.*

---

†Director, Elementary Children's Education, General Board of Discipleship, The United Methodist Church, Nashville, Tennessee.

Tuesday, May 30   Read 1 Kings 8:22-23.

The Temple was a holy place. It contained the Ark of the Covenant—a visible reminder of the promise God had made with the Hebrew people through Moses. The Temple also contained the very presence of God—the Holy of Holies. The Temple was God's dwelling place, though God was not contained by the Temple.

A holy place for us provides a memory or remembrance of God and opens us to the possibility of a renewed awareness of God's presence.

Take time to remember the holy places in your life. Give yourself permission to be aware of the times, the locations, the activities through which God has been very present with you. Were you alone or were people involved in some way? How was God proclaimed through them? What feelings were you aware of? How did you express those feelings? How did those holy places change the way you see and respond to all that God has created, including yourself?

Spend a few minutes writing down or drawing some of these memories of holy places. How has God's greatness been revealed in these experiences?

Suggestion for prayer: *Read Psalm 100. Invite God into your time and space. Give thanks for the holy places in your life. Ask God to open you to the experience of holy places this day.*

Wednesday, May 31   Read 1 Kings 8:41-43.

Experiencing God's presence leads to proclamation. One can never be surrounded by God without letting others know.

In this case, the foreigners in distant lands were going to hear of God's greatness and come to the Temple. So great was God's goodness; so loud was the praise of the Hebrews. Telling one's next-door neighbor was not enough. Indeed, telling someone in the next village was not enough. God could be praised sufficiently only when the word about God's greatness had been shouted into the next state and nation. Then the invitation was to be given: "Come to the holy place and see for yourself."

Experiencing God's presence expands our world view. We are changed by God's presence. No longer can we be content to share our awareness of God with our small circle of friends or our own church group. God's presence in our lives radiates from our very beings—much as Moses' face glowed when he came down from Mt. Sinai. So we become the good Samaritan—being a neighbor, meeting a need, sharing a word of hope, going out of our way to proclaim God's greatness. How far do you need to go from where you are now to where you can praise God with your whole being?

Not all "foreigners" live in distant lands. To whom is God drawing you so that you can witness to your faith?

What petitions are you willing to make before God on another person's behalf, especially when the other person is someone you would rather avoid?

Suggestion for prayer: *Read Psalm 100. Offer to God any unwillingness to go out of your way to proclaim God's greatness. Ask God to guide you to those persons or groups who need the gift of faith you can offer.*

Thursday, June 1   Read Luke 7:1-10.

Can you recall a time in your childhood when there was something you really wanted from someone else, but you just couldn't bring yourself to ask that person for it? However, you did persuade someone to ask for you—on your behalf. To your amazement, your request was granted!

In Luke, a Roman official sends some key persons from the Jewish community to ask Jesus to heal the official's servant. For some reason the Roman officer decides he is not worthy to have Jesus in his home. So he sends some other friends to tell Jesus just to say the word and the servant will be healed. Picture the look on the face of Jesus as he turns to face the crowd and says "I tell you, I have never found faith like this, not even in Israel" (TEV).

Luke precedes this story with sayings of Jesus regarding loving your enemies, not judging others, trees bearing fruit, and the story of the two house builders. So we should not be surprised when Luke emphasizes the theme by providing an account of a Roman soldier's faith. The Hebrews have been upstaged by a Roman.

How big is your world? How open are you to God's working through someone you just tolerate because it's politically smart to do so?

How inclusive are you willing to be?

What keeps you from trusting God's power?

How does your lack of trust in God's power affect the way you live in God's world?

Suggestion for prayer: *Read Psalm 100. Picture a time recently when you did not have enough faith in God's greatness. How could more trust in God have influenced your behavior? Ask God for the gift of trust in God's power.*

Friday, June 2   Read Galatians 1:1-5.

Paul was concerned over what he had heard about the churches in Galatia. He was so concerned that he did not begin this letter with his usual warm greeting. Nor did he give thanks for the kind of witness the churches in Galatia were making.

Paul did three things in the opening sentences of this letter, however. He reminded the Galatians who had called him to be an apostle. He drew upon the support of the Christians who were with him. And he reminded the Christians in Galatia of God's saving grace through Jesus Christ.

Has your congregation known enough or cared enough about another church in any other part of the world to write a letter to them about their Christian discipleship? What would you say? How do you think the receiving church would respond? Would they read the letter in a worship service or small study group? Would they pass it from person to person? Would a translator be needed?

How would your congregation respond to a letter from a sister church? What do you think the letter would say? Who would be grateful for the bond of fellowship and for the reminder of the common foundations of faith? Who would be offended?

How long has it been since you shared with anyone else your own experiences of being called by God to discipleship?

What keeps you from being aware of the struggles of Christians in congegations around the world?

Suggestion for prayer: *Read Psalm 100. Be aware of entering God's presence. Ask God to show you ways to join others in making joyful noises in many lands.*

Saturday, June 3   Read Galatians 1:6-10.

If the Christians in Galatia were excited about getting a letter from Paul, they were suddenly jolted when the words of greeting moved to words of criticism. Paul was chastising them for losing their zealousness so quickly. The Galatians had given up the GOOD NEWS for news. When the churches in Galatia were begun, Paul had spoken with the authority of a faith which came from God. But the Galatian Christians had yielded to the lure of a less powerful authority in Paul's absence.

The reminder for us is that we must continually ask for the gift of discerning the truth and for the gift of God's working through us as we share our faith with others.

We have so much information available today. Television, newspapers, and magazines tout controversy constantly. One research project report is challenged by another research project report. A story about what is happening in another country is followed almost immediately by a report presenting a conflicting viewpoint. And then we Christians have difficulty agreeing on what the Bible says and what the words direct us to do. Who is right—the members of the Dutch Reformed Church of South Africa or the black Christians in that same country?

What is your usual response to someone who is, from your point of view, perverting the gospel? How is God calling you to respond?

What keeps you from being more passionate in living and sharing your faith?

Suggestion for prayer: *Ask God for the ability to know the truth and for the gift of a passionate faith.*

Sunday, June 4   Read Psalm 100.

This is the day of rest and renewal. When we allow ourselves to relax both mind and body, we are renewed. We are made whole, healed of the fragmentation which we experience daily. Our response is to give thanks to the One who made us and to say yes once again to the Covenant which God has initiated. So, we have come full circle. Like Solomon, we find ourselves in a holy place, glorifying God.

Become aware of any tense places in your body. You may tighten and relax those muscles or massage them with your fingers.

With your mouth closed, breathe in deeply. Hold your breath for a brief moment, then let it out slowly through your mouth. Do this two or three times, then begin to breathe normally. With each breath, you are remembering that God has breathed life into you. Thanks be to God!

What else are you thankful for today? What do you want to proclaim before God?

Be aware that this is a holy place. God is with you. You can experience God's goodness amd steadfast love and everlasting faithfulness. Thanks be to God!

What question or concern do you want to share with God? Wait quietly for God's response.

Because you are God's person, you are connected with people you know well and people whose faces you will never see. You are part of a faith community which is here and now as well as in the past and in the future. Thanks be to God for those who have helped shape your faith and for those whose faith you will help shape!

Remain in this holy place as long as you wish. Then go in joy to wherever and whatever God is calling you.

CALL TO WHOLENESS . . . HOLINESS

June 5-11, 1989   **Nan Merrill†**
Monday, June 5   Read 1 Kings 17:17-24.

God is calling each one of us to wholeness . . . to holiness. More than this, we are called to evoke wholeness, holiness in others—to become so transparent that we render Christ's healing love present. How are we to answer this call? Today's scripture reading offers some clues.

The widow woman admits her need. She is humble enough to cry out for intercession on behalf of her son. She recognizes and admits that she herself has sinned and is in need of forgiveness. And, who among us is not in need of healing—be it physical, emotional, or spiritual? Who among us is not missing the mark in some area of our life and is, thus, in need of forgiveness?

Elijah, a holy and whole man, sees her need and has compassion. His life is totally surrendered to God—one sure sign of holiness. He cries out to the Lord and expects his prayer to be answered. He makes himself a vessel for God to use. Out of this healing process comes resurrection—new life. And we can sense great gratitude, joy, and assurance in both the widow woman and Elijah.

Each day, Jesus is dreaming his dream of wholeness and holiness in us. How ready are we to respond? To admit our need for healing . . . for forgiveness? To respond to another's need with compassion? To surrender ourselves without reserve and with confidence to Jesus' dream for us?

Prayer: *O Lord, giver of life, I open my mind, my heart, my sensibility to you. Fill me with a desire for wholeness. Give me humility to admit my need and courage to surrender myself totally to your love—today. Amen.*

---

† Lay pastoral minister in the inner city, St. Agnes Church, Detroit, Michigan.

Tuesday, June 6   Read Galatians 1:11-24.

Every day is a new call to wholeness . . . to holiness. Jesus sees us at each moment of our lives with new eyes. He is always waiting to re-form us as soon as we are ready to say yes to him. We get tired, frustrated, and impatient waiting for others to grow and change. But Jesus is always dreaming his dream of wholeness in us—all the while waiting patiently for us to wake up and begin to live his dream for us.

Imagine how strong Jesus' dream must have been for Paul as he persecuted the early church. Jesus knew how Paul's zeal for legalism, for the tradition of his fathers, was blinding him to Christ's spirit of love and cooperation. Yet, somewhere in Paul's inner being was a deeper yearning. When God called him to wholeness, Paul recognized his blindness and opened the door of his heart to receive new eyes—a new spirit of God's love.

How deeply do we yearn for a new spirit of God's love? Often we are not even aware of our silent, inner cry until we are graced by healing. A woman I know awoke early in the morning each day for six months, went to a window, and stared at one star, aware of a silent, unspoken, unformed prayer being prayed in her. One day, she awoke and was enveloped in God's love for ten days. Surrendered to God's will, she continues to express wonder and gratitude that God took her, a broken vessel, and re-formed her and sent her out in God's name.

Each one of us is a broken vessel. Each one of us is in need of healing, of forgiveness. Unless and until we are willing to allow Jesus to take our brokenness and bless us, we will not know the joy and fulfillment of being sent out to offer ourselves as his body, as his love, as his healing presence to others.

Prayer: *Lord of mercy, Lord of grace, take me and break me. Then, bless me and send me out today to someone in need of your love. Amen.*

169

Wednesday, June 7   Read Luke 7:11-17.

"Weep not," Jesus says to the widow woman of Nain. "Weep not," Jesus says to each one of us. His injunction does not mean, "Do not acknowledge or feel your sadness." Rather, Jesus is telling us that when we weep, we are never alone. He is as present to us in our sorrow as he was with Mary and Martha when Lazarus was dead, as compassionate as he was with the widow of Nain.

When we respond to the call to wholeness . . . to holiness, we begin to sense, to feel, and to live the paradoxes of life. Our own joys and sorrows are experienced at ever deeper levels of our selves. And, the more we are in harmony and balance with our inner being, the more we are called to respond to the cries of others, the more we are able to rejoice and celebrate with another in joy.

Jesus is "the mystery hidden for centuries past and now revealed to us" (Col. 1:26, AP). He makes his home in us. He is the author of the very being that we are—each one of us. And Jesus' life models for us how to carry the divine life, ever hidden within us, to one another in love—his love.

He calls us to be present to others through his cumulative presence in us. Gradually, as we answer his call to wholeness . . . to holiness, he draws us into the universal consciousness, into his identity with people of all races, creeds, and nations.

Each day he invites us to gather together in his name—to weep, to laugh, to take bread and wine, to dance, to pray with one another . . . to become one body, one spirit . . . to BE the whole and holy people of God, to be light for the world.

Prayer: *I thank you, Lord Jesus, for coming and making your home in me. Let me acknowledge your presence in me this day by being present to all those whom I meet along the way. Amen.*

Thursday, June 8 Read 1 Kings 17:17-24.

How easy and human in times of trouble, times when we feel helpless and afraid, to blame someone. The widow blames Elijah: "What quarrel have you with me? . . . Have you come here to bring my sins home to me and to kill my son?" (NJB) In responding to her fear, Elijah recognizes his own powerlessness and blames God: "Do you mean to bring grief even to the widow who is looking after me by killing her son?" (NJB) Then he calls upon God in prayer. And God, ever faithful, answers his cry.

The road to wholeness . . . to holiness, calls us to this kind of faith, to upper room faith. The depth of such faith is born of listening in the silence. T. S. Eliot says it most beautifully in his magnificent "Ash Wednesday" when he suggests there is not enough silence for the word to be heard. Each one of us needs to ask this of ourselves. Is there enough silence in us to quiet the problems, desires, fears, dreams, that live in our hearts and minds so that God's special word in us may be heard? Each of us needs an upper room—whether literal or within our very being—where we can go and rest, go and listen, go and become a whole and holy one of God.

Elijah does not simply cry out to God in prayer. Out of the accumulated silence in his inner being, he hears what God tells him to do and he does it with confidence. He offers himself to the widow's son—his body, his breath, his faith. He becomes an empty vessel, a clear channel, so that God's mercy, compassion and healing can flow through him. And in Elijah's giving, the widow's son receives new life. Is this not the wholeness, the holiness, God calls each one of us to?

Prayer: *O Lord of mercy and compassion, create in me a desire for silence. Give me a patient and steadfast heart to listen for your word in me, and strengthen me with courage to follow your will. Amen.*

Friday, June 9   Read Galatians 1:11-24.

Would that each one of us could recognize God's call to us with the clarity of Paul! He knew that God had set him apart from the time he was in his mother's womb, had called him through grace, and had chosen to reveal Jesus in him. Do we not have that same grace through our baptism? Are we not called by our faith to give Jesus to one another and to take Jesus through the way we live to those who do not yet know him?

What happens when we open ourselves to let God direct our lives? Like Paul, we receive new life—we become more alive and, thus, more enlivening to others. We wake up and see the world and ourselves in a new way. It is almost as if we begin to see, hear, feel with our heart's eyes, ears, and sensitivity. We become unbound to much of what we thought was important and discover new depths of understanding and wisdom within us. The more we abandon ourselves into God's hands, the more peaceful, loving, radiant, trusting, joyful we become.

If all these great things happen, why are so many people waiting until tomorrow or the next day? Perhaps we all know in our inner being that mixing with God can sometimes seem like a mixed bag. Change is usually disturbing and often downright fearful to us. There is no getting around it—when we open ourselves to God, we open ourselves to change, to disturbing what we have learned to call peace within us. Have you ever heard someone say, "It's not a good way to live, I don't like it— but I'm used to it." That is the voice of fear. God is always calling us to new life, life that will move us toward wholeness and holiness. Jesus is knocking at your door. If today you hear his voice, harden not your heart. Great things are sure to happen!

Prayer: *Thank you, Jesus, for showing us the way to life. Thank you for your Spirit to guide us on the way. Amen.*

Saturday, June 10   Read Luke 7:11-17.

The story of the widow of Nain is more than a resurrection miracle. It is one of the many examples of how Jesus is always giving himself to us and giving us to one another. "Jesus gave him [the son] to his mother" (NJB). Just as he gave Lazarus back to Mary and Martha, the centurion back his daughter, so Jesus gives himself back to us through the Holy Spirit, through one another, through the bread and wine of each day.

Scripture abounds with Jesus' invitations to love one another. He gives himself with utter abandon and generosity: "a new commandment I give you—to love one another; my peace I give you; I give you another Counselor; I lay down my life that you may have life." He models for us how we can become whole and holy—and it is by being wholly his.

And even as Jesus gives himself totally to us, he invites us to do no less to others: give them something to eat—ourselves! "Give to the poor, give me a drink, visit those in prison, give light to those in darkness, give to others the knowledge of salvation." Yet, so often we resist his invitation to new life.

Jesus is always asking us through the people, the events, the accidents of our lives to allow him to give himself to us, to others through us. He is always seeking us out, finding us, and inviting us to come back home. Jesus is always knocking at the door of our hearts, waiting for us to open ourselves so that he can make his home in us. So many of us are restless, looking for happiness, for peace, for assurance in our vocations, in our friends and relationships, in our leisure activities—and we find only fragments. Deep within, we know that our hearts will be restless until they rest in God. And only then will we know the wholeness, the holiness Jesus is always calling us to.

Prayer: *I rest in you, Jesus. I rest in you. Amen.*

Sunday, June 11   Read Psalm 113.

"Alleluia! Alleluia! Praise ye the Lord!" What a glorious moment in our lives when we can cry out, "Alleluia!"

Sometimes praise bursts forth from hearts so full that they spontaneously erupt like volcanoes, issuing forth the lava of gratitude, love, and joy. At times, the alleluias in our hearts are quiet, like moonlight shimmering across a still lake on a summer eve—and we smile our thank-you of praise. The first cry of a newborn babe . . . a full rainbow seen amidst sun and rain . . . so many everyday events surprise us with an alleluia expressed as WOW! Praise, more often, wells up as an expression of awe and adoration where words would only diminish the moment. Praise is our only adequate response to the recognition of our own inadequacy in God's presence.

Praise is a gift. We are most whole, most holy, during those times we are lifted up out of ourselves. We glimpse—if only for a moment—the height and depth and breadth of God's glory. We remember that God "stoops to look down on heaven and earth," and that we are called to share in the splendor of creation.

How easy it is to get so caught up in the routine of everyday living that our hearts become constricted, seemingly immune to awe, adoration, and being surprised by the Spirit! Yet, we do not have to wait for a special event to awaken the praise that lives in our hearts. It is our birthright. We were born to praise God!

How rich are those who create time in their lives to remember and to give thanks! Yes, we need to sing our alleluias, for it is in offering praise to our God that we know who we are and who we belong to. Alleluia! Alleluia!

Prayer: *I shall sing praise unto the Lord all the days of my life. Praise the Lord, O my soul! Amen.*

FEARS AND FAITH

June 12-18, 1989   **Bruce A. Mitchell**†
Monday, June 12   Read 1 Kings 19:3-4.

Elijah was rough-and-ready; in the 1980s, we might have called him "macho." But looking at today's scripture lesson, we find a different Elijah, not the man who, a few verses earlier, called for the fire of God to fall upon the armies of kings. Instead, we find a man filled with panic, trying by every device possible to escape human judgment and persecution.

By all rights, Elijah should have been elated. He had been atop Mount Carmel locked in theological combat with the priests of Baal, and Elijah's faith had been rewarded with powerful evidence of God's power. But now he flees in terror. Why?

In many ways our lives are like Elijah's. One minute we find ourselves elated and successful; then suddenly we find ourselves contending with real-life challenges to that faith. Like Elijah, we bask in human successes, but find it difficult—seemingly impossible—to contend with occasional failures that seem to erase every vestige of success (and perhaps faith). Like Elijah, we run, trying to escape failure, persecution, suffering, and sometimes even God.

As we look at Elijah today, we find a human being much like you and me, a person who cries out in anguish, "Why me, Lord?"

Prayer: *Help me, Lord, to realize that solid faith in Christ is my greatest weapon against adversity. Amen.*

---

†Associate pastor, Aloma United Methodist Church, Winter Park, Florida.

Tuesday, June 13   Read 1 Kings 19:7-9.

How far can you run to escape the presence of God?

It seems unlikely Elijah was trying to escape God; rather, it appears he was simply trying to escape human judgment, persecution, and punishment. Often, however, our attempts to escape human judgment coincide with a failure in faith. Perhaps we have a feeling that our actions might not have been pleasing to God. More likely we try to escape because we are not completely sure that God will give us the strength to meet or overcome what other humans put before us. It becomes more a failure in faith than human cowardice.

Inevitably, however, God communicates with the faithful. As we get further from the obvious threat, safety seems more assured. It's a little like the cliché "out of sight, out of mind."

Yesterday Elijah was filled with panic and despair. Today he hears again the voice of God, responds to God, and lets his life become like a new journey with God. His faith becomes strong once again; his body and spirit are nourished by God, and he senses new purpose for his life.

All of us have moments in which we flee, and other moments in which we find ourselves victorious. The 40th psalm talks of fear and faith this way: "I waited patiently for the Lord; he turned to me and heard my cry. He lifted me out of the slimy pit, out of the mud and mire; he set my feet on a rock and gave me a firm place to stand" (NIV).

So it can be for each of us, if we allow faith in God to replace our human fears.

Prayer: *Remind me each day, O Lord, that in my humanity I am weak but that I am offered infinite strength in Christ. Amen.*

Wednesday, June 14   Read Luke 7:36-38.

Have you ever found a point in your life when there seemed no solution to a problem you were facing, a moment when flowing tears expressed deep fears or frustration saturated your soul?

Perhaps you or a loved one has suffered protracted or terminal illness. You've exhausted every possible means of healing; now the only thing left is tears.

Perhaps you have been terminated from a secure position after years with the company. Again and again, your resumés are rejected. The only thing left seems to be tears.

It is unlikely that many, if any, of our readers have lived the lifestyle of a prostitute, but in our own life dilemmas, most of us, at one time or another, have found ourselves as frustrated and fearful as the woman in today's Gospel passage.

We have sought ways in which to change situations in our lives. We have found moments in which we have been ashamed. We have experienced situations of our own making in which we became trapped by what we said or did. Perhaps we became enveloped by thoughts and inner feelings we didn't want anyone to know about, most of all, God.

We go through life fearful of public opinion, fearful of the judgment of twentieth-century Phariseeism. We fear an employer's judgment when we make an error at work. We conform to peer pressure because we don't want to be rejected. We keep secrets from husbands, wives, parents, and children, because we don't want to appear a failure.

Is it possible today's lesson is wrapped up in humankind's difficulty with humility? Is it our unwillingness to trust Jesus? Is it possible that a prostitute understood Jesus better than we do?

Prayer: *All-forgiving God, give me a contrite and humble heart and the trust to know the love of Christ more personally. Amen.*

Thursday, June 15   Read Psalm 42:3, 9-10.

God works in strange ways in the hearts of humans.

Some years ago a highly successful, well-paid engineer left a major company to accept the pastorate of a small country church. His church salary would be 25 to 30% of his engineering salary. Many of his associates in the company questioned the decision, yet the engineer repeatedly responded, "I truly believe this to be a call of God; it is something I must do for God."

It's not uncommon; millions of people through the ages have felt the call to serve God and have responded. That response to God, however, has not always assured an easy lifestyle. The sacrifice of the engineer was small compared to the sacrifices of others willing to risk their life as they volunteered to go into the missionary field, or into centers of poverty or disease because they sensed God had a need for them in that place.

It is difficult to articulate the power of God's call to people who do not understand that call. It is even more difficult to communicate the power of God to others when response to that call sometimes results in serious illness, injury, or death.

The psalmist in today's scripture lesson raises two important questions: "Why does God allow good people to suffer?" and "How can suffering be equated with a holy and loving God?" We experience a psalmist who, like any of us, sheds tears and suffers physical agony when things have gone wrong. As with Job, the psalmist is challenged by those who ask, "Where is your God?"

Everyone, ultimately, faces moments in which faith is tested. Every believer in Christ eventually meets someone who challenges the power of God. But proof of God comes as a product of faith—even when others might seek to destroy that faith.

Prayer: *Merciful Lord, even when life seems darkest, when things seem worst, fill my heart with faith. Amen.*

Friday, June 16   Read Psalm 42:11.

Life is filled with contrasts: Black and white. Day and night. Hot and cold. Fears and faith.

The psalmist sees this clearly. On the one hand, there is a question we ask one another, ourselves, and occasionally God: "Why?"

On the other hand, the psalmist also says that there is an answer to every "why," and that is "God."

Perhaps the most difficult contrast in life is the tension we experience as we try to see life our way, compared to looking at life God's way. Perhaps it is that tension we feel when we attempt a task our own way only to discover that our way is not always Christlike.

All too often we try coming to grips with things apart from God. We try to carry life's burdens ourselves, seeking solutions apart from God. We wonder, then, why situations get worse. We grope for answers. We try to cope with the death of a loved one, illness, or tragedy by ourselves, and we discover we are not very successful at finding answers. Like the psalmist, we find our souls anxious, and we feel our insides churning because we cannot manufacture a solution.

Then we feel that gentle nudge from God reminding us that it isn't our problem alone; that God seeks to comfort and strengthen and guide. God has been there all the time, ready and willing to share the burden we struggle with.

The psalmist is right: all of us face discouraging times, but those discouraging times become bearable, and surmountable, as we trust in God's infinite power.

Prayer: *Lord Jesus, remind us when times seem worst that your power and strength is with us. Amen.*

179

Saturday, June 17   Read Galatians 2:20.

One of the most beautiful things that can happen in any family is true togetherness. It is all too easy today to find members of a family moving in different directions, each toward their own interests, often apart from God.

A husband becomes enveloped in his work. A wife becomes saturated with her job or with activities apart from the family. Children become engrossed with activities of their own to the exclusion of family togetherness.

In short, fragmentation of families often produces hurt and separation.

So it is with our relationship with Jesus Christ. In today's lesson Paul emphasizes the necessity of togetherness with our Lord. Paul reminds us that the real Christian no longer lives with and for himself/herself, but in harmony with—in partnership with—Jesus Christ. The individual's life has been set aside and now that life is one with Christ: "I no longer live, but Christ lives in me" (NIV).

Jesus testifies to this in John 15:5 where he says, "If a man remains in me and I in him, he will bear much fruit; apart from me you can do nothing" (NIV).

Contemporary life is filled with fears and frustrations. We think of job security, peer acceptance, financial security, and wonder what tomorrow will bring. We cannot escape the insecurity of human life.

Today's scripture reminds us, though, that with faith in Christ and others, with Christian togetherness, we can have victory over the fears that would steal our life away.

Prayer: *Lord of grace, replace my weakness with faith to face this day with you. Amen.*

Sunday, June 18   Read Luke 7:36-50.

As we read today's Gospel lesson, we find it telling the story of a woman of ill repute coming to Jesus, kissing his feet, and wiping them with her hair and tears.

She did not come flaunting her faith. She did not stand up in the midst of a crowd and proclaim her faith with a victory sign. Instead, she came to Jesus realizing her human weakness. She came to Jesus recognizing that she was a sinner and seeking some semblance of hope for a life in which virtually all hope was gone.

The beauty of today's scripture passage is wrapped in a quiet, spiritual victory. It is an inner victory in which one comes to know there *is* victory over sin—that the hopelessness of humanity can be overcome through faith.

Thomas à Kempis, in *Imitation of Christ*, summed up this kind of faith-victory thusly: "Faith is required of thee, and a sincere life, not loftiness of intellect, nor deepness in the mysteries of God." The woman who came to Jesus humbled herself to the fullest, giving all she had, even to kissing Jesus' feet and anointing them with her tears.

This week we've shared the tension of fears and faith. Few of us, if any, are immune from fear. However, those whose faith is strong and who trust in Christ are equipped to face the most desolate situation with hope and trust. Through faith the woman who anointed Jesus' feet with tears found peace. Likewise, through faith, we find victory—in Jesus.

Prayer: *O God, replace my fears with faith in Christ. Amen.*

Running Against the Wind

June 19-25, 1989
Monday, June 19

Wanda M. Trawick†
Read 1 Kings 19:4-10.

He was running against the wind, and he was tired of it. His moment of triumph seemed to have backfired. All his efforts to bring spiritual renewal to his nation had failed to produce anything of significant and lasting value. If ever a human suffered from burnout, Elijah did.

Like the best of us, the prophet is ambivalent during this crisis. He expresses a death wish but runs in an attempt to save his life. Whether he is faithless, fearful, disillusioned, or simply physically and mentally exhausted, Elijah's behavior, while understandable, is reprehensible. He has dropped out of the race and lies desolate on the sideline.

And where is the God who was by his side at Carmel? Still at his side. With tender concern God has provided food and rest for the weary runner. Although the prophet has fallen apart completely, God has not given up on him. Nor does he point a finger of judgment at Elijah. He asks a question—a question with a hint of reproach, to be sure—designed to provoke introspection. It is a question that encourages Elijah to get in touch with his feelings.

As Christ's disciples we will always be running against the wind. Jesus warned us we would be a minority. To run against the wind invites exhaustion and failure. But God is not put off by our failures. God is right there when we are sitting with our head in our hands—nurturing us, nudging us toward health.

Prayer: *Thank you, Lord, for caring for us as much when we are the goat as when we are the hero. Amen.*

---

†Free-lance writer, Johnson City, Tennessee.

Tuesday, June 20   Read 1 Kings 19:11-14.

Wind, earthquake, and fire—powerful and dramatic. They were familiar manifestations of God's presence in Elijah's experience. He would never forget the consuming fire of God which fell at Carmel. As an Israelite he had thrilled to the story of the east wind that parted the sea, the story of God at Sinai in the thunder and lightning, the fire and smoke, and the quaking of the mountain. We are both exhilarated and comforted when God shows himself in unmistakable, attention-getting events that prove his existence and presence with us.

But God chooses to show himself in a different way to Elijah—in "a still small voice." It is probably not what Elijah expects, but he is astute enough to recognize it, even in his depressed state.

How often do we miss hearing God's voice or seeing God's hand at work because we have preconceived ideas about how and through whom God will show himself? When we run against the wind, we want big dramatic events to vindicate our faith before a disbelieving, mocking world. We are like John the Baptist who sent his disciples to ask Jesus, "Are you he who is to come, or shall we look for another?" (Matt. 11:3) John had expected the Messiah to bring fire and judgment—to gather the wheat and burn the chaff. Instead, Jesus came teaching, preaching, and healing in a rather low-key ministry. We don't know what John's response was to his disciples' report. We assume he, like Elijah, was able to recognize the voice and purpose of God in quiet, and at times obscure, events. Still small voices worry us. They are easy to miss and can't be verified by others.

Prayer: *Lord, we ask for discernment to recognize your voice in unexpected forms and times and people. Amen.*

Wednesday, June 21　　　　　　　　　Read Psalm 43:1-3.

A question and a plea for vindication begin what is probably the third stanza of a lament composed of Psalms 42 and 43. The writer's vacillation between hope and despair not only gives the two psalms their rhythmic quality but suggest a similar rhythm of moods in a believer. Spiritual giants living in constant victory and ecstacy are indeed rare.

Most of us, like Elijah and the psalmist, find it at times distressingly difficult to answer the questions of those who taunt us, "Where is your God?" We sometimes ask the question ourselves. On the one hand, we can affirm with the psalmist that God is our help, our rock, our refuge. On the other, we become perplexed when evidence against our faith begins to appear incontrovertible and our feelings no longer reflect what we have always accepted as fact. There may come a time (or times) when, if we do possess what we have been promised, we have become incognizant of it. And we question God, "Why hast thou cast me off?" Or we question and rebuke ourselves, "Why go I mourning?"

Sometimes our "whys" are desperate demands for explanation. Sometimes they are simply expressions of perplexity. Saints through the centuries have asked them. Jesus asked and agonized "why?" from the cross. Running against the wind almost demands questions and doubts from time to time. The crucial question becomes, "Will I keep on running if my questions are not answered to my satisfaction?"

Devotional exercise: *Reflect on how your doubts, questions, and desire for vindication affect your commitment to obedience. Is there a way to make those hindrances a positive force in your life? Can you retain hope when you feel faith is gone? Can you find both comfort and example in the one who admitted to Jesus, "I believe; help my unbelief"? (Mark 9:24)*

Thursday, June 22   Read Psalms 42 and 43.

When we are inundated by the forces against us, when we find no evidence that God is for us or with us, we may find ourselves engaged in the same desperate struggle in which the psalmist finds himself. The struggle may be with circumstances, with other people, with God, with ourselves, or with all of the above.

The psalmist has reasons to be depressed and anxious—the oppression of his enemies, seeming abandonment by God in spite of his hunger and thirst for the Lord, and his failure to respond adequately to the taunts and questions of unbelievers. In spite of all these reasons, however, he asks himself, "Why are you cast down . . . and why are you disquieted . . . ?" There is an element of reproach in the question which is repeated as a refrain in the poem—a tacit recognition that in spite of everything his emotional state may not be completely justifiable.

The poet takes a healthy approach to his problem. He makes no attempt to deny or repress his dejection and agitation. He is "cast down" and admits it. He has some "whys" for God and for himself as well. Questioning himself is a step in the right direction, but one period of introspection is not enough. His decision to continue hoping and eventually praising is followed by emotional relapses and must be repeated twice more.

Emotions are powerful and must be dealt with continually if we are to keep running against the wind. The challenge is to acknowledge them but to keep them from controlling us. As the psalmist did, we are to let reason and will question those emotions which can defeat us.

Suggestion for prayer: *Acknowledge and name the negative emotions which absorb your energy, and ask for God's truth and light to help you put them in perspective.*

Friday, June 23   Read Luke 9:18-20.

It was a crucial question, but the time had come to ask it. Jesus had already turned his face toward Jerusalem. If his disciples did not know who he was at this point, the events to follow would certainly put a damper on what little faith and incomplete understanding had been ignited among them. If they did not know who he was by now, his ministry had failed. It was a tense moment for him, and he prepared for it by spending time alone in prayer, as his custom was.

The disciples reported, as Jesus already knew, that the people saw him as a prophet. That was the popular opinion. Jesus then emphasized the "you" in his second question. "But what about you?" he asked. "Who do you say I am?" (NIV) And their answer would forever separate them from the rest of the nation, just as it separates us from the rest of the nation, just as it separates us from those holding the majority opinion today. It set them to running against the wind. They would henceforth be in the world but not of the world—never at home here again. They would be like T. S. Eliot's magi who returned home from their journey but were no longer at ease there in what was now an alien land.

Our answer to a similar question Pilate asked, "What shall I do with Jesus who is called Christ?" (Matt. 27:22) still pits us against the prevailing winds. In an age when the emphasis is on getting rid of anything divisive, we are faced with this awkward question, "Who do you say I am?" We can't escape the question. We all must answer it and then live with whatever complications the answer invites into our lives.

Prayer: *Lord, I sometimes need assurance that you are who you say you are, and always I need courage to live in accord with what I profess to believe. Amen.*

Saturday, June 24   Read Luke 9:21-22.

Just one unexpected thing after another. First of all, they are told to keep quiet about the biggest event in the history of Israel. And that prohibition is followed by a devastating repudiation of nearly everything they had believed about the Messiah. So shocking is Jesus' blunt announcement of the treatment he is going to receive, they don't absorb the information about the resurrection.

They had expected a throne—a seat of honor and power. They are told to expect a cross—an instrument of indignity and death. That kind of 180-degree difference is a shocker. Although Jesus had made allusions to his fate earlier, he saved this plainspoken unequivocal announcement until after their confession of faith. Perhaps they needed to articulate their faith openly before they could handle the consternation they felt on hearing his words.

Those of us who came into the fold because we were told Christ was the answer and later were introduced to his "hard sayings" can appreciate to some degree what the disciples were feeling. My thought upon first reading passages like Luke 9:23-26, the parable of the good Samaritan, and the sermon on the mount with its harrowing conclusion in Matthew 7:21-27, was, "Oh, no. They didn't tell me about all this!" Christ was the answer all right, but he was also going to be a problem.

He is always surprising us—forever introducing us to the unexpected and often to the unwanted. But let's not miss "the rest of the story." The last word is not crucifixion but resurrection.

Prayer: *Lord, shake me loose from my preconceived notions of what the Christian life is supposed to be like, and open me up to the unexpected promptings of your Spirit. Amen.*

Sunday, June 25   Read Luke 9:23-24.

How many evangelists use Luke 9:23 as an invitation? It is remarkably uninviting, and we wish we could explain it away.

The meaning of self-denial continues to be debated. Does it mean to obliterate self, to forget self, to put self second, third, or further down the line, to "just say no" to self, or simply to give up anything that would lessen our commitment to Christ? Whatever it means, it probably doesn't square with most current thinking in psychology. We will be running against the wind again. Perhaps the trick is to have high esteem for the self you deny.

The metaphor of cross-bearing is another area of controversy. In Jesus' day the cross meant death, and it still means that for believers in some areas today. But whatever cross-bearing means to you or me, it is to be voluntary and, according to Luke, daily.

Denying self, bearing our crosses, following Jesus, losing our lives—all these concepts exhort us to give more than get, to do the right thing instead of the safe thing, to do and give the most instead of the least we can get by with, to spend our lives instead of hoard them, and to endure the worst for the sake of following Jesus.

Running against the wind is foolish unless the finish line is worth crossing—unless we "run straight toward the goal in order to win the prize, which is God's call through Christ Jesus to the life above" (Phil. 3:14, TEV).

Devotional exercise: *Reflect on these lines from Melville's* Moby Dick: *"Eternal delight . . . will be his, who coming to lay him down, can say with his final breath—O Father! . . . I have striven to be Thine, more than to be this world's, or mine own."*

IN CHRIST WE ARE FREE

June 26–July 2, 1989
Monday, June 26

Marian Yagel McBay†
Read Galatians 5:1.

We are afraid of freedom

At first glance this week's theme, "In Christ We Are Free," seems to be an obvious truism. However, I invite you to reexamine your notion of freedom through a thorough working of the Galatians text. Though we will not together examine the other lectionary readings, 1 Kings 19:15-21; Psalm 44:1-8; and Luke 9:51-62, I urge you to do so along with the scripture lessons for each day. I think you will find that our study has profound implications for each of these readings, especially for the Luke story.

In today's lection we are told, "For freedom Christ has set you free." These are curious words. What else would Christ set us free for if not for freedom? Yet to be free from one set of ideas or values or beliefs does not necessarily make us free if we replace our earlier set of beliefs with equally or more stringent ideas. Think of the countries of the world who free themselves from fascist regimes only to place themselves in the hands of a despot of another kind. My father used to call this "jumping from the frying pan into the fire."

Devotional exercise: *Examine yourself deeply today. Are there areas of your life in which you are in "bondage"? Write these things down and reflect back on them as we go through this week of study together. You might pencil them in in this devotional guide for easy reference. When you are finished, pray about each one of them. Pray that you will not be afraid to face them and that you will not be overcome by fear when the time comes to let them go.*

† Minister, Nancy Webb Kelly Children's Church/Belle Meade United Methodist Church, Partners-in-Mission, Nashville, Tennessee.

Tuesday, June 27   Read Galatians 5:13-18.

In the law we feel secure

Most of us have lived out a period in our lives during which we have questioned the values with which we were raised. Usually this questioning includes a period of time in which we are essentially without ethical limits. Some individuals, many of them now devoted Christians, have gone out on ethical limbs that would appall many of us. Whether promiscuity, antisocial behavior, or religious doubt is the memorable plague of their conscience, the outcome is likely the same. For a significant period of time following their era of individual anarchy, these people become terrified of freedom. "Freedom", as with the Galatian Christians, was (and may still be) perceived as a suspicious commodity resulting in incredible emotional pain. All too often it brings with it the threat that we ourselves, like the Galatians, might "be consumed."

Paul addresses the fellowship at Galatia with just this understanding in mind. The relatively new church, rich with the spirit of God's saving grace, has been challenged by Judaizers. These Jew-now-Christians are trying to convince the newly converted Gentiles that they must be circumcised and obey dietary laws of Judaism if they are to be true Christians. But Paul said, "The whole law is fulfilled in one word, 'You shall love your neighbor as yourself.' " To press the practices of Judaism upon the Hellenistic peoples of Galatia was tantamount to imposing the Law (Torah) as a means of grace. How dare they!

As devoted Christians, we are consistently faced with the tension between loving freedom and protectionist laws. Paul assures us that if we are living in the Spirit, laws are unnecessary.

Prayer: *Gracious God, deliver us from the bondage to rules and ideas that keep us from your grace. Grant us freedom to love one another in Christ. Amen.*

Wednesday, June 28   Read Galatians 5:19-21.

We are not secure in the law

Laws do not protect us from the human spirit gone awry. They only indict the lawbreakers. Further, law is not necessary for pointing out what is evil and what is not. Along with Paul, we can basically agree about those things which are unacceptable to community life: sexual immorality, impurity, indecency, idolatry, drug use,* hatred, quarreling, jealousy, rage, religious factions, etc. It is only when we choose to live according to impulse that we place ourselves under the law, for the law is only relevant when we are living lives of destruction. Laws may well ultimately protect us from one another, but they can never be a means of grace.

The Judaizers assert otherwise. They believe that the Law (Torah) is a means of grace, though they deny this when it is pointed out to them. When we adopt rigid ideas of morality and behavior (including, especially, customs and traditions unrelated to ethical living/sacrificial loving), we risk asserting the same misunderstanding as that of the Judaizers. We may say we believe that salvation is through the grace of God in Christ, but we live as if it were through the grace of works in our own lives. And so we, too, are in bondage—in bondage to our fear that if we do not control ourselves effectively, we shall be thrown again into chaos. We do not trust Christ to uphold us in love. We turn to our own impulses—and fail. Paul tells us there is another way.

Prayer: *Dear God, help us to know that true freedom is ours when we accept your grace and rely on Christ's love. Amen.*

---

*The Greek word the RSV translates "sorcery" is actually the root word for our present-day "pharmacy." The Greek word refers to any kind of drug use, helpful or no. See *The Interpreter's Bible*, vol. 10, p. 562.

Thursday, June 29   Read Galatians 5:22-23.

Freedom looks different

It takes human beings a tremendous amount of trust to be able to love another. We must work at lowering our walls; we must conscientiously unload our defenses; and we must be intentional in our efforts to give ourselves to others. Until we have done these things, we are incapable of loving others. The average human being can learn to trust another trustworthy human being over the course of time. But only the Christian can learn to love his or her enemies with the same ease!

The fruit of the Spirit are the fruit not of our labor but of Christ's labor in us. We can all recognize them: love, joy, peace, patience/long-suffering, goodness/generosity, faith, gentleness/meekness/humility, self-control: "Against such there is no law." And it is precisely here where the "freedom" to which Christ has set us free is birthed with new meaning. When we walk and live in the Spirit of Christ, there is no need for law.

The really good news is this: "The whole law is fulfilled in one word, 'You shall love your neighbor as yourself' " (v. 14). Not only are we outside the law when loving our neighbor—we fulfill the law without even trying!

Well, maybe it isn't that easy. It isn't easy to put to rest our fears and hurts. It isn't at all an easy thing to love one's neighbor as oneself. We live in a world where we don't really know what it means to love oneself. We also live in a world in which we are often confused about who indeed is our neighbor. But neither of these is the real obstacle to our hope. The greatest obstacle to our hope is our inability to believe that God in Christ is immanent in us. We fail to trust the Christ who lives within our very selves.

Prayer: *Dear God, help us to hear Christ's still small voice within us. May we finally be truly open to the guidance of the Spirit. Amen.*

Friday, June 30   Read Galatians 5:24.

Christ makes freedom possible

If we are one with Christ, then we have united ourselves with Jesus' life, death, and resurrection. But what does that mean in everyday life, and how does that effect the freedom of which Paul speaks? Primarily Paul's words are a profound statement of the conviction that we who are in Christ need no longer be on guard against our "passions and desires." Christ has taken care of them for us.

If you are like me, though, there are days when feelings that seem like "passions and desires" are overwhelming. They begin subtly in the form of daydreams and unfulfilled aims. Other times you feel depression, hopelessness, or mental fatigue. Yesterday I wrote that we live in a world in which we often do not know how to love ourselves. We have learned to ignore our own destructive lifestyles as well as the destructive acts made against us by our own government and economy. We have in many ways lost the basic instinct of self-preservation. Because we have lost this sense of being in danger at conscious levels, we experience many negative feelings without understanding. Depression, mental fatigue, and hopelessness may not be signs of selfishness at all. They may be signs that point to our deepest inner selves and so to our neighbors' needs also. Learn to tell the difference between impulse and deep struggle.

When Paul tells us that we have "crucified the flesh with its passions and desires," he is telling us that narcissism, impulsiveness, and greediness prevent us from loving our communities, our families, and our God. In some real way we are not free to see ourselves until we are profoundly free of ourselves.

Prayer: *Dear God, free us of ourselves so that we may pray like St. Francis that you will make us instruments of your peace. Amen.*

Saturday, July 1   Read Galatians 5:25.

To believe in Christ is to be free

Somewhere years ago I saw a poster of a ballerina shimmering around the edges. A soft glow emanating from the darkness set off her pale and delicate features. The poster read, "If you can think it, you can do it; if you can dream it, you can be it." Oh, how I wish it were as easy as it sounds! The statement is true, but behind that statement can be a lifetime of hard work. The ballerina was a fitting image.

The same is true of walking in the Spirit. We begin by living by the Spirit, but the task of fulfilling that vocation is one filled with great effort and learning. We discipline ourselves in prayer; and like the supple gymnast or perfectly balanced dancer, we slowly, ever so slowly, achieve rhythm and intentionality in our daily lives. Years or decades may pass before our way is as clear as the yellow brick road, but we do not give up and we look less and less behind us.

We are Christians. We are a people who seek meaning and purpose in our daily lives. Let this be our purpose: to live as Christ lived, going about our everyday tasks and taking time to care for our neighbors along the way. Let us live with the commitment to discernment that is so characterized by Paul. Let us not take lightly the words of anyone, but let us take very seriously the inner voice that yields good fruits in its labor.

Prayer: *Almighty God, teach us to walk in your Spirit. Fill us with the fruits of a Christ-filled life. Make us to others the light you have been and will always be for us. Amen.*

Sunday, July 2   Read Galatians 5:26.

Do not be afraid of freedom

In the movie *Julia,* Lillian Hellman is a woman of deep compassion and intellect. Her best friend, Julia, is an exceedingly bright and intrepid character who becomes involved in the secret movement of Jews out of Nazi Germany. Because Julia is known, she is unable to carry financial resources to underground organizations inside Nazi Germany. She asks her friend Lillian, a writer and world traveler, to carry money into Germany for her. At first, Lillian says she is afraid. Julia reflects for a moment on their childhood days and then replies something along these lines: "It is not fear which will keep you from doing this. It is the fact that you have always been *afraid of being afraid.*"

Those lines have haunted me to this day. How many times in my life have I avoided my Christian responsibility because I have been simply afraid of being afraid? Paul is telling the Galatians that they do not need to be afraid of freedom, that freedom in Christ is a comforting, fruitful experience. But they have been afraid before, and now they are afraid of being afraid again.

Do not be afraid of freedom in Christ. A thoughtful and dedicated teacher of the arts once told me that the only real freedom is in structure. Christ provides the perfect structure for freedom. Through the Holy Spirit we are filled with the love necessary to use our freedom in "kingdomly" ways. We may usher in peace and joy in our daily lives and we may contribute to a society, community, family, or world which is a much better place to be. Meanwhile, within our deepest selves we find safety and comfort in the arms of our Savior.

Prayer: *O God, keeper of all your children, teach us the true meaning of being free in your Spirit. Grant us the courage to stand tall in your love and to walk proudly in your ways. In Jesus Christ's name we pray. Amen.*

BECOMING AN ACTIVE NEW CREATION

July 3-9, 1989   **Hugo L. López†**
Monday, July 3   Read Psalm 5:1-8.

From setting to focus

This psalm is traditionally classified as an individual lament. Hurt by the wickedness of evildoers, the psalmist seeks divine justice.

The setting for the occasion includes both time and place. The time is the morning (v. 3), a symbol of a new beginning and, in this case, a beginning with God. The place is the holy temple of the Lord, either within its walls or facing it from a distance (v. 7).

The focus of the psalmist is God. He turns to the Lord fully convinced of God's holiness and justice. His understanding of these divine qualities is that "evil may not sojourn with" God and that God "hatest all evildoers." According to this understanding, God makes no distinction between sin and sinner. Even God's own creatures are rejected when they become instruments of evil.

But there is more in the psalmist's worship than pleading his case before a just God. He comes to this sacred moment "through the abundance of thy steadfast love" and "in the fear of thee." Indeed, this is an affirmation of God's love as well as of God's justice. Then the psalmist prays for God's guidance on the road of life, fully trusting divine righteousness.

Suggestion for meditation: *How does the setting of your prayers help or hinder your perception of God's presence and answer?*

---

† Pastor, Homer United Methodist Church, Homer, Illinois.

Tuesday, July 4   Read Galatians 6:7-10.

From clarification to affirmation

In this concluding section of his epistle, Paul sees the need for an important clarification. The new Christians in Galatia need to realize that God knows all our intentions and actions. Furthermore, God has created us in such a way that in our social lives every action of ours brings about a reaction from other people.

To make his point Paul uses the fertile image of sowing and reaping. Since the beginning of creation, God has established that all vegetation yields seed and bears fruit, each according to its kind (see Gen. 1:11-12). This principle applies also in human life.

The two options open before us are reaping corruption when we have sown "to our own flesh," that is, to our self-interest, or reaping eternal life when we sow "to the Spirit," that is "to fulfil the law of Christ" (v. 2). In view of this, we affirm perseverance in well-doing. We will be rewarded at the time that God has set and which only God knows. This is the *kairos* of God (which the RSV renders as "due season"), that is, the time of God's final action in this world. In the meantime, we are encouraged to recognize and take every God-given opportunity (*kairos*, this time translated as "opportunity"). We should be especially alert to do this with "those who are of the household of faith."

Prayer: *Help me, O God, to recognize the times and opportunities that you provide in my life. Give me the faith and love to do good to others at those times. In the name of Christ. Amen.*

197

Wednesday, July 5   Read Galatians 6:11-14.

From observance to commitment

Verse 11 indicates that what follows is important. For this reason, Paul writes it with his own hand, instead of dictating it to the scribe.

The believers of all religions—Christianity not excepted—need to be aware of an ever-present danger. This is the danger of allowing the observance of religious forms to take the place of personal faith and commitment. The Greek phrase that is rendered "to make a good showing in the flesh" literally means "to make the person look good in the flesh." Here the emphasis is clearly on the believer, who thus becomes the center of attention.

The focus needs to be shifted back to where it belongs. As Paul puts it, the glory belongs in "the cross of our Lord Jesus Christ." Absolutely no religious form can take the place of the cross for the Christian. This sacrifice is sufficient as the application of justice for the sin of the whole world.

Circumcision is a physical mark which identifies a man as a member of the chosen people of God, according to Old Testament tradition. Baptism and Holy Communion are Christian sacraments which point out the centrality of the cross of Christ. But they were never meant to take its place. As Christians we appropriate the cross of Christ by dying to sin and being raised to life with the risen Christ. Two of the functions of the sacraments are to reenact that sacrifice for us and to help us reaffirm our commitment to God and God's kingdom.

Suggestion for meditation: *"Far be it from [us] to glory except in the cross of our Lord Jesus Christ." May this be our personal prayer and commitment.*

Thursday, July 6   Read Galatians 6:15.

From rites to new creation

Paul does not rule out circumcision as meaningless. Being a Jew himself, he has great appreciation on the human level for the whole meaning of this ritual (see Phil. 3:4-5). What he is saying is that there is now for those who believe in Christ a new reality that supersedes the rituals of the Jewish tradition. This is *a new creation*!

The Greek word that has been translated in most English Bible versions as "creation" really encompasses a variety of related meanings: first, the concept of the coming into existence of individual creatures; second, the totality of the created world as an initial and an ongoing act of God; third, the Christian's conscious state of being in the new faith.

All of this is implicit in the way Paul uses this term. But there is in his thought a new dimension. This is more explicit in Second Corinthians 5:16-20. The newness of this creation over-flows onto all aspects of the believer's life situation. He/she never again regards other people from a purely human viewpoint but as God's creatures who, in Christ, become new creations with boundless possibilities before them.

The new or spiritual creation does not cancel or invalidate the old or natural creature. Through the new creation in Christ the old creature is transformed and is given an opportunity for a new beginning, a new vision, a new purpose in life, and a new power to pursue it.

Prayer: *Eternal God, help us to prepare our whole selves to follow up on this new reality: In Christ we are new creations! Amen.*

Friday, July 7   Read Galatians 6:16-18.

From doctrine to practice

After reaching the climax of the new creation in Christ, Paul summarily brings his topic—and with it the epistle itself—to a close. He wishes peace and mercy to "all who walk by this rule." In this context, "walking" is a meaningful symbol. It points to a continual advance towards a new goal, a steady improvement of life in pilgrimage, and a constant renewal of our vision due to an ever-changing horizon.

However, this movement forward does not imply the negation of everything that is left behind. Out of the many expressions and experiences of the Old Covenant, Paul uses here "the Israel of God." He applies this name to all who are blessed with the new creation. The name Israel was first given to Jacob after he struggled with God's messenger (see Gen. 32:24-28). "Israel" actually means "he who strives with God" or "God strives." This has also proven to be a description of the history of Israel, that is, Jacob's descendants as a nation. The whole history presented in the Old Testament can be seen as Israel's constant struggle to choose between the only true God and the many false gods that appealed to their selfish inclinations. That history also reflects God's constant struggle to keep the wayward chosen people faithful.

Now Israel is included in this new opportunity of peace and mercy in the new creation in Christ. Paul, as a Jew who has gone through this experience himself, offers his readers a proof of its reality. He "bears on [his] body the marks of Jesus."

Prayer: *O God, may the grace of our Lord Jesus Christ be with us as we bring this new creation to active manifestation in our lives. Amen.*

Saturday, July 8   Read Luke 10:1-12.

From empowerment to action

The new creation must receive the power it needs to transform faith into action.

At this time, Jesus is aware that the days are drawing "near for him to be received up" (Luke 9:51). Therefore, he wants to make sure that whatever time he has left will be used in the best possible way. He has already sent the twelve apostles "to preach the kingdom and to heal." As preparation for their mission, he "gave them power and authority over all demons and to cure diseases" (Luke 9:1-2).

Now he sends "seventy others . . . two by two . . . into every town and place where he himself was about to come." He gives these seventy lay evangelists detailed explanations about the situation, as well as specific instructions for their ministry. His instructions present an excellent model of stewardship of time and talents in evangelization. The evangelists must not worry about their needs or about the dangers they will face or about those who may not accept their message.

"Peace be to this house!" is more than just a greeting. The word *peace* gives it content and purpose. This peace is intended to stay in the listener and start transforming his/her life and circumstance ("house"). If this opening statement is well received, the messenger can stay in that house and accept that hospitality. He will bring to those people healing and the announcement of the coming of the kingdom. But if it is not well received, he must move on. Neither time nor faith are to be wasted on nonreceptive lives.

Prayer: *Lord, we want to be your messengers. Empower us and guide us to bring your message to those who need it. Amen.*

Sunday, July 9   Read Luke 10:17-20.

From action to integration

During this week together we have gone from the setting of our worship to our focusing on God; from the clarification of the consequences of our actions to the affirmation of our good actions; from the observance of religious rites to the genuine commitment of our lives to God; from our participation in rites to the climax of becoming new creations of God; from the acceptance of our doctrines to the practice of our faith; and from our empowerment by Jesus to the action of evangelization.

Now we consider the disciples' joy of returning to Jesus and to one another. All of them bring an excellent report: "Lord, even the demons are subject to us in your name!" This is at the same time a report of what they have accomplished and a recognition that the power for it has come from Jesus. The reality of their report is joyfully confirmed by Jesus, who has had a vision of the fall of Satan.

The moment of integration comes in the following words of Jesus. First, he reassures them that he has given them authority (and power with it) to overcome all forms of evil, even "serpents and scorpions" (cf. Ps. 91:13), which are symbols of Satan's powers. Furthermore, they have done this as members of teams of evangelists, which creates a union among them. Finally, he reveals to them that their "names are written in heaven," which establishes a communion between all of them and God.

Prayer: *We thank you, O God, for a vision of spiritual development. Help us recognize where we are now, and bring our lives to fulfillment as integrated parts of your plan. Amen.*

GOD'S PRESENCE

July 10-16, 1989   **Michael J. O'Donnell**†
Monday, July 10   Read Psalm 139.

The response of the Lord in our lives is a mixed blessing at times. We have a strong need for God to be with us always. Human nature also calls us to be completely independent of any outside entity. We have a continuing conflict with these two needs.

With God by our side we can never go completely wrong. God is always there to help us through whatever situation we find ourselves in. This does not mean that God just bails us out of our foolishness but that God is available when we call in faith.

But part of us resists that closeness. Our society dictates that we be "self-made" persons. While in our hearts we realize that we are God-made, we still find ourselves bending to the will of society.

The psalmist reminds us that we are utterly dependent upon our Lord for our life, our strength, our hope. God knows us deeper than we can know ourselves. God hears our thoughts even before we think them, our prayers before we utter them, our direction before we turn toward it.

Our independence is an illusion. Our faith links us to the ultimate reality—God. When we can get that perspective right, we can view the pressures of society in a new light and have new life in Jesus Christ.

Prayer: *Most gracious and ever-present God, who knows us better than we know ourselves, we thank you that you love us so much that we can never escape your presence. Amen.*

---

† Abbot of the Order of St. Luke; Director of Resourcing, Dayton North and South districts, West Ohio Conference, The United Methodist Church; editor, *Sacramental Life*, Dayton, Ohio.

Tuesday, July 11   Read Psalm 139.

The presence of the Lord in our lives is quite reassuring. We can approach all the cares of our world with confidence, knowing that God is here with us and with all persons. We can rest in the assurance of a God who cares.

This presence gives us confidence, builds our faith, allows us to look beyond our problems to a truth that is greater than even our own lives.

We can look upon the tragedies of the world—famine, war, substance abuse—without falling into utter despair. Of course, this does not mean that we can ignore those afflictions, but we can see that there is a hope that transcends the situation.

God's presence reminds us that we have a responsibility in the midst of the world's heartache. We cannot view the problems without being compelled to do something about them. God's ever-present nature frees us to accept God's power to address those issues.

Were we to have to go it alone—without God's presence, without God's power, without God's direction—it would be hopeless indeed. But we know through Jesus Christ that God does give us power and authority to address every issue there is.

As individuals we can help do the job in the context in which we live. When Christian individuals come together as the church of Jesus Christ, then the power of God comes in full force and nothing is impossible.

For that to happen, we must all do our part, for it is in the corporate nature of the church that Christ is incarnated, made flesh again in our world.

Prayer: *Increase our faith, O Lord, that we may move beyond the possible to use the power you have given us, that your will may be done on earth as it is in heaven. Amen.*

Wednesday, July 12   Read Psalm 139:10-12.

The psalmist assures us that God is always present with us. For many people, however, it is God's absence that is felt more than God's presence. There is often a void in our lives that we can identify as the absence of God.

As we grow in faith we reach certain levels of development. These are plateaus of acceptance of who we are in God's life and who God is in ours. We may have struggled greatly in order to reach that level, and once there we rest in the everlasting arms of our Lord.

We may rest there too long. Taking in the rich fragrance of God's sweet love, we become comfortable and spiritually content. This is dangerous to our spiritual health, for after a period of rest we are called upon to begin the climb to the next level.

If we do not take the initiative, God may choose to prod us. One way is by withdrawing, not from us but from our consciousness of God's presence. This serves as a bitter reminder of what it is like not to have God in our lives. It creates in the faithful a hungering for the Lord. Out of that hungering comes a search for spiritual nourishment. That nourishment does not come easily, however, for we must leave the comfort of the plateau we have been resting on and move along. It is out of God's great love for us that we may feel God's absence but for a little while.

Prayer: *O Lord, in your absence may we feel your presence, that we may strive to discover you anew on your terms rather than ours. Amen.*

Thursday, July 13   Read Psalm 139:6.

For many people the absence of God is felt not because God is actually absent but because God has intentionally become temporarily less accessible. The reason for this may be that we need to alter our perception of who God is or what God wants us to be or do.

As we grow, we develop specific concepts of who God is. While these understandings may have truth in them, they are not the total picture. God is greater than anything we can ever comprehend. There comes a time when the picture of God that we hold dear is no longer what we need in order to continue to mature.

As children we learned to pray asking for specifics, "God bless Mommy and Daddy . . . " We also learn visual and aural cues that tell us that God is present. This occurs in Sunday school, worship, and most especially the sacraments.

We carry this concept of God's visibility as we go through life. Then we pray for God to show us what our purpose is and why we are in this place at this time; and we expect a clear answer.

That may be just the time that God says, "I'm not going to tell you. I have given you the answer already through your faith. Don't ask—listen."

It is when we stop praying by asking God and expecting answers in a specific way that we open ourselves to new understandings, to deeper faith.

Sometimes it is through silence that God speaks the loudest.

Suggestion for meditation: *Pray today by not saying any words at all but by closing your eyes and visualizing God reaching down to lift you up and hold you.*

Friday, July 14   Read Psalm 139:1-6.

While the presence of the Lord in our lives can be quite reassuring, it can also be frightening. We are like children who want to have their parents present—but not too present. We prefer to have them in the background, just out of sight until we call upon them.

We expect them to be watchful of our every need while at the same time not noticing when we do something wrong or bad. We want them to bail us out of situations we get ourselves into but not to interfere with our decision to do wrong.

We have similar expectations about God. We expect God to somehow be a holy presence in absentia; we want God to be absent and present at the same time.

This confusion often throws us into a spiritual whirlwind of uncertainty and despair. We are not sure what we want or what God wants for us. A major part of our faith journey is trying to sort out how much of God we want in our lives; how close we want God to be.

The real question for us is how much we will allow God's presence to influence us rather than inviting God in. God is present, whether we like it or not. What we do with that presence will have a strong impact on our life and the lives of those around us.

Prayer: *Help us put our trust in your holy presence, O God of life. Grant us the wisdom to use your presence for your will and not ours, in the name of the holy and blessed Trinity. Amen.*

Saturday, July 15   Read Psalm 139:1-6.

Is it possible to get too close to God? If so, how close is too close?

In many relationships, we tend to back away from intimacy. Intimacy is viewed as a threat, "If you knew who I really am, you would hate me." Our fear of being found out prevents us from accepting the very love we need. So we try to keep an acceptable social distance. We do not want our personal space violated.

We also fear that God will find us out. We mistakenly believe that God knows us as people know us; that is, only what we reveal of ourselves. But God, who created us through the power of love, already knows us better than we know ourselves. And yet God loves us and God wants to be intimate with us. Jesus came as one of us to show us God's desire for intimacy. Perhaps our problem is that we tend to see the judgmental side of the parent rather than the loving, nurturing side. Much of our relationship with God operates out of a sense of guilt.

But God does not want us to wallow in guilt. The best thing for us to do is to confess the guilt and accept the love that is open to us.

As long as we feel that God is judging us, then God will continue to be too close for comfort for us. When we are able to shed the guilt through repentance, then we are able to rest in the bosom of our loving parent.

Thanks be to God who forgives us and loves us.

Prayer: *Most loving Parent, we are your children who need to come closer to you. Help us to shed the barriers of guilt and remorse that we may accept your unconditional love for us. Through Jesus Christ our Lord. Amen.*

Sunday, July 16   Read Psalm 139:7-10.

God's ever-present nature appears to be both good and bad news for us. On the one hand we rejoice in the consistency and intimacy of God's love. On the other hand we rebel against such closeness.

This conflict comes from our need for autonomy and security. The two are not mutually exclusive. God has given us enough freedom to develop in the way we choose. There are many paths we can travel. Through Jesus, God has shown us the best way, the path that will bring us closest to the Lord, the route that will lead us correctly. God has left us with the decision.

If we choose the wrong path—and we often will—God is always present, ready to help us change our direction and start our journey anew. However, it is not simply a lifting us up out of the wrong itinerary and plopping us on the right one. It is the giving to us the constant opportunity to discover what we have been doing wrong and to correct ourselves.

For us this is repentance; for God it is called grace. It is that fine balance that our Sovereign gives us to maintain our spiritual health. This does not come easily for us, for repentance means that our autonomy is not total. Ultimately we come under the lordship of Jesus Christ. It is only when we realize that as a blessing rather than a restriction that we can accept God's loving grace.

Praise be to God who offers us autonomy and grace!

Prayer: *Most loving God, we thank you for caring so much about us that you allow us to come to you over and over. Guide and direct our ways, now and forever. Amen.*

KNOWING OURSELVES AS GOD'S OWN

July 17-23, 1989   **Janet McNish Bugg†**
Monday, July 17   Read Psalm 139:1-18.

This psalm of praise and thanksgiving tells us why the psalmist knows he can call on God in his current situation. God knows us, the psalmist writes. God knows everything we do. God understands our thoughts. God knows what we will say before we say it. God is everywhere; there is no place we can go to escape God. God created us; God "didst knit [us] together." God knew us in our mother's womb, saw us before we were born. The psalmist is awed by such a God and in wonder knows he can turn to this all-knowing, always-present God for help.

Like the psalmist, we know that there is no facet of our lives that does not belong to God. Therefore, we know that we can turn to God in whatever situation we find ourselves. Why hide our thoughts from God? God already knows them. Why hide our actions from God? God already knows everything we do. Why hide ourselves from God? God made us, and God is everywhere. Why pretend we are something we are not before God? God knew us in the womb.

How fortunate we are, then, that we can share in the psalmist's wonder at our Creator, that we can affirm, "How precious are your thoughts to me" (TEV), for it is in the thoughts of God and in our awe-ful response that our noblest dreams for ourselves and humanity are born.

Knowing ourselves as God's own means that we acknowledge and rejoice at God's place in every facet of our lives.

Prayer: *How precious are your thoughts to me, O God! Let me remember that no part of my life escapes your loving and just attention. Amen.*

---

†Editor, *Pockets,* the magazine for children published by The Upper Room, Nashville, Tennessee.

Tuesday, July 18   Read 2 Kings 4:8-17.

This would be a very different world if all of us who acknowledge God as our creator were as open to serving others' needs with no thought of personal gain as were Elisha and the Shunammite woman. People need to hear God's word. Elisha accepted the call to become God's prophet and in doing so committed himself to a "nonprofit" lifestyle—a lifestyle of existing on the barest essentials. Jesus clearly outlined such an existence in Luke 9:3: "Take nothing with you for the trip: no walking stick, no beggar's bag, no food, no money, not even an extra shirt" (TEV). The Shunammite woman, open to another's need, provided Elisha with a room whenever he came to town. In her openness, she asked nothing for herself, and God was able to work through her to meet the needs of the prophet.

Elisha's concern for the people of the land extended not only to preaching the word of God to them but also to meeting the needs of their daily existence. In Second Kings 4:1-7, Elisha helped the poor widow; Elisha recognized that a wealthy woman has needs, too. In a time when a woman's worth was measured by how many children—sons particularly—she could give her husband, this woman's childlessness would have been a great personal tragedy. Because Elisha brought God's word to the woman, she did indeed conceive and bear a son.

God often meets our needs—although not always in the way we expect—through the actions of other people. Knowing ourselves as God's own, then, means being open enough to others' needs that God can work through us to meet those needs.

Devotional exercise: *Sit quietly and picture the people who are part of your life every day—people in your family, in your workplace, in the places you frequent. What are their needs, spoken or unspoken? Are you able to let God work through you to meet those needs?*

211

Wednesday, July 19 Read Psalm 139:13-18.

If God formed me in the womb before I had the chance to call God's name, did God not form others in like manner, no matter what name they give to God?

If God knitted my bones together before I ever heard the Creation story, the words of the prophets, or the story of the baby in the manger, did God do any differently with a child born to Hindu parents or Muslim parents or parents who are citizens of an officially atheistic nation?

If God knew me before I was born, before I had ever heard, much less understood, words like *incarnation, redemption, salvation,* and *forgiveness,* did God not know others whose theologies may not include similar concepts?

If we do, indeed, acknowledge God's activity in all of human birth (and not to do so severely limits God's power), then this activity is the bottom line for us; it is where all of us, no matter who we are or where we live, have our identity. All of us have the same basic identity as children of God—formed in God's own image, Genesis tells us. Any search for self-identity that does not acknowledge both this basic identity for ourselves and all others and the resulting ties with all of humanity is a spurious search fueled by an individualism not in keeping with God's wishes for this earthly family.

Knowing ourselves as God's own means that we know others as God's own.

Prayer: *Dear God of all people, help me remember that my brothers and sisters are Everyman and Everywoman. Amen.*

Thursday, July 20   Read Luke 10:38-42.

Most of us are neither wholly Martha nor wholly Mary. Often when we stop to hear God's word or to experience the beauty of God's creation, we are aware that there are tasks we need to be about. And when we are about those tasks, we yearn for a time apart, for time to hear God's word for us. Living with these Mary-Martha tensions often allows only glimpses of God's love and the beauty of creation. But perhaps in the midst of those tensions we become part of that love and beauty.

In his book *A Way in the World*, Ernest Boyer tells of a busy homemaker and mother of two who declared to her minister, "I'm never going to read the New Testament again." She pointed out many of the New Testament passages that seem to speak against home and family in favor of more dramatic action. Then she asks, "What of Mary and Martha? It's Mary, who spends her time adoring Christ, rather than Martha who works to keep him fed, who Jesus says has the better part. Where do I fit in?"

Most of us, I think, feel more like Martha. Our time is spent in seemingly mundane daily tasks which so consume us that it is difficult to see ourselves as a vital part of God's kingdom. Yet it is in the very giving of ourselves in countless small acts to others that they and we experience the kind of love Jesus talked about. Perhaps we need to ask ourselves how those daily tasks serve others. We may be surprised to find that, like Brother Lawrence, we can know God's presence in the midst of sweeping floors and baking bread. And we can know that God affirms us in the midst of our routine.

Knowing ourselves as God's own means that we understand even our most mundane task as service to God.

Prayer: *Dear God, help us to see our everyday tasks from a fresh perspective and to feel your affirming presence with us. Amen.*

213

Friday, July 21   Read Luke 10:38-42.

How many of us have silently thought that Martha has taken a "bum rap" for almost two thousand years? After all, somebody had to feed Jesus, and Mary was obviously not going to do it! Welcoming and feeding a guest was the honorable, courteous thing to do in Martha's time. So where did Martha go wrong?

"Martha, Martha!" [Jesus said.] "You are worried and troubled over so many things, but just one is needed" (TEV) . This one thing may refer to the amount of food Martha is preparing. "Just a sandwich will be fine." Or this one thing may have a spiritual reference: "The only important task now is to hear what I am teaching you." Either meaning tells us that Martha has lost the perspective out of which she needs to examine all of her activity. Martha has in this instance chosen activity over hearing and understanding the word of God.

We, too, can become so busy trying to live out our understanding of God's word that we neglect to have that word present with us, refreshing us. And we do not let it sustain us. When the results of our work are much less than we expected, we become angry, or bitter, or self-deprecatory; we become "worried and troubled over so many things." It is only when God's word is with us, when we are able to see ourselves acting in God's larger purpose and in God's own time that we can turn loose of the results of our work and give them to God.

Recognizing ourselves as God's own means renewing ourselves constantly in God's word so that we can not only carry out the many mundane tasks that make up most of our existence but also dare to become "busy" with the problems of nuclear proliferation, homelessness, hunger, and pollution.

Prayer: *Dear God, I stay so busy, often too busy to hear you. Forgive me, and keep nudging me to stop to listen. Amen.*

Saturday, July 22   Read Colossians 1:21-29.

In this epistle, Paul appears to be addressing some of the false teachings that arose in the early church. Nowhere does Paul tell us what these false teachings are, but his statements on the pre-eminence of Christ and his assertions that the gospel is for everyone and that salvation does not mean separation from the created world lead scholars to believe that Paul was combatting an early form of Gnosticism.

In answering these false teachings Paul restates for the Colossians what their reconciliation in Christ means. "At one time you were God's enemies because of what you did and thought" (AP), Paul writes. And who should know better what it means to be God's enemy but the one who was the archenemy of early Christians, the one who "tried to destroy the church"? (Acts 8:3, TEV) But now, Paul writes, by means of Jesus' physical death, "God has made you his friends." Recognizing ourselves as God's own, allowing God to befriend us, means recognizing God's authority and becoming, like Jesus and Paul after him, a servant. In a world seemingly gone mad with power—power measured in dollars and megatons—we must learn to wield another kind of power, the power of the servant, the power that comes from "using the mighty strength which Christ supplies" (TEV), and which works in us. The secret, then, of this kind of power is that "Christ is in you," that our lives conform so to Christ's life that we become Christ's presence in the world.

Knowing ourselves as God's own brings friendship with God, and that friendship is a demanding one.

Prayer: *It is difficult, dear God, to live in this world and not conform to the world's definition of power. Help me remember, God, that you are the all-powerful one, and the only truly powerful people are those who are your servants. Amen.*

215

Sunday, July 23   Read Colossians 1:21-29.

"God has made you his friends" and "Christ is in you"—we tend to lose sight of both of these messages. Again, it is Paul, who as Saul of Tarsus had been God's enemy, who can speak so forcefully of being reconciled to God. After his experience on the Damascus Road, Saul—who had been responsible for so much persecution and death—could have been so overcome with guilt, so burdened with the weight of his actions, that he could not hear the message: that because Christ died for all, sin had no power over Saul, that Saul now lived in fellowship with God in Christ. Had Saul not been able to accept his sanctification by God's grace, he would not have become the apostle Paul, the carrier of the message to the Gentiles—to us. He would never have written so powerfully about justification by grace through faith and about the indwelling Christ. What guilt immobilizes us? Have we accepted God's forgiveness? What great thing is guilt preventing us from accomplishing?

Being reconciled with God means our being in Christ and Christ's being in us. Thus, even when we are alone, we are not really alone. In a world where so many are lonely in the midst of a crowd, where we are nameless, identified by a computerized number, estranged from family, so mobile that we have lost our roots, living in a society that so highly prizes individualism, what a welcome message this is. Christ is in us; we are never truly alone.

Guilt and loneliness are debilitating states of mind. Knowing ourselves as God's own does not mean we are strangers to guilt and loneliness, but it does mean that through God's reconciliation of us, we can free ourselves from their effects.

Prayer: *Thanks be to you, God, for the freedom from guilt and loneliness that you offer us. Amen.*

A GOD WHO CARES

July 24-30, 1989   **William E. Smith†**
Monday, July 24   Read 2 Kings 5:1-7.

The contrast between the two principals in this international drama is striking. Naaman, the powerful Syrian army commander, and Elisha, the humble, unpredictable prophet of Israel, seemingly have little in common.

Naaman was a leper. That reality not only forced him to face the limitations of his power but led him into a relationship with the God of Israel that brought both healing and faith.

There is a paradox here. Healing is possible only for those who are ill and admit their need of help. Declared Paul: "I will . . . gladly boast of my weaknesses, that the power of Christ may rest upon me . . . for when I am weak, then I am strong" (2 Cor. 12:9-10).

Notice how once again God used ordinary people through whom to work his will: a Hebrew servant girl in Naaman's household captured during a military incursion into Israel; a prophet who prefers obscurity to public display; and two kings who unwittingly become spokespersons of the divine will.

Can we believe that God is at work in all circumstances in ways we cannot possibly know, and that if we but trust, God's grace will see us through? " God moves in a mysterious way His wonders to perform; He plants His footsteps in the sea, And rides upon the storm."*

Prayer: *Lord, deepen my faith in your care, and help me to love all persons even as you love me. Through Christ our Lord. Amen.*

---

† United Methodist minister (retired from West Ohio Annual Conference), teaching at the Divinity School, Duke University and living in Pinehurst, North Carolina.

* William Cowper, "God Moves in a Mysterious Way."

Tuesday, July 25   Read 2 Kings 5:8-15*a*.

Naaman was stunned. He had arrived with his horses and chariots and considerable wealth before the house of Elisha. Not only did the prophet not offer Naaman a cool drink; he did not even show up to welcome him. A strange reception for such a high-ranking guest. Instead, Elisha sent word to Naaman to wash seven times in the Jordan river.

Naaman was hoping for something more dramatic (5:11). Besides, how could one be cleansed by bathing in a muddy stream? There were far more impressive rivers in Syria. "So he turned and went away in a rage."

Once again cool heads prevailed. His servants convinced him he should at least give the prescribed remedy a try. After the seventh dip in the Jordan his flesh was restored "like the flesh of a little child, and he was clean." But whatever benefits may have come from washing away diseased scales from his body, the primary cure was the transformation of Naaman's soul. Naaman returned to the man of God and exclaimed, "Behold, I know that there is no God in all the earth but in Israel."

It is an amazing declaration. The greatness of God is affirmed by a non-Jew, by definition an unbeliever. Here is a dawning universalism that is to find its culmination in the coming of Christ and the proclamation of the Good News to all the nations. And Elisha's role as a prophet in Israel, as God's personal envoy, was affirmed.

Make no mistake about it: to God belonged the glory. Always it is so. Benjamin Franklin is reported to have remarked to a friend recently recovered from illness: "God heals, and the doctor takes the fees."

Prayer: *How great thou art, O God of the universe! Help me to be receptive to your healing presence always, through Jesus Christ our Lord. Amen.*

Wednesday, July 26   Read Psalm 21:1-7.

This is a psalm deeply rooted in the worship life of the Hebrew people. It was probably sung in celebration of the anniversary of the king's coronation. The king was "the unique channel through which God poured his blessing upon his people."* It is this special relationship between monarch and the God of Israel that inspires the psalmist.

"In thy strength the king rejoices." Is it presumptuous to seek God's gracious protection for our lives? Not as long as we remember the Source of all our blessings:

Know that the Lord is God;

he has made us and we are his own,

his people, the flock which he shepherds.

(Psalm 100:3, NEB)

Thou dost meet him "with blessings and prosperity" (NEB). The image is that of a caring God far more willing to give than we to ask, who goes out to meet us, like the father of the prodigal son, to shower blessings upon us.

For the king trusts in the Lord. Professor Leslie translates the final phrase: "And of the lovingkindness of the Most High he has no doubt."

Through the disciplined life of prayer and Bible study we need to cultivate a childlike trust in a loving God that will sustain us at all times: "Underneath are the everlasting arms" (Deut. 33:27).

Thanks be to God!

Prayer: *Grant, O Lord, the vision to see your power and love at work in the lives of others, as well as in our own lives. Help us always to give thanks. Through Jesus Christ our Lord. Amen.*

---

* Elmer A. Leslie, *The Psalms* (N.Y., Abingdon-Cokesbury, 1949), p. 89.

Thursday, July 27   Read Colossians 2:6-10.

The church at Colossae was in trouble. Some of the newly-converted Christians still clung to pagan beliefs and practices which were undermining the supremacy of Christ and creating bitter divisions within the church. Could they understand that "Christ is all in all," and that we are saved not by good works or by esoteric wisdom, but by "faith in the working of God, who raised (Christ) from the dead?" (2:12) It was to meet these challenges that Paul wrote to the Colossians from prison.

In today's reading Paul meets the opposition head-on. The personhood of Christ cannot be compromised: "He is the image of the invisible God, the first-born of all creation . . . in him the whole fulness of deity dwells bodily" (1:15, 2:9).

In Jesus of Nazareth who walked the hills of Galilee, who healed and taught and forgave his enemies, who died a martyr's death, who rose from the dead and is alive forevermore we see "all the fulness of God" (1:19). This "scandal of particularity" is what distinguishes Christianity from the other religions of the world. There is much that is good in each of them, but the supremacy of Christ stands alone.

Remember who is writing this letter: not an armchair theologian but a former enemy of Christ determined to stamp out every vestige of the Christian "heresy." Then he encountered the risen Lord who called him to be "a servant of Jesus Christ . . . set apart for the gospel of God" (Rom. 1:1).

Paul reminds us that theological doctrines will not save us. The life-transforming grace of Jesus Christ will.

Prayer: *We thank you, O God, that your grace is greater than our sins and our stumbling faith. Amazing grace indeed! Amen.*

Friday, July 28   Read Colossians 2:11-15.

The Christians at Colossae were being corrupted by a strange syncretism of Jewish legalism and pagan philosophy which is not surprising, considering the social context in which they lived.

Nor should we be surprised today by the popularity of cults (e.g. the Krishnas, the Moonies, the Children of God, etc.). Or by the dawning of the "New Age," which combines faith healing, fortune-telling, and meditation (we, too, believe in prayer!) with distinctly un-Christian doctrines: the transmigration of the soul to name but one.

So what else is new? We long for God: "Our hearts are restless till they find their rest in thee" (Augustine). If our lives are not rooted and grounded in Christ, we become easy targets for the purveyors of "every wind of doctrine," and deluded by "the cunning of men (and women), by their craftiness in deceitful wiles" (Eph. 4:14).

It has been said that anything is permissible if there is no God. That is precisely what Paul is combating in ancient Asia Minor and modern America. God has revealed God's nature supremely in Christ. God offers power and peace and purpose to all who are joined with Christ in baptism and raised by him to newness of life.

New life. In Christ. Now.

Prayer: *Gracious God, Father of our Lord Jesus Christ, forgive my halfheartedness. Save me, and save our spiritually starved generation, from the folly of following false gods. Amen.*

Saturday, July 29   Read Luke 11:1-4.

The disciples saw Jesus praying. So they asked him to teach them as John (the Baptist) had taught his disciples.

Father: Behind the Greek *Pater* is the Aramaic *Abba* which Jesus characteristically used. It is a very intimate term which some have translated "daddy." What is important is not so much the word itself as the relationship that is implied. God/Father/Abba is not a transcendent being dwelling in cold and distant splendor, but One who is intimately related to and lovingly concerned for each of God's children.

Hallowed be thy name. Thy kingdom come: "May the time come when the holiness of God's being will be universally acknowledged."* Then, surely, God's kingdom will have arrived. Meanwhile, we are to revere God's very being.

Each day: To trust God is to know that our basic needs for life will be met daily. That does not mean we are to be extravagant or wasteful, but that God is dependable. We are not to worry about the unknown future, but live one day at a time.

Forgive our sins as we forgive: Forgiveness and repentance are interdependent. We cannot forgive others until we, ourselves, have been forgiven.

Lead us not into temptation: We can hardly expect to be spared trials when our faith and even our integrity will be tested. There is comfort in knowing that God will not let us be tempted beyond our strength. (1 Cor. 10:13) It is even more reassuring to know that God is always near and God's power is ever available to those who ask.

Prayer: *Thanks be to you, God, for love beyond measure and power—love that enables us to overcome all that would defeat us. Amen.*

---

* The Interpreter's Bible, vol. VIII (New York, Abingdon-Cokesbury Press, 1952), p. 201.

Sunday, July 30   Read Luke 11:5-13.

In a world of no refrigeration and entire families sleeping in one room, with the door to the house closed for the night, it is a lot to expect a neighbor to get up, waking several members of the family in the process, and provide fresh bread. Besides, everybody knows that bread baked early in the morning was expected to last only that one day. Who would ever have three loaves left over? But the neighbor kept pounding. Hungry guests, arriving unexpectedly at midnight, needed food, and Eastern hospitality demanded nothing but the best.

Very reluctantly the father got up and stepped gingerly over curled bodies. Cursing under his breath for having to share his family's precious food, he opened the door and thrust three loaves of bread into his neighbor's hands.

Is God like that, finally and begrudgingly giving in to our incessant pleas? Of course not! We do not have to bombard heaven with cries for help. God knows our needs even before we ask. And if a loving human parent gives a child only good gifts, how much more lovingly will our parent in heaven give to those who ask?

Does this turn God into a celestial Santa Claus waiting to answer our every request? No. God is not to be cajoled or manipulated. If we continue to think only of ourselves, we will shut both God and our neighbors out of our lives. We are to begin our prayers by focusing on God: "Hallowed be thy name. Thy kingdom come. . . ." Then we are to ask for personal blessings.

The thrust of Jesus' words is unmistakable: we are to seek, knock, and ask. God is to determine what is best for us. Because God truly cares, we are in for some major surprises!

Prayer: *Thank you, Abba, for your providential care. Help me to trust at all times, even when you seem to say no. May your will be done on earth through me. Amen.*

THE WILL OF GOD

July 31–August 6, 1989   **John W. Bardsley†**
Monday, July 31   Read 2 Kings 13:14-20.

Chronic question

Knowing the will of God has been of great concern ever since our Creator breathed the breath of life into Adam and Eve. When the prophets, respected holy men, spoke, "Thus says the Lord!" people listened because these holy persons were close to God.

In today's reading, we hear of Elisha, now an old man. He has not been heard from since he sent a prophet to anoint Jesu (2 Kings 9). Though on his deathbed, Elisha must do one more act of power and might. As so many have when a leader is about to die, Joash weeps and says, "What will I do now?" Joash uses the exact words Elisha did when telling of Elijah's death (see 2 Kings 2:12). For Joash, Elisha is more important to the nation than all their chariots and armies.

Elisha tells Joash to shoot an arrow out the east window to show that the victory would be in the east, where Syria had taken Israelite territory. Guided by Elisha, Joash takes on power and authority he never thought possible.

People still look for leaders who represent the highest ideals of commitment and service. For believers, these ideals mean holiness—living close to God so that our acts reflect God's will and purpose.

Doing the will of God, we ride God's chariot to victory!

Prayer: *O Lord, help us to know your will. Then give us the courage to do it. Amen.*

---

† Pastor, The United Methodist Church, Huntington, New York.

Tuesday, August 1   Read 2 Kings 13:14-25.

Accepting the will of God

Elisha commanded Joash to strike the ground with the arrows. Joash perfunctorily struck the ground three times without enthusiasm. Elisha was furious! He had spoken for God, and Joash had not really paid attention. "You didn't go far enough! You didn't go all the way!" Elisha said (AP). "Therefore, the victory is limited, incomplete." A golden opportunity had been presented to Joash, and he had blown it.

How often have we gone only part of the way with God? How often have we stopped just short of the goal? God's enemies and opponents do not. To paraphrase verse 19, "Keep shooting the arrows until you've won!"

A young woman spoke about her multiple sclerosis and the effect it was having on her ability to live life as she wanted to. This Christian mother, now speaking to others in groups about her faith, said, "I would not change anything in the past year, including MS. Oh, I wish I didn't have to deal with it, but it has caused me to spend more time seeking the will of God. I should have done that much sooner."

Victory is achieved with complete commitment, persistence, determination, and enthusiasm. Joash stopped short of these. When we focus totally on knowing the will of God, the results are always surprising and boundless.

Prayer: *Lord, let me know and understand that when I work with you, we can do anything. Amen.*

225

Wednesday, August 2   Read Psalm 28.

The will of God sought from the source

This psalm is divided into two sections. The first portion, verses 1-5, dramatically expresses the psalmist's desperate need for God. The urgency is probably an illness caused by or blamed on certain godless and reprehensible persons.

The problem has reached such a critical stage that if aid does not soon come, the writer will end up in the pit—i.e., the grave, Sheol. There is no place to turn but to God, the Rock. "Rock" is used several times in the Old Testament to indicate the strength and protection the Lord offers.

God's help is needed so the psalmist will not suffer the evildoer's punishment. We can almost hear the psalmist plead, "Listen to me, Lord! Don't turn a deaf ear to me! I don't want to end up like them!"

Then he lifts his hands, begging for help and mercy. Uplifted hands are a prayerful posture and signify a reaching out to God, eagerly awaiting some sought-after blessing. The psalmist does not wish to overlook anything that will convince God to hear him in this crisis.

In Luke 11:5-8, Jesus speaks of the friend's boldness—persistence. James says that the prayer of a righteous person is "powerful and effective" (James 5:16, NIV).

The psalmist pleads directly to God and waits confidently for a positive answer, for it is assuredly the will of God that believers be saved.

When we consider God's readiness and ability to hear as well as God's love for us and willingness to answer, we find good reason to direct our pleas to the "Rock of our salvation."

Prayer: *Lord, help us to realize that you have already begun to act on our behalf even before we ask for your help. Amen.*

Thursday, August 3   Read Psalm 28.

Found in answered prayer

The desire to have prayer answered is as deep as the desire to know the will of God. We hold out all sorts of promises if God will just answer our request. Implied in such promises is that the answer given must be the one we want.

Whatever the threat that occasioned today's psalm, it is now gone. God has answered the psalmist's prayer. Prayer and praise go hand in hand, and the psalmist moves rather abruptly to praising God. He responds not in any irrational emotional way but from the depths of a saving experience (v.6). Then follows a powerful affirmation: "The Lord is my strength . . . shield . . . a fortress of salvation" (NIV).

The psalmist cannot contain his joy and happiness. His heart trusts God and "leaps for joy." Our God is a great God. The psalmist offers words of gratitude and thanksgiving.

The psalms have been a help and encouragement to many and were understood and used by Jesus. We can understand the psalmist's prayer and spontaneous exultation. When the danger is removed, when the crisis is past, when we realize, once again, that God can be trusted, there is relief and happiness. A song of boundless happiness replaces the cry of distress.

Others benefit from the witness of a happy spirit and a joyful heart. The miracles of God's answers to our prayers should not be kept a secret. "Let the redeemed of the Lord say so" (Ps. 107:2).

Prayer: *O God of all, open our eyes to your miracles that come to us in our deepest need. Amen.*

Friday, August 4   Read Colossians 3:1-11.

In the resurrected life

Too often we speak of resurrection only in terms of the future. But for Paul the resurrection life begins in the kingdom of God here and now.

"If then you have been raised with Christ, seek the things that are above" is not a philosophical abstraction. It is guidance to the Colossian church which is being threatened with dangerous doctrinal differences that would divert them from their faith in Christ as the Son of God (1:15-19; 2:3, 8-23).

The answer is to "set the mind on things above." This is a deliberate act, a conscious spiritual discipline. We are surrounded by much that entices us away from faith in Christ. Some tend to think that once we are saved, everything falls into its proper place. We have nothing to worry about. Not so. Paul says, "Put to death . . . your earthly nature" (NIV). This means new values, new priorities, new motives. To be "in Christ" is to be in the *real* world—now. Freed from the magnetic power of sin, the new life is now ours and we are being renewed. Resurrection begins now!

Individually and collectively we are called to live in the victory of Christ over those things that would enslave us as persons and prevent us from interacting as loving members of the human family of God.

Finally, there is no distinction of race or color in this family. "Christ is all, and in all."

Prayer: *Lord, help us to put our feet, our hearts, our minds, and our spirits on higher ground. Amen.*

Saturday, August 5   Read Luke 12:13-15.

In how we handle possessions

More than once, Jesus answered a question with a teaching, a parable. In this case a man had asked about the proper division of an inheritance. But Jesus makes it clear that he is not interested in this kind of thing, or, at the least, has no time for what he considers to be trivial pursuits.

The wealth that the inquirer seeks is vanity and transitory. Jesus is concerned with the lasting riches that bring abundant living. He says not a word about clever investments, only that life is more than "abundance of . . . possessions." We can wrap ourselves in a big house with all the accessories, but in bad times, if we have lived only for self, we will have no soul to face life with. We will be empty, without foundation.

Jesus turns the question around and raises an altogether different but more meaningful issue with which the man must deal. The man's mind was preoccupied with worldly or physical things. Jesus points out that life does not depend on amassing a huge fortune (v. 23). The noblest work can restrict and retard our growth and development in life if we invest our efforts in it only.

The antidote for such selfishness is Christ—his life, his teachings. "For where your treasure is, there will your heart be also" (v. 34). To be "rich toward God" is to put the heart "in Christ." The practicality of Christ's teachings is awesome.

Prayer: *Lord Jesus Christ, help us to keep the things of life in their proper perspective. Amen.*

Sunday, August 6   Read Luke 12:15-21.

Found when we wake up

Searching for wealth and possessions is wasted effort because death always comes when we don't expect it, despite all sorts of warnings. And it comes too soon. In the final analysis, wealth is irrelevant to entering the kingdom of God.

The rich man gathers all his possessions in one place, tearing down old barns to build bigger ones. Jesus calls him a fool because the man has focused only on collecting "things." To be "rich toward God" means living selflessly and being in close communion with God through prayer and following the example of Jesus.

If we are wrapped up only in self, our horizons are extremely limited. We may live on a high when things go well, when a project is successfully completed, when others tell us how good we are, how talented. But unless life is balanced between the physical and the spiritual—in their proper perspective—we pay for our shortsightedness with depression, obsession, and the longing for a "change"—something different to expand our narrow world.

When Jesus is Lord, we do not have to be overly concerned about taxes or money market rates. The tragedy that Jesus pointed out was that his questioner really believed that riches consisted of what he had accumulated. Jesus was upset because that man had his priorities so out of place. What about us? Christ wants us to remember it is by our God's pleasure that we receive our inheritance.

Prayer: *Father, help us to live so that all we do will make us rich toward you. Amen.*

A Love Relationship with God

August 7-13, 1989   **Brandon I. Cho†**
Monday, August 7   Read Jeremiah 18:1-3.

The metaphor of pottery has a profound significance in our understanding of God as our Creator. In today's passage, God is compared to the potter who fashions vessels out of the formless clay. It is interesting to note that in the Old Testament Hebrew, "creator" and "potter" are expressed by the same word.

Being a potter is not easy. In order to make good pots out of clay, the potter must devote his/her talent, energy and time. It requires a creative imagination, an undivided attention, patience, and a skillful coordination of hands and feet. The potter must know how to mix the clay evenly, shape it with hands while turning the potter's wheel, bake it in the oven just right, and put an appropriate paint on it. Making a pot involves both mind and body. It is a work of art, creating something out of nothing.

Likewise, when God created the heavens and the earth, God devoted all of the divine creative imagination, energy, power, and time. Therefore, when we look upon God, the origin of all creation, we think of God's extraordinary creative presence.

Even while you are reading this meditation, God is busy creatively working in you and in many other lives. Now can you hear the turning sound of the potter's wheel? Can you see God's busy hands and feet?

Prayer: *God, our Creator and Giver of Life, this is the day that you have made, and we will rejoice and be glad in it. I know your creative work is done even now as I pray. Thank you for being my potter today. In Jesus' name. Amen.*

†Pastor, North Long Beach United Methodist Church; president, Alumni Board, School of Theology at Claremont; president, Transgeneration Ministry of Korean-American United Methodists, Long Beach, California.

231

Tuesday, August 8   Read Jeremiah 18:4-6.

Jeremiah proclaimed God's message: "Like clay in the hand of the potter, so are you in my hand, O house of Israel" (NIV).

In biblical times, clay was one of the most common natural resources available. Consequently, it was widely used. It was used to make bricks. It was also used for homes as a cheap plaster, a floor surface, and a roof covering. Later in the New Testament, Jesus was found using clay when healing the blind man (see John 9:1-7).

A lump of clay has small monetary value. Yet it becomes beautiful and highly valuable when it is discovered, molded, shaped, and painted by the potter. As an enthusiastic student of art, I have been increasingly amazed at the beauty of Korean pottery that has been made over the last 5,000 years. It is hard for me to imagine that those beautiful art pieces were once formless lumps of clay. Now they shine with beauty, not because of their own merit but because of the masterful touch of the potter.

We were once like formless lumps of clay. But when God touched us with love, we became like beautiful pottery. And we are not done yet. God still wants to take yet undiscovered potentials within us and mold them in such a way that can bring the best out of us.

Once we were just lumps of clay, but now we are God's masterpieces who have inherited God's image. Can we live up to that image? Are we willing to let God mold us in the shape which seems best to God?

Prayer: *Dear God, my master potter, I thank you for creating me in your own image. I am your clay, Lord. Mold me as you will. I dedicate my will and life to you in the name of Jesus Christ. Amen.*

Wednesday, August 9   Read Psalm 14.

This psalm of David makes a direct condemnation of Jews who led ungodly lives despite their God-fearing religious tradition. According to the psalm, these Jews are the fools who say in their hearts, "There is no God." Because of their denial of God's presence in their lives, they are corrupt and do abominable deeds. "They shall be in great terror, for God is with the generation of the righteous." The psalm clearly warns that they have to face the consequences for the choices they have made.

This psalm speaks to contemporary Christians as well. In spite of our good intentions, we are often tempted to let our own ego, pride, and self-interest take precedence over the kingdom of God. In our busyness we put God under the piles of papers, behind appointments, and out of our minds. We may be good-hearted Christians, but we forget God, who is the very essence of our being. As one of my colleagues said to me today, "Busyness in the Lord's work does not make up for neglect of the Lord."

God deserves more than sporadic attention and indifferent responses from us. God yearns to commune with us every day. A love affair with God is the purest, most rewarding and everlasting relationship we could ever enjoy. It begins with the acknowledgment of God's presence in our lives. "The fear of the Lord is the beginning of knowledge" (Prov. 1:7, NIV). In our devotion and ministry, therefore, we must take time to reaffirm God's presence in us and humble ourselves before God.

"The Lord looks down from heaven to see if there are any that act wisely, that seek after God." Are you such a one?

Prayer: *Thank you, God, for reminding me that you are looking for willing hearts that seek after you. I acknowledge you as my eternal God in each moment of life. Accept my devotion as I pray in the name of Jesus Christ. Amen.*

233

Thursday, August 10　　　　　　　Read Luke 12:32-34.

It has been said that everyone is born into this world empty-handed and leaves this world empty-handed. Nothing we possess on earth can be eternal. Then why should we work so hard for things which by nature cannot last?

In the Gospel of Luke, Jesus tells us that we need to focus on the things of eternity. However, our mind tells us to be rational and practical. It tells us to live for here and now. It reminds us that we only have 24 hours a day to take care of our jam-packed schedule. Time is gold, and we shouldn't waste our precious time thinking about intangible things like the business of heaven. The here-and-now can give us an immediate and concrete satisfaction. It sounds convincing, doesn't it?

But our loyalty to the here-and-now will eventually be worn out, exhausted, and short-lived, unless it is tied to eternity. Our efforts for the here-and-now can find true meaning and purpose only when they are inspired and directed by the treasure of heaven, God's will and way.

Thus, Christ invites us to put our treasure in heaven. He is calling us to transform ourselves from a self-centered, self-serving lifestyle to a Christ-centered, other-serving discipleship. He is challenging us to reorganize our priorities based on God's perfect and eternal purpose for us rather than our on own short-sighted desire.

Let our treasure be in God's eternal hand, and let us live each day responsibly and joyfully as Christ-centered, other-serving disciples.

Prayer: *Loving God, help me to put you on the top of my priority list this day so that I may learn to place my treasure in your eternal kingdom. I pray in the name of Jesus, who has shown me the way of eternal life. Amen.*

Friday, August 11   Read Hebrews 11:1-3.

"Faith is being sure of what we hope for and certain of what we do not see" (NIV).

This well-known verse describes well the meaning of faith. Here, faith is understood in light of Christian hope. Faith is not blind trust or wishful thinking. It is anchored to the unending hope in the risen Lord. Therefore, it is based on the absolute certainty of the things we hope for and the things we do not see.

How reassuring these words must have been to those Christian martyrs who had suffered trials and tribulations because of their uncompromising faith and witness! To them faith did not need to be proved by scientific data. What they needed was inner assurance, peace, joy, and strength derived from their faith in Christ, and they received them. Thus, they were able to stake everything on Christ, even their own lives.

Faith is really a verb. This action-oriented word is the very foundation of our existence and ministry. Faith brings to us certainty and God's eternal promise. Therefore, faith gives us a clear sense of purpose, direction, and meaning. With faith we can boldly plunge into the ocean of an uncertain and unknown future, for our future belongs to God. In fact, our past, present, future, and everything else belong to God who created this world out of nothing. If we are in God's eternal hand, then there is nothing to be afraid of. We can take another giant step of faith forward and upward today and the next day and the next day until we come to meet God face to face.

Prayer: *Loving God, thank you for showing me once again the beauty and power of faith. So when I am in doubt, I will rely on that faith. Thank you for giving me your assurance and hope. I joyfully pray in the name of Jesus Christ, my Lord and Savior. Amen.*

Saturday, August 12   Read Hebrews 11:8-10.

As it was written in Genesis 12:1, Abraham left behind the security of familiarity and risked plunging into the unknown.

What is the secret of Abraham's bold action? The Hebrews writer asserts that it was his faith. By faith Abraham responded to God's call. By faith he obeyed God's instruction. By faith he became a sojourner, living in tents day in and day out. Because of his unyielding faith and complete obedience to God's call, Abraham has become the ancestor of our faith. His life story reminds us that faith is the foundation of our life, and that adventure, however risky it may seem, is often a necessary ingredient of being God's faithful people.

But most of us tend to prefer safety and security rather than adventure. We are more apt to place our trust in the known and familiar than to venture out to experience the unknown and unfamiliar. We thus become cautious of our actions and decisions. We see numerous examples of this in our relationships and ministries. Abraham's story warns us that our dependence on the known and familiar for the sake of our safety and security may stagnate us, keep us from experiencing the fullness of faith, and restrict the work of God in our lives. We cannot limit God in the box of our own security and safety. We need to liberate God from such bondage and let God freely lead us according to God's perfect will, even into the unknown and unfamiliar.

We do not know what tomorrow will bring, and yet the God of Abraham invites us to follow with faith. Can you see God waving at you? Can you hear God calling your name?

Prayer: *Loving and faithful God, I place my trust in you rather than in my own security and safety. Only then can I be truly free to venture out in faith to the unknown and unfamiliar and do your will. Lead me on, my eternal God. In Jesus' name I pray. Amen.*

Sunday, August 13   Read Luke 12:35-40.

"Let your loins be girded and your lamps burning . . . . You also must be ready; for the Son of man is coming at an unexpected hour." It would seem that the theme of today's passage is: "BE PREPARED!"

"Be prepared!" By using the example of prepared and watchful servants waiting for their master's return from a wedding banquet, our Lord admonishes us, "Let your loins be girded." In Middle Eastern culture, servants wore long, flowing robes and out of necessity gathered them up under their girdles in order to work freely and efficiently. To use today's language, Jesus is calling us to roll up our sleeves for work.

Jesus also said to "let your lamps [be] burning." The Middle Eastern lamp had a cotton wick which floated in a round sauce of oil. The servants, therefore, had to keep trimming the wick in order to keep the lamp burning through the night. This meant that they had to be up and alert until their master's return.

Only the alert, prepared, and faithful servants will be able to welcome Christ and meet God. We are called, therefore, to be prepared constantly. We are also called to be faithful in our service, not out of fear but out of joyful anticipation. It will be a glorious day when we meet our Lord face to face.

So let us be mindful of God's presence in our lives always. Let us think of God's will for us in each waking moment. Let us dedicate our lives for servant ministry every day.

Prayer: *Loving God, who has called me to be your faithful servant, I come to you this day rededicating my life to you. May your will be done through me today. So be it.*

Rhythms of Faith

August 14-20, 1989
Monday, August 14

Elwyn M. Williams†
Read Jeremiah 20:7-9;
1 Corinthians 9:15-16.

The rhythm of uncertainty

If we expect our faith to be sustained as one sustains a high note on a musical instrument, we deceive ourselves. There are rhythms of faith, from high to low and vice versa, which, if accepted creatively, provide a fuller dimension for our religious experience.

Our scripture today describes one of Jeremiah's lowest notes of faith. The *Interpreter's Bible* goes even further and says, "Here we have the bitterest and saddest laments of Jeremiah in all the series of his 'confessions'."

Jeremiah feels that he has been duped, enticed, deceived, even seduced by God, that his ministry somehow has fallen into untenable paths. It is not that he would abandon his prophetic role but that God's mastery of him and God's presence within does not give Jeremiah the kind of motivation he feels he must have. Paul feels the same kind of necessity laid upon him.

Our yearning to serve is from time to time embedded in uncertainty which haunts and snarls our ministries. Only when we honestly face this inner, burning uncertainty will we realize that this particular rhythm of faith will not last forever.

Prayer: *O thou who art immeasurably stronger than we are, help us to take those difficult, halting steps through the dark recesses of our faith, acknowledging our doubt and our need. At the same time help us open our spirits to the possibility of change and growth and light. Amen.*

---

†Retired United Methodist minister/college administrator, member of Oregon-Idaho annual conference of The United Methodist Church, Palm Coast, Florida.

Tuesday, August 15   Read Jeremiah 20:10-13;
                                          Psalm 6:8-10.

The rhythm of renewed hope and faith

It is truly a dark night of the soul when you feel that even your friends watch for your fall. The low note Jeremiah touched in yesterday's scripture reading does not seem to be responding to his anguished pleas to the Almighty—until verse 11. Then suddenly, in a burst of faith, he asserts that God is with him as a Dread Warrior.

To agonize over our ineffectiveness in the face of overwhelming need is to empathize with Jeremiah. He calls upon God and receives a new sense of faith. In the next breath he invokes vengeance upon his persecutors. I do not commend this. When strength and direction return for us, as they will in due time, we are called to translate this renewal of faith into creative and positive patterns. This is no passive God Jeremiah experiences, but One who is actively involved in our human struggles. The rhythm of anguish and doubt has been broken for the prophet. Likewise, God can refine our faith through tragedy, loss, doubt, and darkness of all shapes and sizes in a continuing process.

These passages from Jeremiah and the Psalms assure us that when we seek to recover our stability, composure, and effectiveness, a renewal of faith and hope is possible. With this certainty that we will never be abandoned by God, higher notes of faith are clearly heard.

Prayer: *Dear God, may we accept and appreciate times of light and dark, along with other opposites which possess our spirits. May we rejoice in the assurance that we are not alone through these rhythms of faith. Amen.*

Wednesday, August 16   Read Psalm 10:12-18;
Hebrews 10:31.

The rhythm of mystery and awe

The God the psalmist experiences is one who sees, who does not forget us, who hears the desire of the meek, who is intimately aware of our need. There is a sense of awe and mystery about God for the psalmist similar to that described in Hebrews. "It is a fearful thing to fall into the hands of the living God."

There is too little of this in contemporary faith—almost a chuminess which relates to the Almighty in casual terms. The transition from "thou" to "you" reflects this attempt to approach the Eternal more personally. However, for the psalmist, "The Lord is king for ever and ever."

It is more than respect we pay God. It is awe, reverence, openness before perfection. Awareness of strength above all strength sets the stage for newness. This is a much higher note of faith than we commonly experience, precisely because we do not sense the uncommonness or true distinctiveness of the Almighty. The psalmist did not have the ultimate redemptive example of Christ to meld with his God relationship. Despite that, I perceive a more solid, healthy, personal relationship with the Eternal than is reflected in some of our casual prayers.

The psalmist experienced a God of finality and wholeness in the face of his mortality and incompleteness. Yet this Lord, the Eternal, was intimately concerned with humankind. This is awesome! In our rhythms of faith, let us be sure that this note of awe and reverence is realized.

Prayer: *O Eternal God, deliver us from ourselves, and help us, we pray, become mightily aware of your completeness and awesome presence. Amen.*

Thursday, August 17
Read Hebrews 12:1-11;
Ephesians 6:18.

The rhythm of perseverance

There are times when we feel devastated by circumstances and relationships, temporarily overwhelmed by life's impedimenta. Is it not usually our own baggage which impedes us rather than the obstacles we encounter?

When our home burned to the ground in 1985, I did not quickly perceive this to be an opportunity for spiritual growth. In due time I came to see that if an experience like this is borne with faith, not despair, it has enormous redemptive possibilities. It is not the event itself which prevents our spiritual progress but our basic orientation which plays the redeeming role.

In five different translations of verse 1 there are five different words used to describe *how* to run the course which lies before us. The words are: patience, perseverance, steadiness, resolution, and patient endurance. These are rhythms of faith which actively describe our response to the strokes of destiny which come to us all.

As we proceed through this marvelous letter written to a persecuted church, our own personal "races" are placed in perspective. Difficulties, the author says, are not indications that God is displeased with us but rather evidence of God's love. It is a considerable step beyond the God-person relationship in the Old Testament—centering upon what God can do for us. It reaffirms the recurrent theme in the New Testament—how we can best serve God through Christ.

Suggestion for meditation: *What difficulties do you presently face? Place these in a framework of faith and opportunity with steadiness, patience, resolution, perseverance, and patient endurance.*

Friday, August 18   Read Hebrews 12:12-17;
                                                        Isaiah 35:1-10.

The rhythm of "follow through"

Therefore—notice how many times this word is used in Hebrews—three times in chapter 12 and liberally in the early chapters. It is appropriate, for it is the most precise word to describe the direct conclusion of logical reasoning. The author of Hebrews follows through with periodic admonitions based on elaborate proof of the superiority of the Christian faith.

One of the keys to a successful golf swing is "follow through." It is not less true with our faith. By faith, the author says, all kinds of results are possible. Therefore, lift, strengthen, make straight paths, strive for peace—follow through. These are the strong suggestions in today's scripture.

Isaiah's perspective illustrates a different kind of follow through, the marvelous testimony of God's wondrous works. All creation will experience God's glory, those in impossible situations will receive new life and courage, with the closing image of a new highway beyond all human expectations. It is the affirmation that God continually follows through in the blessings bestowed upon humankind.

This is a variation of yesterday's rhythm. It is perseverance translated into resolve, a completeness of discipline so that we do not make Esau's mistake, the classic example of an irrevocable and long-term decision made in a moment of desire for sensual satisfaction.

Yesterday we referred to the race of life, requiring active perseverance; today we look beyond the immediate race to the journey of life. *Therefore*—"follow through" with your faith.

Prayer: *O God, grant unto us the faith we need rather than the desires we seek. Amen.*

242

Saturday, August 19   Read Luke 12:49-53;
                                           1 Peter 4:12-19.

The rhythm of challenge

Sometimes we are tempted to think that if we accept Christ and follow in his footsteps, life will be blessed with serenity. Difficult passages like this bring us back to the reality of our discipleship. The challenge to become a mature Christian is not all sweetness and light. There will be times of conflict, of division amidst the basic serenity of faith. Addressing difficult practical problems is an integral dimension of the Christian life.

Jesus was keenly aware of the implications of his life and teachings. Division and unrest are necessary elements of change. Jesus simply wants his followers to be sure they understand both sides of the Christian coin—comfort *and* challenge.

If the Gospel of John is immersed in the idea of individual eternal life, the Gospel of Luke provides a necessary balance of concern for suffering humanity. Whenever such practical problems are faced effectively, the peacemaker may be the occasion for conflict. We are reminded in the passage in Peter that this creative confrontation of faith in relationship to society is to be done not in a spirit of self-righteousness or self-pity but as sharing in the ministry and mission of our Lord.

Jesus chose a course which led to death upon a cross. That course resulted in incredible faith, strength, and change for his followers. To become a part of this continuing visitation of God in Christ to the world, we as disciples must boldly declare ourselves willing to take the possible consequences of challenge and change. We are called to serve!

Prayer: *O God, let us rejoice in the challenge of our faith, that we may translate the difficult experiences of life into opportunities for service. In the Spirit of Christ. Amen.*

Sunday, August 20   Read Luke 12:54-56;
                                          Matthew 16:2-3;
                                          Genesis 28:16-17.

The rhythm of the commonplace

How can there be any rhythm of faith in the commonplace, the ordinary? The routine of ordinary existence far outweighs peaks of religious faith. The signs of the weather are obvious, commonplace. It should be just as obvious, Jesus said to the Pharisees and the Sadducees and the crowds, that the far-reaching importance of the kingdom be perceived.

It may not seem appropriate to think of Jesus as being frustrated, but these passages indicate a considerable degree of dismay that the obvious fact of the kingdom in the midst of life was being missed by so many. To Jesus the kingdom was everywhere, nearer than breath itself. Perhaps we too miss the miracle of the kingdom in the common places of life, thinking too much and praying too little to be renewed by the power and Spirit of Christ.

St. Augustine heard the voice, "Take up and read," in a monastery garden. John Wesley's "strange warming of the heart" took place at a prayer meeting. These were not unusual places. They were common places in which, with an openness to receive, the kingdom within was experienced in fullness and strength.

When Jacob woke up at Bethel he said, "Surely the Lord is in this place and I did not know it." God's unexpected presence and the kingdom within is always much nearer than we think.

Prayer: *O Lord and Master of us all, help us to touch you in life's throng and press, and make us whole again.* Amen.*

---

*Adapted from "Immortal Love, Forever Full," by John Greenleaf Whittier.

JUDGMENT AND TRUST

August 21-27, 1989   **John Carmody†**
Monday, August 21   Read Jeremiah 28:1-9.

This story purports to date from 593, when Babylon had been harassing Judah for some years and a prophet such as Jeremiah could sense the coming disaster of complete conquest that occurred in 587. The prophecy of Hananiah bespeaks hope that God would restore the vessels and royal prisoners taken away in the first Babylonian raids. This prophecy ran counter to Jeremiah's own inklings and in fact did not occur. So we find two prophets clashing in their sense of what God is about to do.

Jeremiah is happy enough to contemplate Hananiah's prophecy coming true—no rivalry will keep him from welcoming news that is truly good and carries God's grace. But he has been impressed that, traditionally, prophecy has dealt in predictions of war—because traditionally the prophets have charged the people with having sinned and so merited divine punishment. The golden age, by contrast, will be the prophecy of peace come true, for that will imply a people meriting God's blessings.

We cannot fully accept the equation of wrongdoing and punishment that we find in both Jeremiah and Joshua through Kings, because it seems to scant God's disposing as God wishes and the abounding of grace over sin. But we can join the prophets in thinking that God guides history for our correction and sanctification. We can recall that God numbers every hair of our heads and always wishes only our good.

Prayer: *Dear God, we want to place our lives and our times in your hands. Give us your Spirit, who can perfect our trust. Amen.*

---

† Senior Research Fellow, University of Tulsa, Tulsa, Oklahoma.

Tuesday, August 22   Read Psalm 84:1-7.

Scholars of the Psalter have distinguished several psalms that focus on Zion, the holy mountain in Jerusalem where the Temple stood. The Temple was the center of worship and thus the center of life under the Lord who had formed Israel as a unique people—God's own special portion.

The first lines of Psalm 84 celebrate the beauty of the Temple where the Lord dwells. Such beauty is more than gold, incense, and song. It is the splendor the spirit feels when in the presence of the divine holiness. Verse two makes this point unforgettably: the longing that can bring the spirit close to fainting, the joy no other presence can produce. It reminds us of C.S. Lewis's phrase, "surprised by joy." Only God can give true joy, which is like an overflow of acceptance into the divine embrace. But longing for God, making true joy our desire, our petition of God, is quite legitimate. Indeed, those who pray regularly and well are nearly bound to feel such longing.

For the devout, the house of God is what a nest is for a bird. The courts of the temple are like the home a wayfarer glimpses from afar and rushes toward with lightened feet. To be with God in church, to be consumed with singing God's praises has been many a saint's deepest desire. As lines five through seven suggest, such prayer is no enemy of action and strength. A busy time like our own needs much reminding that without contemplation its busyness quickly becomes superficial, even counter-productive. Work and prayer ought to be complementary.

Suggestion for contemplation: *Imagine Jesus in the temple, praying Psalm 84. Picture his face. Hear his melody. Touch the hem of his garment.*

Wednesday, August 23   Read Psalm 84:8-12.

The God to whom the psalmist prays is the Lord of hosts—the commander of legions of angels, the king of all creation. Yet God is also the God of Abraham, Isaac, and Jacob, who has kept the promises to make Israel a nation fertile in children and lands. God will look upon the shield, the emblem of this people. On the king who sums up the people the Lord's face will shine. Such is the psalmist's hope: God will make the people prosperous, because the people are God's own inheritance.

When we pray to God for help and blessing, we imply such a covenantal bond. If we ask our God for bread, will we get a stone? Can God be other than faithful to the love shown in the Exodus, shown in the passover of God, which we can never be certain is not simply communication too pure for us to fathom? The problem is our own amnesia, the way we keep forgetting what God has been for our predecessors in faith, what God once and for all showed divinity to be in raising Jesus and pouring the Holy Spirit forth in our hearts. A day in the courts of this God is better than a thousand days elsewhere because the presence of God is everything we desire: healing, meaning, the substance of heaven. Blessed indeed are those who trust in God, for their trust opens them to the divine presence. Just as Jesus depended on faith to work his miracles, so God depends on trust to make the divine presence felt. The love of God poured forth in our hearts by the Holy Spirit is a down payment in the coin of trust.

Prayer: *O Holy Spirit, comforter and advocate, move in our hearts, over our gifts, and through our world, to stir up our trust. Amen.*

Thursday, August 24   Read Hebrews 12:18-24.

The Epistle to the Hebrews is the fullest New Testament typology, showing how Christian faith finds Jesus to have fulfilled the promises unfurled in the Hebrew Bible. Here the argument is that the Christian sense of God takes away the terrors of the divine manifestations on Mount Sinai, when the Torah came down from heaven, and brings people to a heavenly Jerusalem aglow with the triumph of the new covenant that Jesus, the new Moses, has mediated. Where once there was fear and no surety of salvation, the author now finds peace and confidence through the work and merits of Jesus.

This typological contrast is lovely in a Christian context and rightly contemplated should issue in great praise of God. Like the scenes of the heavenly Jerusalem in Revelation, it ought to move us to praise unceasingly the gracious mercies of God, who for no merits of our own has called us children and held out the promise of eternal beatitude. But we have to be alert to the dangers, both historical and theological, of painting the God of the Hebrew Bible as vindictive and legalistic so that we might magnify the mercy of "the Father of our Lord Jesus Christ," as Paul so frequently calls God. These dangers have come home to roost in hatred of Jews and the shameful history of Christian anti-Semitism. They have helped Christians think themselves a New Israel, elect and predestined, who might lord it over both the Old Israel and any others they thought less elect than themselves. No such bigotry could ever be from God.

Suggestion for meditation: *Reflect on the connection between this passage from Hebrews and Christian rejection of Jews as passé.*

Friday, August 25   Read Hebrews 12:25-29.

These verses continue the typological argument laid out in the prior verses. Note the contrast between what was earthly and has become heavenly. God is the one who is speaking in the present. Hebrews is much given to stressing that when we hear God's voice, we must not harden our hearts (see 3:7, 15; 4:7). On the other hand, the victory of Christ, whose sacrifice has secured a salvation that will never fail, takes some of the terror from God's voice. If we inhabit a kingdom that cannot be shaken, we can approach God's throne in confidence. Still, God is a fire consuming all sin and hypocrisy. Indeed, the love shown in Christ ought to inspire the purest worship and service human beings can generate.

While many of the figures of Hebrews may be foreign to our present-day mentality, we should not miss the continuing significance of its reflections on sacrifice and priesthood. Sacrifice is the exchange of gifts that makes us holy. Priesthood is the mediation between divinity and humanity that came to a peak in the incarnation of God's Word. Both are gracious condescensions of God, accommodations to our human enfleshment. We need symbolic acts and material mediations, as we need sights and sounds, because we are embodied spirits. A little less than the angels, we should rejoice that God has fashioned from Christ a whole alphabet just to converse with us. While we wait for the full, heavenly revelation of the consummation accomplished through the love of Christ, we may rejoice in all gift-giving.

Suggestion for meditation: *What return can we make to God, except the sacrifice of our hearts, the gift of our faith, hope, and love?*

Saturday, August 26   Read Luke 13:22-24.

The Lukan Jesus is always under way toward Jerusalem, where he will defeat the Satan who has been dogging him and usher in the time of the church, when salvation will open out to the whole world. In Luke the ministry of Christ, and so the life of Christ's followers, is a journey, a pilgrimage, a being under way. The advice to enter by the narrow door is interesting, even daunting. The same Jesus who tells the stories of the good Samaritan and the prodigal son, who cannot overstress the largess of God, warns us not to be presumptuous. Although we cannot exaggerate the goodness of God, we need to bear down on our own recalcitrant wills. The narrow gate presumably is the path of discipline, strict accountability, keeping the law. Jesus certainly criticized the law when it had become heartless, but he continued to reverence each jot and tittle. This reminds us that the instructions that have come down the Christian tradition may be seen as either blessings or burdens. When we get inside the tradition, come to know and love it from the heart, we can understand why many saints have been punctilious in keeping not just the commandments but also all the rules of the church.

The many who seek to enter could be humanity at large. God and the way of Christ are universally attractive, until people learn that embracing the gospel entails restrictions on their sensuality, their pursuit of mammon, their pride. These are trifles compared to the treasure of God's love, but many of us continue to hanker after them.

Prayer: *Create in us, O God, a clean mind and a clean heart, that we may gladly put aside what keeps us from following you. Amen.*

Sunday, August 27   Read Luke 13:25-30.

The remainder of this Lukan pericope is a warning in view of the coming judgment. God, the householder, will not know those who cry God's name from lives of wickedness. Even if they have accompanied God's Christ, their evil deeds will bring them distress on the day when the fates are sorted. The complement of heaven is not those who cry, "Lord, Lord," but those who do the divine will. Here we have one of the several biblical foundations for liberation theology, which is founded on the primacy of praxis (doing, action).

Those who do the truth come to the light (John 3:21). Faith is a holistic venture, not something we can accomplish by thought alone. Probably this is so primarily because faith is a venture in love, a commitment of whole mind, heart, soul, and strength. Just as one only learns who the beloved is by years of living together, so one only learns who God is by years of living together. The illuminative way, as Christian spiritual masters have called it, is the understanding of faith that comes after one has for some time been a steadfast practitioner. The language of faith is metaphorical, symbolic, coded. Until one is an insider, a steady practitioner, words such as *mystery, hope,* and *sacrament* have only half their proper resonance. It takes time and cooperation for the Spirit to teach us their proper import. It takes much doing—praying, sacrificing, serving—to light them up from within. But each week of fidelity should beget confidence that judgment will prove merciful.

Suggestion for contemplation: *Imagine that you and your friends have come before God for judgment. What would you most want to have changed?*

A GODLY LIFE

August 28–September 3, 1989 **Martha W. Hickman†**
Monday, August 28 Read Ezekiel 18:1-9, 25-29.

The scriptures for this week describe a variety of ways in which a godly life is to be lived. The first two are from the Old Testament, and, while they contain some surprises, they are variations on the theme of justice and moral behavior. When we move to the New Testament readings on Wednesday, the tone changes. Justice is still required, but now there is a whole new theme of compassion for the Self and for the Other.

At first reading, this passage from Ezekiel may seem naive— if not outrageous. In our time we have seen babies born addicted to drugs, infected with the AIDS virus. We know the effects unemployment, poor housing, inadequate nutrition, and psychological scarring have on the lives of the innocent young. All of us know in our own lives the ways in which we are scarred—and blest—by the personal histories of parents, grandparents, communities. And often—though we want to do better—we, too, pass it all on to our children.

But it can be an easy out, this attitude. It can breed passivity and an unwillingness to try, railing instead against the injustice of God. It is said that psychiatrist Sigmund Freud was once asked whether, in view of all the conditioning to which we are subjected, we are responsible for our own lives. He is reputed to have answered, "Who else?"

So part of the message of Ezekiel here is, You are responsible for your life. You can change. And, it is never too late.

Suggestion for meditation: *Think of one critical aspect of your life in which you would like to see change. For a few minutes, hold it in the light of God. Write down any insights that come to you.*

---

† Professional writer, Nashville, Tennessee.

Tuesday, August 29   Read Psalm 15.

The psalm begins with a kind of poetic question, "Lord, who may enter your Temple? Who may worship on Zion, your sacred hill?" (TEV) Then, on a much more prosaic note, the psalmist goes on to describe in arbitrary fashion one version of a godly person—legally upright, full of moral virtue. Unexceptionable qualities, for the most part, though we might balk at a few: The godly person "despises those whom God rejects" and "makes loans without charging interest" (vv. 4-5).

Some of these prescriptions seem harsh, but we need to see them in historical context. Interest rates in the ancient world could be as high as 50 percent; the Jews were forbidden by Mosaic law to charge interest to the poor (Exod. 22:25). We might also remember that a code of moral justice was in itself an achievement in Old Testament times. Before the Hebrew understanding of monotheism, gods were to be appeased, placated as creatures of whim, with all the foibles of human beings.

Maybe this description of moral behavior could be considered as a basic set of "entrance requirements" (the knowing of good from evil, the habit of being careful in speech so as not to spread rumors or slander other people). This may be analagous to the membership vows United Methodists take when joining the church: "Will you be loyal . . . Will you support . . . ?" "Yes," we say, knowing this is just the beginning of our relationship with the community.

But, fine as it is, there will come a deeper understanding of the nature of God.

Prayer: *Eternal God, as we stand at the gates of your temple, may we do so with expectation and with willingness to be surprised. Amen.*

Wednesday, August 30   Read Hebrews 13:1-2.

When we move to the New Testament there seems to be a whole new assumption about the nature of the religious community—that its members will care for one another, that they will "let brotherly love continue" and, we assume, sisterly love as well! There is, of course, already a history of the believing community caring for one another as an expression of their love for God. Earlier in Hebrews, the author has said, "God . . . will not forget the work you did or the love you showed for him in the help you gave and are still giving to your fellow Christians" (Heb. 6:10, TEV).

This outpouring of love is a new thing. Where did it come from? From their response to God's love in Christ. And from where else? Partly from empathy for one another and out of a bonding strength that came through persecution and suffering.

So their empathy extends also to the stranger. Not only because, having suffered themselves, they know what it is to feel unwelcome, disdained, and turned against. But also because we do not know in what form God will be found. Who would have thought that a carpenter from Galilee would turn out to be the Messiah?

There is a Tolstoy story about a shopkeeper who dreamed the Lord would come to visit him. But the only visitors he had were an impoverished old man, a poor woman with a hungry child, and a wary shopkeeper berating a would-be thief. To each of these the shopkeeper gave food, clothing, and wise counsel. And at the end of his day, he realized that in these visitors he had received the Lord.

Prayer: *Eternal God, ever present, as we move into the day that is ahead, may we see your face in the faces of those we meet. Amen.*

Thursday, August 31   Read Hebrews 13:3-7.

We have here a collection of admonitions—around prison, marriage, and the love of money! Perhaps each of these has either explicitly or implicitly the threat of abandonment. The admonition, "Remember those who are in prison, as though you were in prison with them" (TEV) arouses our empathy for the person who, for one reason or another, is away from the community and could certainly feel abandoned.

The admonition for honoring one another in marriage warns against abandonment of the other in our most intimate, and therefore most potentially painful, relationship.

The love of money. Are we fearful of being abandoned to poverty? We have seen many people whose financial needs are not met. It would be mockery to tell them to be satisfied with what they have. That is not what is being suggested here. The writer of Hebrews is writing to a specific people whom he knows. The admonition against being swept up in "the love of money" is wise counsel for anyone.

Is there a fear more terrifying than the fear of abandonment? To what, for ultimate security, are we to give our love, our ultimate love? To the God who says, "I will never leave you; I will never abandon you" (TEV).

Prayer: *O God, you who hold creation in the hollow of your hand, be our security and our peace. Amen.*

Friday, September 1   Read Hebrews 13:7-8.

When we falter, when we lost sight of our goals, when we feel the threat of abandonment, what will rescue us, bring us around, show us the way again?

Each of us has models of faith. Maybe historic figures we have read about; maybe a loved parent or teacher, a special friend who told us of God's love. "Consider the outcome of their life," reads Hebrews 13:7. The words in the Greek mean the manner of their leaving life, the mood of their dying. Surely death is a moment of truth. If, in the face of imminent death, a person remains radiant in the faith, that is a strong witness. Perhaps you have in your family or acquaintanceship stories of dying people who seem even before death to have been entering some transcendant experience. In my family we love to tell how my grandmother greeted her sisters who had already died and of the surprise in her voice as she greeted them and exclaimed at the beauty of these who had come to welcome her home.

Or the story of Dietrich Bonhoeffer, going to his martyr's death under Hitler, proclaiming that for him death was the beginning.

And what else will sustain us in the dark times? What embodiment of love, what surging assurance of goodness? The model of Jesus, who in all times and under all circumstances reveals to us the essence of God's love and power.

Suggestion for meditation: *Go over in your mind your own "sacred stories," of people who have died in the faith. Feel the strength of their witness as it enters your life now.*

Saturday, September 2   Read Luke 14:1, 7-11.

The readings for today and tomorrow are from Luke, and they are about food, about the customs of table seating and whom to feed. The very mundaneness of the subject—its everyday presence in our lives—brings this part of the gospel close to our daily experience.

We are told that Jesus went to have a meal on the Sabbath with a Pharisee. This is no violation of Sabbath law, since food would have been prepared ahead of time.

But then comes this piece of advice on how to behave at a wedding feast. It is a droll story, and we can all feel the embarrassment of the man who chose too fine a place for himself and then was asked to move to make way for a more notable guest. Far better, says Jesus, to sit in a more humble spot and be asked to move up.

Well, yes. One would not like to be put in the position of being demoted. But is this a spiritual precept or just a piece of political wisdom? There's nothing wrong about political wisdom, but we don't usually think of it as parabolic teaching.

But then, the capstone: "For every one who exalts himself will be humbled, and he who humbles himself will be exalted."

So it's not just a matter of whether or not to embarrass yourself. The story stays in the mind as an example of appropriate humility being a wise attitude in the long run to gain the spot you would like.

Enlightened self-interest as well as political expediency—and all, says Jesus, infused with the wisdom of the gospel.

Prayer: *Eternal God, who wishes fullness of life for each of us, guide us through the thickets of motives and goals so we may abide in your wisdom. Amen.*

Sunday, September 3   Read Luke 14:12-14.

Having suggested a proper attitude toward who sits where at the banquet, Jesus now moves to the issue of whom to invite—not exclusively your friends, relatives, or rich neighbors, who will invite you back. But invite those who can't—the poor, the lame, the maimed, the blind. One assumes this invitation is extended to these people because they need food, but that's not the motive described. No, feed them, and you will be rewarded at the resurrection.

Another appeal to self-interest. Nowhere does Jesus decry self-interest—it is in our interest to be in good favor with God in the long run—"at the resurrection of the just."

But in the meantime, until the resurrection, the blessing is inherent in the act. Ask those who have tried it.

In Nashville, Tennessee, there is a church which has a "Luke 14:12" program. On Tuesdays and Fridays the church bus picks up clusters of homeless, hungry, and destitute people and brings them to the church for a hot, fresh-cooked meal, served with enthusiasm and mutual respect by a core of church folks. This story is surely repeated in many churches around the nation. Obviously these street people are in no position to return the invitation. The preparers and servers know they are following Jesus' admonition, and in the fullness of God they will have their reward.

But they have it already—the blessing. You can see it in their faces as they talk.

Prayer: *Eternal God, may your love for us move us to compassion for all your creation, especially for those in greatest need. In Jesus' name. Amen.*

FOLLY OR FAITH?

September 4-10, 1989   **Thomas P. Harp†**
Monday, September 4   Read Luke 14:25-33.

On what basis do we make a decision for Christ? Some people follow Jesus assuming it isn't going to cost them anything. That's folly, like a person building a tower without first counting the cost. When their faith is severely tested, they disappear. Others calculate the cost of following Jesus and choose not to; the cost is too great. Faith hasn't figured in either of these decisions.

Have any calculated the cost of following Jesus and found it affordable? Lest we be smug, who among us really knows the cost? And who among us really can pay the price? Sooner or later we must face the truth that the ultimate cost is too great for each of us. When we face our "crucifixion," our spirits may be willing, but our flesh will be weak.

One doesn't come to faith by counting the cost. Faith isn't reasoned or calculated. The issue is this: take Jesus' warning seriously. Discipleship demands much. If we don't believe that, we are foolish. Our crosses won't come equipped with a wheel like some I've seen being "carried" cross-country. Yet if we had let a simple warning deter us, we wouldn't be here. If we think we can handle whatever comes, we will learn otherwise. So who can be faithful? We can! Coming up short, we choose to follow Jesus anyway. Why? Because that's faith.

Prayer: *Lord Jesus, you demand that we carry our cross. Empower us with your Spirit, that we may follow where you lead us. Amen.*

---

† Pastor, Kenmore Presbyterian Church, Kenmore, New York.

Tuesday, September 5   Read Philemon.

Take a walk with Onesimus on his way "home" to Philemon. Think his thoughts for a moment. What do you think Philemon will do? How will he respond? You don't really think he will let you off, do you? Surely Philemon's other slaves will run away if he doesn't punish you—what else would deter them? But maybe he'll respond the way Paul expects. Maybe he'll even go beyond what Paul asks. No, freedom is too much to expect. Or is it? You have no guarantees. Is it folly or faith that leads you back to Colossae?

Perhaps it was folly for Onesimus to go back. We don't know how Philemon responded. Agreed, the place of Philemon in scripture suggests that Onesimus was freed. Onesimus, the Bishop of Ephesus, presents us with an attractive possibility. We don't know. Surely anyone walking towards Colossae with Onesimus would have thought him crazy. An escaped slave returning to his master voluntarily, instead of in chains? What folly!

What faith! What else? Like Onesimus, we walk into our future, minds racing with anticipation and hope, fear and trembling. What will our futures hold? What enslavements have we fled that we must face before we can be set free? Remaining "escaped" isn't really freedom, it is a life of fear, of hiding. The one God, who has power over both our former master and us, wills our freedom. We must face the sources of our enslavement, that we may be set free.

Prayer: *God who sets people free from slavery, we live in fear of the powers that once held us captive. Grant us faith to face those powers, trusting that you will indeed set us free. Amen.*

Wednesday, September 6   Read Psalm 94:16-22.

In New York State, we are in the midst of an experiment with TV cameras in the courtroom. The other day a courtroom scene showed a young woman on her knees in front of the judge. She was testifying against a man who had shot her in the head and left her for dead about a year before. She demonstrated how he had forced her to kneel in front of him. She said that while she knelt, she prayed and prayed that God would deliver her from the man. The attorney asked her if the accused had said anything to her. She said he had laughed, saying that praying wasn't going to do her any good. I couldn't help but wonder if he still believes that. I am sure of this: she believes even more firmly now than before.

The words of this psalm kept running through my mind as I watched the brief account of the trial: "The Lord defends me; my God protects me" (TEV). That gunman may have thought her prayers were folly. I believe otherwise. She would likely say as the psalmist, "If the Lord had not helped me, I would have gone quickly to the land of silence" (TEV).

Unfortunately, few people have such dramatic and ready evidence of God's power to deliver the innocent from the wicked. That doesn't prevent us from believing the psalmist's words: "[God] will punish them for their sins; the Lord our God will destroy them" (TEV). Indeed, God does hold us accountable for our actions. Sometimes, God even allows us to see that accountability in action.

Prayer: *Righteous Judge, who will not allow the guilty to go unpunished while the innocent suffer, we thank you for every time we catch sight of your justice in action. Amen.*

Thursday, September 7   Read Philemon.

What's the difference between a demand and a strongly worded request? Paul seems to have stated his case very clearly. Yet he stopped short of telling Philemon what he must do. Instead, he respected Philemon, trusting him to make the right decision. "I could be bold enough, as your brother in Christ, to order you to do what should be done. But because I love you, I make a request instead" (TEV).

Is it folly to trust another with a decision, to express your own preference, yet allow another the final say? Some think so. After all, there is no guarantee that the "other" will do as you wish. Is it not better just to legislate (to order) the desired action? The ordination of women is still an issue in many churches. Other issues have appeared or will appear—abortion, euthanasia, pornography, homosexuality, marriage for Catholic priests. People on each side of these issues will seek to force the other to yield. Would it not be better to take Paul's approach seriously?

Some will assume this means taking no action on controversial issues. Not so. Did Paul take no action? Hardly! That would have been to allow Onesimus to remain with Paul or to send him back to certain punishment. Instead Paul took amazing action, some would say foolish action. He chose to become involved— even to take sides! But he did so with love, a love that refused to impose itself on the other, yet beckoned invitingly. Isn't that the way God loves us?

Prayer: *God who loves us, how hard it is for us to trust your love, to allow it to shape our love of self and others. Strengthen our faith, that we may love as you love. Amen.*

Friday, September 8   Read Ezekiel 33:1-11.

I have heard people claiming to speak for God, warning against practically everything. And I am weary of self-righteous watch guards pretending that they and they alone know God's will. The current libertine ethic seems to me in part to be a reaction to the proliferation of people who trivialize evil by warning against everything from playing cards to nuclear energy. If God has a credibility problem these days, perhaps it is because there are too many watch guards speaking their piece in the religious marketplace.

So where does that leave us? It is folly to tolerate evil in the interests of pluralism. Do we care about our sisters and brothers enough to speak a word of warning? Or do we really believe it's everyone for himself/herself? As Christians we are bound to speak a word of warning to those who do evil. But our word of warning must be credible. To trivialize sin to the point that people adopt an attitude of, "Why bother? It doesn't do any good to change!" is to fail our Lord completely. God is a God of the living. God will forgive those who repent.

If I read Ezekiel right, our silence on issues will speak thunderous volumes on the day of reckoning. Our choice is to take seriously our responsibility to communicate, to recognize that there are, indeed, other points of view within the faithful community, and that God's word has power to win others to its wisdom.

Prayer: *God, grant us wisdom as we speak a word on your behalf. May our attitude be governed by your love. Amen.*

Saturday, September 9   Read Psalm 94:1-15.

Here are the words of one like the watchman in Ezekiel who realizes where his people are headed and tries to teach them a new way. A former member of the ruling caste (dare we make that assumption?), he now knows what end lies ahead. It is folly, and not faith, that deceives the oppressor into believing all is well while people suffer poverty and political powerlessness. It is folly, not faith, that leads a society to destruction.

God will not tolerate corruption forever, though God has demonstrated far more patience than many would like. Neither does God act in the immediacy of the demanded now, to suit those whose impatience waits for nothing. God will punish evildoers. Those in power must take God seriously. Not only does the oppressor risk the fury of the oppressed; the oppressor risks the fury of God.

So the frustrated watchman speaks: "My people, how can you be such stupid fools?" (TEV) How foolish it is to think God will long allow one people to oppress another! How hard it is to understand how we oppress others! How necessary that we have faith, trusting God to instruct us and others in the ways of righteousness! "The Lord will not abandon his people. . . . Justice will again be found in the courts, and all righteous people will support it" (TEV).

Prayer: *How easily we can see injustice in other lands, O God. How hard it is to recognize it in our own lives, especially when we are the oppressors. Grant us eyes to perceive the needs of those around us, and give us faith to work for justice everywhere. Amen.*

Sunday, September 10   Read Luke 14:25-33.

We assume everybody wants into the kingdom of God. Not so! Check out the preceding story (Luke 14:15-24). Everyone who was invited to the party chose not to come. Can you imagine all the invited guests staying away? Contrary to our assumption, nobody who was invited was allowed to taste the feast. Instead, those who were obviously excluded from the initial invitation are welcomed at the table.

Contrast that with this paragraph. Here everybody is following Jesus, but Jesus seems to want to put them off. He tells them to count the cost. "Whoever comes to me cannot be my disciple unless he loves me more than he loves his father and his mother, his wife and his children, his brothers and his sisters, and himself as well" (TEV). What's going on here anyway? First it seems many are invited, but they choose not to come. Then it seems those who come are being put off.

This story is similar to the story in Matthew where the one guest was thrown out for not wearing a wedding garment (Matt. 22:13). It appears that we are expected to make certain preparations. Following Jesus is not as simple as joining a church. Perhaps that is the focus of these difficult sayings. There is a difference between folly and faith. It is folly to assume we can follow Jesus without making difficult decisions about ourselves and our lifestyles. The life of faith demands hard choices and clear priorities.

Prayer: *Lord Jesus, your sayings are sometimes hard to understand; and when we undertand them, hard to follow. Grant us faith to clarify our priorities, that we may love you with our whole being. Amen.*

September 11-17, 1989 **Mary Lou Redding†**
Monday, September 11 Read Isaiah 6:1-5; 54:1-4.

This week of *Disciplines* is about sin. I have struggled with the
lectionary readings and with what to say about them. Maybe my
difficulty with the assignment says something about the subject.
I'll bet it's easier for most of us to commit sin than to carefully
consider what sin is and does. Part of my difficulty probably
comes from my reluctance to face the sin in my own life. But part
of it has also to do with my not wanting to point a finger at you.
Who am I to judge?

Sin is not as much talked about—even in church—as it once
was. About 20 years ago Karl Menninger wrote a book titled
Whatever Became of Sin? Some would quickly say sin is alive
and well and thriving in Brazil. Some would say there's lots of
sin in New York City. And possibly in some of the houses on the
other side of our town. But what about on your street? Or mine?
It seems to me we're more likely to call our own failures just
that—failures, weaknesses, foibles. But not sin.

The first step in getting help with alcoholism is said to be
admitting the need for help. Perhaps the same is true with sin.
Perhaps we must name and face what for us individually is sin.
The Book of Amos makes sin the failure to live up to God's
demand for righteousness. Hosea makes it the breaking of covenant, turning our backs on covenant love. What do you think sin
is? Write your definition here: _____

_____

Prayer: *Holy God, help me to recognize and honestly face the sin in my
own life. Amen.*

---

†Managing Editor, *The Upper Room*, Nashville, Tennessee.

Tuesday, September 12   Read Hosea 5:15–6:6.

I'd hate to be a weather forecaster. One day last winter we were told there was a 20% chance of snow, no accumulation expected. About lunchtime our 20% began falling furiously, and soon we were getting someone else's 80% as well. As temperatures plummeted, the melting snow froze on the roads. Hundreds of cars were stuck on the highways, and the next day schools were closed. But by midmorning the bright sun began burning off the ice and snow. At lunchtime my daughter said derisively, "They could have had school! The roads are dry."

That episode reminded me of verse 4 from today's reading, where love for God is compared to the morning mist. As that snow and ice were burned off by the sun, so is the morning mist. And all too often our love for God seems like that. We resolve to show our love for God more, to live better lives, to change. We promise ourselves and God (from the best of motives) that things will be different. But when the heat is on, like the morning mist those resolves burn away.

Most of us have at least one area of our lives that seems to be an arena of continuing struggle. We want to follow God's ways, but somehow we cannot seem to do it. Such weaknesses are sometimes called a "besetting sin." Sin can be deeply rooted, and our lives can be hard ground. We need God's repeated, gentle rain to soften the places where we have become hard and resistant. Some sins are deeply ingrained patterns of hurtful and self-destructive behavior that cause us and others continuing pain. What is your arena of continuing struggle? Where do you find yourself starting over, again and again?

Prayer: *O God, you know me on this one. You've heard me say it before, but I say it again today: I want to do things your way. I want to follow your will in _____. Make my love for your ways stronger than my inclination to sin. Amen.*

Wednesday, September 13   Read Hosea 4:1-14; 5:15.

One way we deal with our sin—or avoid dealing with it—is by isolating ourselves. We may say our personal choices are not hurting anyone. But the truth is, sin always has consequences.

We may recoil from theology that says God brings sickness or hard times on us to get our attention, but what is the truth here? Suppose we overeat and get fat. Is the fat punishment? Or we abuse our bodies in other ways and become ill. Is the illness punishment? Or we treat people badly and relationships deteriorate. Is the misery of those troubled relationships punishment from God? Or is God simply allowing us to feel the consequences of our acts?

Hosea does not see sin as an individual problem. Though each one must face his or her sin and accept responsibility for it, when God's people "break all bounds," the consequences go far beyond personal discomfort or misery: "bloodshed follows bloodshed," the land mourns, people waste away, even the animals are dying. Sin harms not only the sinner but also the community of which the sinner is part. All of life is interwoven, one piece of fabric made up of the threads of individual lives.

Sin hurts me. It hurts you. When we sin, we block our own deepest needs being met. It may seem we're "getting away with it," but because our deep needs go unmet we will eventually become miserable. Yet there is a Godly sorrow "that worketh repentance." This sorrow draws us—and through us our communities—toward God. Every action you and I take either moves God's kingdom closer to reality or hinders its coming. Your life and mine are part of the same piece of fabric. Whether we like it or not, your sin harms me and mine harms you.

Suggestion for meditation: *Consider the fabric of your community. How do your strengths, gifts, and sins show in it?*

Thursday, September 14   Read 1 Timothy 1:12-17.

One Sunday not too long ago our church was S.R.O.—standing room only. We had a "superstar" Christian to speak to us. People are often eager to hear the famous athlete or entertainer. It's as if their fame is a stronger-than-usual argument for following God. If those superstars have led lives of obvious sin (sometimes it seems the more obvious the better), we welcome them as witnesses.

The Epistle to Timothy contains a familiar phrase, "Christ Jesus came to save sinners, of whom I am chief." That phrase always strikes me as strange. It's like bragging: "I'm the sinningest sinner, the worst of the bad." Though we've all played "Can you top this?" in one way or another, it seems ridiculous that competitiveness could extend even to sin, that we want to outdo one another even in the magnitude of our failings.

But the fact is, most of us are *not* terrible sinners. We haven't committed the "big ones"—murder, adultery, grand larceny, apostasy. We are not "chief among sinners," and we know that—which deceives us about the reality and the gravity of our sin. We slide into a sense of ease. We may even adopt a stance of relative adequacy—"I do about as well as the next one."

Yet as ordinary as our sin is, we cannot remove it from our lives. We cannot heal the hurt it has inflicted on us or others. Most of us have long ago left behind worm theology—"for such a worm as I"—but perhaps with it we have left behind the sense of our very real need for forgiveness. Jesus Christ came into the world to save sinners. That is each of us in our daily, unspectacular, eternally significant need to be put right with God.

Prayer: *Dear God, sometimes I forget that I am a sinner, absolutely dependent on you for all that is good about me and in my life. Thank you for loving me enough to save me. Amen.*

Friday, September 15   Read Luke 15:1-2.

These Gospel stories reveal some basics about God's ways with us and with our sin. The first is this: Jesus was not a man who shied away from sinners. What do you think it was about him that made sinners want to be with him?

In my youth I occasionally wanted to go to places that the church disapproved of. "Can you take Jesus with you? If you can, then it's okay to go there." That question was supposed to make us decide not to go. Clearly, Jesus would be repelled and stop at the door, and so should we.

That isn't the picture of Jesus presented in these verses. Sinners were not put off by Jesus. Quite the opposite—they seemed drawn to him. They engaged him in conversations and invited him into their homes. Some of the devout Jews could not understand Jesus' willingness to be close to sin. The Pharisees were sometimes among these. They were a devout sect, praying and working for a renewal of holiness within Judaism, praying for God's Messiah to come. Perhaps some of them had even been hoping Jesus was the one. But when he began mingling with unclean people, they knew it couldn't be. They knew God wanted purity, holiness, separation. Surely the Messiah would not hang around with sinners.

Like them, we have difficulty seeing God welcoming us just as we are, loving us and coming to us even with our sin. But God longs to be close to us, to eat and drink with us. It is not necessary that we clean up our act in order to approach God. We simply invite God to be part of our daily activities. We will be changed by this relationship, just as we will be by any relationship. But the place of beginning is where we are.

Suggestion for meditation: *Where are you reluctant to invite God into your life? How can you begin to extend that invitation today?*

Saturday, September 16   Read Luke 15:3-10.

Several months ago in worship, preparing to take Holy Communion, I was painfully aware of a recent sin. I was struggling about whether to commune, because I wasn't ready to give that sin up and I knew it. I prayed, "O God, I don't feel worthy to take Communion this morning. . . ." Quick as a flash I heard God say in my heart, "Oh? And all the other times you have been?" I was startled. Are we worthy? Never. Are we welcome? Always. That is the nature of God's dealing with us.

In Wesleyan terms, that is called prevenient grace. The word comes from two Latin roots, *pre*, "before," and *venir*, "to come." It is the grace that bears us toward God even before we decide to begin the journey. It is God wooing us, beckoning to us, searching for us.

God does not usually come into our lives like a demolition expert, razing old structures with one spectacular explosion. That might actually be easier—to walk away from one way of life with its problems and spoiled relationships and start over fresh. But more often, God changes us the way opening windows changes stale air inside a house—little by little, displacing the old with something fresher, healthier, more appealing.

And God is persistent. Like a shepherd with willful and stupid animals, God follows us into our ravines, saving us so that eventually we may cooperate in the process of our being saved. We may pat ourselves on the back for our resolve to be better, but there is a prior question: What (or Who) made us dissatisfied with where we were? God, our faithful lover. And when we turn from self-destructive ways and choose something healthier, who is our happiest cheerleader? Again, God.

Prayer: *O God, for your grace that seeks me even when I don't want to be found, I give you thanks. Amen.*

Sunday, September 17　　　　　　　Read Psalm 77:11-20;
　　　　　　　　　　　　　　　　　　　　1 Peter 3:8-18.

When was the last time you talked to anyone about God? Not theology and theory, but about your personal encounters with God? For some of us, it has been a very long time. This is not lack of proclamation in the first degree; there has been no premeditation. It happens incidentally, usually because we aren't aware that God is doing any "mighty deeds" in our lives.

Years ago when I filed for divorce, I considered myself both to have failed and to have sinned. I felt sure that I had missed God's will for my life. But a spiritual friend said, "How do you know *this* is not God's will for you?" I was astounded. How could he even suggest such a thing? He went on to say, "Perhaps there were lessons you needed to learn that you could learn no other way—and God knew that." He began to talk about God's subtle working. At the time, I could not accept what he said. I could not see God in those events. God's "footprints were not seen." But as I have talked with others about my weaknesses, needs, and failures, I have seen just how much God has done, how far God has brought me.

Our personal stories of God's working speak to people. Nothing you have to say is more compelling than your own experience of the grace of God. Nothing makes God real for others like hearing how God has been real in the lives of ordinary people. But many of us keep God's acts in our lives a carefully guarded secret. What is the reason for "the hope that is within you"?

We are redeemed from our sins for a reason: that we may glorify God. How has God changed you? How has God "saved" you? Who can you tell?

Prayer: *O God, place in my path people who need to see and hear you, and help me to proclaim how you have acted in my life. Amen.*

GOD'S NEVER-FAILING LOVE

September 18-24, 1989   **Stacy A. Evans†**
Monday, September 18   Read Psalm 107:1-9.

This psalm begins Book V of the total number of the Book of Psalms. It begins this section of the Psalms with a shout of thanksgiving. In the Revised Standard Version the first verse ends with an exclamation point:

> O give thanks to the LORD,
>> for he is good;
> for his steadfast love
>> endures forever!

We begin this week on a positive note. The psalmist is saying that we have something to look forward to. Even if we have had desert or wilderness experiences, even if we have been hungry and thirsty (literally), if we turn to God, God will deliver us.

God's love is described as "steadfast," something that can be depended upon when all else fails. In fact, God's love can be depended upon even before all else fails. We can turn to the Divine long before disaster threatens. God wants to lead those who turn to the Divine in a "straight way," or as another version puts it, in a "direct way."

What we are being told through the psalmist is that God will see us through any trials or tribulations. The hope that this psalm gives is that God not only sees us through but also provides a clear path to the other side of our experiences of pain or disappointment. We can depend on God's steadfast love.

Prayer: *O God, thank you for loving us beyond and through our trying times. May your steadfast love keep us steadfast in daily living. Amen.*

---

† Pastor, Broad Street United Methodist Church, Columbus, Ohio.

Tuesday, September 19   Read Hosea 11:1-7.

An underlying theme of this week's scripture selections is hope. Hope is found in God's caring for Israel, and we can find hope in God's caring for us as well.

God cared for Israel in the way a mother cares for her helpless infant. As the mother must not only feed and clothe the infant but also give the baby tender caresses and much nurturing attention, so God tended Israel. But like so many in our world today, in spite of that care the son/daughter goes away from the parent. Of course, some of this is as it should be. The child must mature and learn to have a mind and will of her/his own.

But God is an unusual Parent. Unlike the human variety we have known (or perhaps are), God is all-wise. In turning away from God, Israel turned its back on the source of life and wisdom for itself.

Sometimes we, too, turn away from God, thinking that God is too strict or too far removed from the petty concerns of our lives. We, too, turn our back on wisdom, on the Source of goodness and clear thinking for daily living.

The assurance we receive from this passage is, however, that even if we turn away, God does not retaliate in like measure. We can depend on God's continuing care in season and out of season.

Prayer: *When times get tough and you seem far away, remind me, O God, that your love is steadfast and is for ever. Amen.*

Wednesday, September 20 Read Psalm 107:1-9;
1 Timothy 2:1-7.

Yesterday we found there is hope in trusting God even during the tough times. Today's readings reinforce the steadfastness of God's love and care and emphasize the naturalness of prayer.

For the Christian believer, praying can be second nature. Nothing is more common or self-expected than frequent prayer.

God does not require elaborate words or complex concepts. There is no necessity for *thees* and *thous*. What God wants is for each of us to have a full, rich way of life. Such a life involves a constancy of reaching out beyond one's own world to touch the resources of the Divine.

Praying for others—those in authority or those next door—is not a burden but simply an ordinary part of daily living. In living life this way, the Christian finds hope not far away but always close "at hand."

List here the concerns and people you will hold before God as they come to mind today:

Prayer: *God of hope, help me be steadfast in my faith, one day at a time. Amen.*

Thursday, September 21   Read Luke 16:1-13.

Well, we're "over the hump"—this week is half over as of yesterday. It's all moving toward the weekend now.

What a jolt to have to read this passage from Luke when the big part of the week is already behind us!

But being a good steward is what dealing with time is all about. Clock time has no meaning in and of itself. So the last several days have been time that has passed. So what? If you have not invested yourself in the time that has passed, this is the exact question that needs to be asked: So what?

Each one of us is given the exact same amount of time to experience each minute, every hour, every day. How we spend our time is one of the great litmus tests of who we are as persons. Do you spend most of your leisure time alone? Do you spend it with family or friends? Do you take time to improve your grasp on life itself by doing things that are designed to enhance your daily life?

The dishonest steward was commended for his compassion toward his fellow debtors. Will we not be also judged by what we do in relation to those over whom we have some influence and authority? How do you spend your time with those who depend on you? Do you need to forgive their debts?

Prayer: *O God, help me forgive my debtors as you forgive my debts to you. Amen.*

Friday, September 22   Read Psalm 107:1-9.

It's Friday again! Another busy week in our lives is coming to a close.

As you look back over this past week, what strikes you as most important? Have you improved your relationships? Has your job gotten a little better? What about your home life? Have you been kinder, more understanding?

It impresses me that God often speaks to us more through questions than through answers. The life of spiritual growth is a life of reflecting carefully on what is really happening in our own daily walk. When we ask ourselves questions and reflect honestly in finding answers, we open ourselves to the Divine speaking in and through us.

The psalm that has become our companion for this week says in part: "Let them thank the LORD for his steadfast love, for his wonderful works to the sons of men!" What do you have to be thankful for at the end of this week? Take some quiet time now and ruminate over the events of the week. Muse about them slowly and deliberately, trying to discern how God has been present to you in the midst of your actual daily living this particular week.

Then give thanks that God has been with you!

Prayer: *O God, you are my constant companion. Help me to see you and feel your presence in more and more of my life each day. Amen.*

Saturday, September 23   Read 1 Timothy 2:1-7.

This date is the birthday of a very good friend of mine. It happens that his life and mine have diverged over the years so we rarely get to see each other. But this is still an important date for me each year, as I savor what this friendship has meant to me and what his life has contributed to my own.

One thing I can do is to pray for him and his loved ones. And I do. The constancy of my praying for my friend is often more subconscious than conscious. I am sure that as the years have flown by, in some ways we have less and less in common. But still I pray for him.

Praying for my friend is one of God's "means of grace" for me. I am closer to a "quiet and peaceable life" by remembering my friend in prayer than if I ignored him. You see, it is not just praying for the President and for world peace that counts. For the object of our praying is not only what the requests do to influence God but also how our lives are affected.

When Paul writes to his friend Timothy that "supplications, prayers, intercessions, and thanksgivings be made for all," he is urging his colleague and pupil to value the spiritual contact that can be kept current by practicing ongoing prayer for others.

If you have not done so, make a list today of persons you want to pray for in an ongoing way. Then, pray for them, starting today. I believe it will be a "means of grace" for you, too.

Prayer: *God, thank you for the others we know by name and by life circumstances for whom we can pray. Amen.*

Sunday, September 24
Read Psalm 107:1-9;
Hosea 11:8-11;
Luke 16:1-13.

Today is the Lord's Day! We have journeyed together through this week and heard again about God's never-failing love. Sometimes we turn from it, but God never turns away from us. God is always waiting for us, welcoming us back with outstretched arms. Think of it in this way: God reaches out loving arms in order to hug us gently but firmly. God wants us each to know that even if we have trouble accepting ourselves, our Creator does accept us. As the saying goes, "God don't make no junk!" We are God's creations; we have been reminded of our goodness this week.

God speaking through the prophet Hosea promised to "return them [us] to their [our] homes." This is a statement of strength and comfort for us all. Not only are we accepted but God also takes an active interest in our welfare. God will not forsake us even in the most dire of life's circumstances. *That* we can depend upon.

We are reminded by the Gospel lesson that we cannot depend on the changing items of this world (such as money), but we can depend on the unchanging love and care of the Divine. We need to make our faith available to God's faithfulness. What we cannot do for ourselves, God can and will do if we seek God and allow God to be the senior partner in our life's unfolding.

My hope is that you and I can experience today as truly the *Lord's* Day so that our day today will be much better than any other Sunday in memory!

Prayer *Come, Lord Jesus, be my guest in my life today; and stay with me in all the days to come. Amen.*

The Gospel of Peace with Justice

September 25–October 1, 1989   **Ada María Isasi-Diaz†**
Monday, September 25   Read Luke 16:1-3.

This chapter in Luke begins with the parable of a steward who is not only wasteful but who gives away money that is not his by pardoning debts owed not to him but to his master. And this "dishonest steward" wins the praise of his master because of the way he used the money, even if the money was not his.

The parable makes it very clear that the steward is a dishonest man. But the main point of this account emphasizes that money is not to be an end in itself but a means to achieve an end. The steward is praised for understanding this point. As a means to an end, money is to be used by whoever needs it to attain "the eternal habitations." This is indeed difficult for us to understand.

Though the early Christian community described in Acts 2:42-47 held everything in common, we tend to dismiss this by insisting that their behavior was due to the mistaken idea that the end of the world was coming right away. We argue that our accumulation of earthly goods and our insistence on private ownership are made acceptable by the "delay" in the coming of the reign of God. But Luke 16 continues to be the word of God for us today. The reign of God is not yet here but we are called to witness to it, to participate in making our world believe in it by the very way we live. The important thing, then, is not the *when* of the coming of the reign of God but its meaning in our lives. Our use of money, our behavior in general, has to witness to and make possible our participation in the reign of God.

Prayer: *Divine Friend, open our hearts so that we may be challenged ever anew by the words of your gospel. Amen.*

---

†Associate General Director of Church Women United; lecturer and writer, New York, New York.

Tuesday, September 26   Read Luke 16:10-13.

There are two interconnected themes in this short paragraph of the Gospel of Luke. First, one cannot be trusted except with what one has committed oneself to. If it is money or business, then that is what one can be trusted with. If the commitment is to struggle for justice, to be about the gospel message, one can be trusted with that. So what we must look at first of all is what it is that we have given our allegiance to. Is it to God? Or is it to attitudes and understandings that will make us rich and famous even at the expense of others?

The second theme here has to do with the gospel's demand for a radical decision—an either/or proposition. It is not possible for us to be "a little bit" about God, to be somewhat committed, to choose sometimes to be about justice and to put it on the back burner other times. But once we start, once we choose God, we must keep that commitment central in our lives. Who we are, what our values are, what we do—all of it must be analyzed and chosen insofar as it helps us to carry out our commitment to God. The Book of Revelation makes it clear: "I know your works: you are neither cold nor hot. . . . So, because you are lukewarm. . . I will spew you out of my mouth" (Rev. 3:15-16).

Of course we are going to waver; at times we are even going to be "dishonest"—we will betray our allegiance to God. The living out of our commitment to God and the gospel message of justice and peace is an ongoing process of conversion. In the long run we do know that we will always need to turn to God once again. What makes it possible is knowing that God will not only always receive us anew, but that our Divine Friend will always be calling us, bidding us to be honest, trustworthy, and to choose God and not mammon.

Prayer: *Help us never to be lukewarm, O God! Amen.*

Wednesday, September 27   Read Luke 16:19-26.

What is choosing God all about? How do we know/show that we are committed to God and to the gospel of justice and peace? We find the answer to these questions in the parable of Lazarus and the rich man. In scripture nameless people are the ones not considered important. But Jesus uses the poor man's name to make it very clear that his importance had nothing to do with what he had or did not have. His name was Lazarus.

What Lazarus longed for was to share in what the rich man had. The rich man ends up in Hades not because he was rich but because of what he did with his wealth. The rich man was not willing to share with Lazarus, so in Hades he cannot expect Lazarus to share with him even a drop of water. In life the rich man had chosen to be radically separated from Lazarus. Most probably he had not even noticed the poor man by whom he walked day after day. Now in Hades, the separation continues: a great chasm makes communication between Lazarus and the rich man impossible. In life the separation had benefited the rich man; after death the separation works against him.

It is important to notice that in this parable nobody condemns the rich man. In reality Hades for him is a continuation of choices he had made in this life. He chose to be apart from the poor; he chose not to share—and those choices become his lot for all eternity. The chasm keeps Lazarus from going to the rich man. It is not that Lazarus is taking revenge. It is not that Lazarus does not want to quench the thirst of the rich man. Lazarus does not reject the rich man even if the rich man had rejected him. But the rich man had never gone to Lazarus, and now when he so wants to do it, he cannot. The chasm that keeps the rich man from Lazarus is his attitude toward the poor.

Suggestion for meditation: *How do I use my "riches"?*

Thursday, September 28   Read Luke 16:27-31.

Getting to know God and what God calls us to do is not a mystery beyond our grasp. Matthew 25 makes it very clear: when we see the hungry, the naked, the sick—we see God. Our excuses have to do with not wanting to know instead of with not being able to know. Our excuses have to do with our lack of willingness to make the radical choice of being people of justice and peace.

This is what the last verses of this parable are about. Like the rich man and his five brothers, if we finish in Hades it is not because God has not told us what to do. God speaks to us loud and clear. But many times we do not hear because we do not want to accept God's revelation expressed in the poor and the oppressed. But even if we do accept God's revelation made known in the poor and the oppressed, how do we answer?

The parables of Lazarus and the rich man and the dishonest steward tell us how to answer. We are called to use what we have—riches, status, influence, contacts—on behalf of the poor and the oppressed. That is what sharing is all about.

We share to enable others to live their lives fully. Therefore, our sharing has to bring about structural change. We must ask ourselves why our society blames the poor for their poverty instead of blaming the system for not providing enough jobs and opportunities. We must ask ourselves why we continue to blame women for their oppression when patriarchal power is what keeps them from full participation in our churches and society. To share is to bring about radical change; it is to be willing to question how our society operates so as to exclude a great number from resources we all need to live life fully.

Prayer: *Make us courageous, O God, as we share the radical gospel of your Son. Amen.*

Friday, September 29   Read Joel 2:23-30.

To be in solidarity with the poor and the oppressed is not a matter of agreeing with, of being supportive, of liking, or of being inspired by them. Instead, solidarity is the sense of togetherness, of oneness which arises out of the common responsibilities and interests we have in our world today. Our world has shrunk; what happens in any part of the world affects all other areas. Two world wars, multinational corporations, the threat of global atomic annihilation, the global spread of AIDS, the political influence/control of different nations in any part of the world by the superpowers, the threats to the ozone layer, acid rain—all of these are examples of the interconnections in our world today. It is precisely this interconnection which calls us to stand in solidarity with each other, to understand that my own economic and social status are related to the poverty and oppression of Rosa, a poor woman in Lima, Peru, who has only tea to give her children on weekends when the church pantry is closed.

Understanding and embracing this commonality of interests is both the basis for and the first step in expressing our solidarity with the poor. Another step we must all take is to do away with the mentality that we are the givers and the poor are the receivers. We must move from this kind of mentality to a sense of creating community with the poor and the oppressed. But there is no community without justice. To embrace the poor as part of our community or, better, to become part of their community, is not a matter of "generosity" but of justice. Biblical justice is not giving to each one her/his due. Biblical justice has to do with living in such a way that every person has what is needed to live life fully. Not just survive but live life fully—development of our bodies, our minds, our creativity, our dreams.

Prayer: *Divine Friend, help me to understand how I am connected to the poor of this world. Amen.*

Saturday, September 30   Read 1 Timothy 6:6-10;
Luke 16:19-31.

Solidarity is an expression of the interconnections that exist among love of God, love of neighbor, and love of self. Jesus reminds us that love of self is the starting place for all of our loving. Love of God and love of neighbor cannot exist without love of self. Love of self is not selfishness; selfishness has to do with a self-centeredness that excludes love of God and love of neighbor. Jesus tells us that we cannot be about what is best for us if we are not about what is best for our neighbors.

True love of self is an intrinsic part of solidarity with the poor. We are not isolated individuals. The human person is a social being who needs others not only to help with the minimal—food, housing, clothing—but also as persons with whom to be in relationship. The other that Jesus points to in this parable is Lazarus: the poor and the oppressed. The other for the rich man are not his friends or his brothers—people from his own world. The other for the rich man is the beggar at the door, the one he totally ignored. The rich man could not become the person God intended him to be because he ignored Lazarus. The rich man could not be saved because he did not love his neighbor Lazarus, and his lack of love for Lazarus was in reality a lack of love for himself and God.

Prayer: *Divine Friend, give me the courage to face myself and answer these questions with sincerity and without fear:*

How do I show my love of self as a social person? Who are those with whom I stand in solidarity?

How is their world related to mine? How is their poverty maintained by my lifestyle?

Concretely, how can I more lovingly stand in solidarity with them?

285

Sunday, October 1   Read 1 Timothy 6:11-19.

In order to stand in solidarity with the poor and the oppressed we need to have a commonality of interests with them, to see the interconnections that exist in our world today, and to understand that we should act out of a self-interest that is part of true love of self. We also need to understand that the poor and the oppressed have a privileged way of looking at our world today. From the fringes of society they can see possibilities which are often veiled for us. Why? Because we need to protect the way things are in order to continue to enjoy the privileges which are ours.

I have often wondered how the poor whom Jesus spoke about and spoke to saw the world, how they dreamed the world could be. None of the poor in Jesus' parables and in his world wanted to impoverish the rich and take their places. All of them simply wanted to participate, to share the crumbs from the table, to stop bleeding, to stand upright, to see. And their need to have others share with them shaped their vision of what the world should be like: a world in which all could share and share alike.

How do we bring about this world the poor can so clearly envision? In my family relationships, how do I treat my husband, my wife, my children? Are we as a family a real community which takes time for each other? Do we challenge each other? In my workplace, how do I treat my employer, my employees? Do I act responsibly and fairly? Do I go beyond the sense of "to each her/his due"? In society, do I get involved in social issues like homelessness, drug abuse? Do I know what is going on in Central America, Africa, and try to influence how the USA acts in other countries? Do I act out a sense that the poor and the oppressed are my community, that I must stand in solidarity with them for my sake as much as for their sake?

Prayer: *Help me to know, O God, that as I stand with the poor, I am standing with you. Amen.*

THE EXERCISE OF FAITH

October 2-8, 1989   **Stephen L. Baines†**
Monday, October 2   Read Psalm 101.

Faith is a much abused word. It suggests vague feeling and sentimental devotion. We often think of faith as believing that, in the end, things will turn out all right for God's people.

Things will turn out all right for believers, but such a belief doesn't do justice to the muscular faith presented in scripture. Faithful followers of the way of Jesus Christ were intensely bent on both living and proclaiming God's good news for Christ's coming again. Paul, for example, looked forward to the next world, but he spent his life laboring for God.

This week's readings stress being faithful in a sinful world. Psalm 101 is a declaration of commitment to faithful living. The speaker, Israel's king, declares that, as God's representative, he will imitate the attributes of God. This means loving justice and avoiding all evil. This involves more than keeping his hands clean. A blameless life involves actively rooting out evil and protecting good: "My eyes will be on the faithful in the land" (NIV).

Duty is important here, as in the other scripture readings this week. The faithful person has a duty to serve God in any way possible. The king in Psalm 101 could, with his faithful zeal, serve well as a model for all believers.

Suggestion for meditation: *Meditate on this quotation from Martin Luther: "The right, practical divinity is this: Believe in Christ, and do your duty in that state of life to which God has called you."*

---

† Free-lance writer, Nashville, Tennessee.

Tuesday, October 3   Read Amos 5:6-7, 10-15.

"Hate evil, love good" (NIV). Amos, the faithful prophet in a wicked age, was telling the people of Israel to change their unrighteous lives or God would devour the nation like a fire. The prophets spoke often of God's love for Israel, but they knew too well that the people had grown presumptuous. They saw themselves as God's chosen, people whom God would always shield from harm. The prophets knew that faithless living, manifested in the rich trampling on the poor, would lead to calamity.

Amos paints an appalling picture of the idle rich, a picture that seems painfully contemporary. The rich take bribes and deprive the poor of justice in the courts. They hate truth and hate goodness.

Contrast these people with the righteous king of Psalm 101. Here is unfaith contrasted with faith. Amos warned the people of Israel that they must seek to live righteous, faithful lives, else they would inevitably be punished. His words offer judgment, but also hope. The people can be spared *if* they will serve as dutiful people of God. They have turned God's order upside down with their perversion of justice, their pride, their abuse of privilege. To ward off disaster, they must seek the Lord.

Again, duty is important. The people of God have a duty to act like God's people, people of faith. This was true in Amos' day. It is true in our own. The faithful people must act faithfully, or God is not truly with them.

Prayer: *Merciful God, forgive us for not dutifully seeking the good. Remind us constantly of the joy of serving you and serving all humanity. Amen.*

Wednesday, October 4   Read Luke 17:7-10.

Self is the name of a popular magazine. The title seems to typify the magazines I see in the supermarket checkout lines. An alien visiting our planet might well wonder if our only concerns in life are keeping our weight down, coping with romantic spats, and advancing our careers. The magazines—and, in fact, the media in general—talk much about duty, but it is always duty to self.

Jesus was like a dart aimed at the balloons of pride and self-centeredness. He understood humanity's inclination toward self-ishness, and he knew that even the faithful could be guilty of pride and presumption. Today's parable is a slap at such arrogance. According to Jesus, when we have done our best we can expect no special rewards. We have only done our duty. We have fulfilled an obligation, and so we cannot boast or carp. God never owes us anything, no matter how nice we are. Salvation is free, not earned.

Paul spoke of how salvation is by grace, not human works (see Eph. 2:8-9). He knew that humans tend to boast of good deeds. But preaching, teaching Sunday school, and singing in the choir score no extra points with God.

Today's passage is more than a jab at pride and arrogance. It is a caution against resting on our laurels. We are to joyfully serve God, but we can never assume that we have finished our work. Duty never stops, and the faithful know they can never do too much for God.

Prayer: *Gracious God, thank you for saving us. Deliver us from our pride and selfishness, and never let us tire in serving you. Amen.*

Thursday, October 5   Read Luke 17:1-6.

The disciples asked Jesus for an increase in faith. They wanted the kind that would help them meet the high standards of conduct in verses 1-4. But they wanted the faith given to them, apparently with no effort on their part. Jesus tells them to use the faith they already have, which—even if his words about uprooting trees are an obvious exaggeration—indicates that whatever faith we possess is a potent thing.

Psychiatrist Garth Wood wrote a popular 1986 book, *The Myth of Neurosis*. In it he criticizes therapists who allow clients to drift for years while they make excuses for their behavior and blame it on their past. Wood frequently emphasizes the importance of having obstacles to overcome in life. "Never," he says, "should we underestimate the importance of difficulty."* He recognizes, as most mature believers do, that the old values of hard work and sacrifice are still important.

In the life of faith we graciously receive the free gift of salvation, but we follow it up with hard work. Much of the sorrow in our life with God and our life with each other stems from outright laziness.

"Increase our faith," say the disciples. "Use what you have, and you will be astonished at the results," says the Lord. There is no place in the kingdom for lazy faith.

Prayer: *Lord, teach us to use the faith we already have. Help us work out our salvation with fear and trembling. Help us be grateful children who never cease to exercise our faith. Amen.*

---

* Garth Wood, *The Myth of Neurosis* (New York: Harper & Row, 1986), p. 97.

Friday, October 6   Read 2 Timothy 1:1-7.

General William Booth, founder of the Salvation Army, knew much about muscular faith. He labored in the London slums for many years, and his followers carry on the tradition of witnessing through word and deed to the down-and-out.

Booth understood the tendency of believers to let their faith lie dormant. He once said, "The tendency of fire is to go out; watch the fire on the altar of your heart."

Paul, who dearly loved the young pastor Timothy, must have known that Timothy had an inclination to be timid. The young man possessed a sincere faith, a faith no doubt nurtured by his mother and grandmother, both believers. But Timothy needed more boldness in his faith. Like the disciples in yesterday's passage, he did not need more faith—he needed to "fan into a flame" what he already possessed.

Timothy had a good role model in Paul. Here was someone who stressed again and again the impossibility of earning God's favor. Yet this was the same man who modeled boldness, tirelessness, restless duty to God. Paul himself possessed the spirit of power, love, and self-discipline he mentions in verse 7. His was a passionate, robust faith, a faith available to all believers, including the sincere, but sometimes timid, pastor of the church at Ephesus. Like Timothy, we would all do well to fan into a flame the fire that is in our hearts.

Prayer: *Lord, teach us about a faith not only sincere but powerful. Remind us of your saints—William Booth, Mother Teresa, and others like them who burn with an eager and brawny faith. Amen.*

Saturday, October 7　　　　　Read 2 Timothy 1:8-12.

No one likes to suffer, not even the children of God. Not Jesus, not Paul, not anyone in the New Testament exhibited a martyr complex. Yet the holy people always understood that in a world riddled with sin, the good will inevitably endure sorrow.

Paul, happy because he was able to preach and teach the gospel of eternal life, was in prison in Rome. From his prison cell he tells young Timothy not to be ashamed of this imprisonment. More important, he tells Timothy not to be ashamed to speak about Christ. This may lead to suffering, but the gospel must be preached. How can we remain silent when God so graciously retrieved us from eternal separation from him?

Sometimes muscular faith involves acting—teaching, preaching, healing, helping the poor. Sometimes, as in today's reading, it involves patiently enduring the pain. "Join with me in suffering for the gospel," says Paul to Timothy. That is, witness to the world, even though witnessing may bring on hurt.

Novelist James Fenimore Cooper ended *The Deerslayer* with these words: "We live in a world of transgressions and selfishness, and no pictures that represent us otherwise can be true." In such a world, the faithful must act, although their deeds so often lead to grief. It is still God's world, and God still watches over the dutiful servants. This assurance of God's care for the faithful was a comfort to Paul, and is to us.

Prayer: *Loving God, you are always with us, whether in triumph or in sorrow. When we suffer because of our faith, remind us that you are in control of the universe, and that you will hold to us forever and ever. Amen.*

Sunday, October 8   Read 2 Timothy 1:13-14.

Doctrine plus faith plus love—these are the core of verse 13. Paul tells Timothy that sound doctrine must be lived and proclaimed with faith and love. Teaching alone is abstract and sterile. With faith and love it is rich, dynamic, world-changing.

Scholars are not sure what the "good deposit" of verse 14 is. It may refer to the sound teaching mentioned in verse 13. It may refer to good deeds. Whatever it is, the Greek word (*paratheke*) refers to something entrusted to someone else, as one might leave valuables with a friend when one makes a journey. Paul was prepared to die, so he was entrusting a sound gospel—and the vigorous, Christ-centered life rooted in that gospel—to Timothy. The passage is touching—a great man of God entrusting good words and deeds to a follower.

This week we have looked at passages focused on commitment and duty. We have seen that true believers trust God for their salvation, but live vibrant, active lives as they seek to witness to a sin-stricken world. In today's reading we see the logical conclusion of muscular faith: the faithful person leaving his teaching and deeds behind as models for others.

What a way to crown a life! To leave behind the greatest treasure of all, a good example of Christlike living. Even after death, the saints' hardy faith goes on and on.

Prayer: *God, thank you for the great examples you have given us. Keep us so active and zealous that we, like Paul, will leave behind something worth keeping. Amen.*

AM I GUILTY, LORD?

October 9-15, 1989   **Barbara W. Short†**
Monday, October 9   Read Micah 1:2; 2:1-10;
            Psalm 26;
           Luke 17:11-19;
          2 Timothy 2:8-15.

"Hear ye! Hear ye! The court is now in session." The people everywhere—across time, national boundaries, racial lines—are summoned to trial.

We are the accused—charged with breaking our covenant with God; and we recognize familiar figures who have taken key positions in the courtroom to speak for and against us.

Micah is ready for the prosecution, with both general and specific acts of which humankind is guilty in this broken relationship.

From Luke comes the defense. Yes, we are an ungrateful people, he acknowledges, but still there are some among us who thank God and return to the Creator.

The psalmist is the character witness. He pleads the case for humanity, in a profession of integrity and loyalty to God.

But, from Paul's letter to Timothy comes the precedent that may allow us to go free. Herein, Paul says to all: Remember Jesus Christ; remember that he accepts the penalty for our sins and gains our release.

The courtroom is filled and noisy; all would speak at once. But the babble is hushed as the Judge enters. He raps the bench but once, and humanity grows quiet.

God breaks the silence: "Let the trial begin."

Prayer: *Am I guilty, Lord?*

---

† Lay Leader, McMannen United Methodist Church; president/CEO, Info-Marketing Inc., a marketing communications agency, Durham, North Carolina.

Tuesday, October 10   Read Micah 1:2; 2:1-10.

Micah is well known in God's court. He has the reputation of being the country lawyer; but those who know him well know that he has associated with the keen legal minds of his time.

When he bids all people to harken to his message, he speaks with the authority of one in close contact with the living God, who calls God to witness to the word proclaimed. He reminds us all that we have failed our personal responsibility in covenant with God.

As a true prophet, Micah has the vision to see the big picture and the power to envision it for others. He sets us up as the guilty party, as he graphically testifies that our false spirituality does not recognize God's covenant as relevant for all aspects of our lives—in business, in dealings with others, even in court.

Lest those who hear Micah's outcry against sin think that he is speaking only of another generation or of sin in general, he becomes very specific in his oratory. Those whose desire for land or power leads them to greed and covetousness are directly responsible for the breakdown of the social structure. And sin of such magnitude invites—no, demands—action by God.

Micah is not one to plea-bargain; his is a tough message of sin followed by judgment. Those who err can expect punishment befitting the act. For it is only those who remain faithful, those who recognize that the covenant requires obedience and righteous action, that God will gather at the time of judgment. So rests Micah's case.

Prayer: *Am I greedy, Lord? Amen.*

Wednesday, October 11　　　　　Read Micah 2:6-10;
　　　　　　　　　　　　　　　　　Psalm 26:4-10;
　　　　　　　　　　　　　　　　　2 Timothy 2:14-15.

As the testimony against us mounts, we turn inward and begin to ask ourselves, "How did I get here? How could I have so neglected my part of the covenant? How could I have broken the most important relationship in my life?"

As disappointed children, we may even cry out, "But, Father, you promised," forgetting that the promise held expectations of faith and love on our part.

Perhaps we fail because we listen only to God's promise to us and not to the full message that calls our actions and our beliefs into account. Perhaps we listen to false prophets who speak the words that rest easier on our consciences.

Micah warns us of preachers with the easy message, those who take our part in sin rather than confront us with it. They spoke against Micah in his day, and they speak in every age. Unlike the true prophet, they have vision only for the moment, and we are tempted to accept their short-term view.

The psalmist, in another age, recognizes the threat to his faith that exists in wrong associations. The faithful strengthen one another as they listen with one mind to those who speak from a relationship with God. It is in this house, with God and God's people, that the psalmist would dwell.

Timothy, likewise, is admonished by Paul to stick to the truth, and to avoid words without foundation in God.

As we face God in judgment, we look around us. The false prophets are nowhere in sight. Jesus is our only hope.

Prayer: *Am I listening only to the easy word, Lord? Amen.*

Thursday, October 12   Read Luke 17:11-19.

It is mid-week and mid-trial. We are ready for someone to speak a good word for us, for our self-esteem suffers greatly when God's righteousness confronts our sin.

With relief and gratitude, we hear Luke defend us. As a physician, he may not be the skilled orator that Micah is; but Luke speaks in love for all people. He cares for the underdog, for he is a Gentile and knows what it is like to be an outsider.

He tells the story of the ten lepers. We know it well, but we listen as if the words were all new. They, like us, were bound together in their suffering and brokenness. Their common affliction made them fellow travelers in life, even though they had different beliefs. Indeed, the only one of the ten who showed gratitude for the healing that Jesus provided to all was the Samaritan.

"Is there hope here?" we ask. "If the Samaritan could turn back to God in gratitude, why can't we?" But then, there were ten who were healed, and only one remembered. "Can I be that one?" each of us agonizes.

Any of us can be the one who accepts God's cleansing, Luke says. It matters not if one is male or female, black or white, Jew or Samaritan. And any one of us can be grateful. By God's grace, each person carries within the strength to pause in life's pursuit and take time to say, "Thank you." And, in so doing, we too can hear the words we so desperately need to hear: "Your faith has made you well."

Prayer: *Am I the one in ten, Lord? Amen.*

Friday, October 13   Read Psalm 26.

In awareness of God's grace, the psalmist steps forward to plead the case for humanity. In his lament, his faith as one of the chosen people shines through. In the tradition of the Old Testament, he is bound to us as representative of the whole of humankind. When he professes his loyalty to God and his trust as God's follower, he is seeking God's mercy for us all. He is our character witness.

Still, he recognizes that his integrity is not of his own doing but is possible only because God has acted first in his life. It is God who has enabled him to be a whole person, to resist the temptation of associating with evildoers, to seek God's house and God's way.

He claims God's strength as his own to the point that he asks God to test him, to see if he is found wanting.

But isn't that what is happening at this very moment? Aren't we, and the psalmist as our representative, being put through a time of trial? Is it possible, we ponder, that by God's faithfulness to us we can be restored to a right relationship, that the covenant can be reestablished between us?

If so, what are the conditions which will make this possible? If we believe the words of the psalmist, then we must begin by accepting God's grace and faithfulness as the miracle that makes restoration possible. And we must move on from there to worship at God's altar, to studied avoidance of sin and sinful situations, and never-ending prayer for continued gracious acts in our lives.

This is our restitution.

Prayer: *Am I a person of integrity, Lord? Amen.*

Saturday, October 14   Read 2 Timothy 2:8-15.

In a court of law, a precedent is a prior decision that has been made, which serves as a rule in future legal determinations.

In our days of trial, much testimony has been expressed regarding our broken covenant, but nothing has yet been put forward that makes the case clear-cut.

But now, in the writings of Paul to Timothy, we find the precedent that will set us free. For Paul writes, "Remember Jesus Christ."

In our response to that simple command is all we need to receive God's mercy. Jesus Christ took all those sins of which we are accused—greed, covetousness, ingratitude, forgotten promises, broken relationships—and he took our punishment as his own.

Paul, from a prison cell in which he was placed because of his Christianity, writes to Timothy in a way that is both personal and universal. Although physically confined, Paul writes to free Timothy, spiritually, from problems he faces in the early church; and he writes to free us from twentieth-century problems with faith.

The message is the same now as then: Remember Jesus Christ; remember him risen from the dead; remember the gospel more powerful than chains; remember the salvation made possible by Jesus Christ.

Of course, God did not need to draw on this precedent in dealing with our sins. God knows full well the saving grace manifested in Jesus Christ. It is for our spiritual growth that God uses trial, testimony, witnesses, and precedent in our lives.

Each time we sin we are at risk of alienation, until we seek the mercy of the court in the kingdom of God.

Prayer: *Am I really free, Lord? Amen.*

Sunday, October 15   Read Micah 1:2; 2:1-10;
Psalm 26;
Luke 17:11-19;
2 Timothy 2:8-15.

Am I guilty, Lord?

Unquestionably, the answer is yes. And yet, a verdict has been returned in our favor. Micah might question if this is justice, since the innocent Lamb is the one who suffered for our sin.

The psalmist would not be surprised, for he, like us, has experienced the power of God in transforming a sinner into the accepted child of God.

Luke recognizes that we are not acquitted as an innocent party but forgiven in spite of our guilt, just as the leper was forgiven by faith.

And Paul would have us always "remember Jesus Christ," without whom our sins would lead to death.

There is one thing more, however, and that is the word of Jesus Christ himself. He said it to sinners of old, and he says it to us: You are forgiven, but . . .

Our forgiveness is not without expectation, just as our original covenant with God was not without expectation. Jesus would add to that forgiveness: Go and sin no more.

Our restored, re-formed lives are now to be lived in regular contemplation and in prayer to God. We are led to live lives "worthy of the gospel of Christ" (Phil. 1:27) and to serve God and others in love.

All this, and more, cannot earn us freedom. But it can bring us closer to the Power that makes freedom possible.

Prayer: *I am guilty of sin, Lord. Help me also to accept that I am forgiven, and that there is a new covenant in my life. Amen.*

THE JUST SHALL LIVE BY FAITH

October 16-22, 1989   **W. Paul Lanier†**
Monday, October 16   Read Hab. 1:1-3; 2:1-4.

The short book of Habukkuk begins, "An oracle which the prophet Habakkuk received in a vision" (NEB). Habakkuk possessed a quality necessary for creative leadership: vision. He conveyed for God a vision of divine justice. At the time Habakkuk wrote, powerful nations were vying for dominance.

Habakkuk asked God, "Why dost thou countenance the treachery of the wicked?" (Hab. 1:13, NEB) and the Lord answered, "There is still a vision for the appointed time . . . it will not fail. . . . wait for it" (NEB). Here is the guidance given to the prophet: be faithful to God. Then we read the "woes" to those who heap up wealth not their own (see Hab. 2:6). Habakkuk is writing about the unfaithfulness of a nation.

This week we will be reflecting on divine justice, our need for confidence in a God who is just and who feels for the troubled and oppressed. We will think about our commitment to justice and those who taught us the precepts of right and wrong. Because we know that God is just, we can delight in this and know calmness in our soul.

Can a nation be a righteous nation? Some have argued that this is not possible, that individuals can be other-centered, but nations are always self-centered. Even if nations cannot be other-centered, individual leaders can have a powerful effect on the direction a nation takes.

Suggestion for meditation: *Who, in your memory, was a powerful leader for good in a nation?*

---

† United Methodist minister (retired), Florida and North Arkansas conferences, Sumner, Georgia.

Tuesday, October 17   Read Hab. 1:1-3; 2:1-4.

This prophet of the 7th century before Christ is very much aware of the violence about him. In the face of threats from one powerful nation after another, how should Habukkuk react? Should he cry out for help? And when will relief be on the way? Babylonia and other godless nations were taking over and ruling Assyria and the prophet's people. Habakkuk asks why.

Martin Luther was profoundly disturbed by what he saw going on in the church of his day. He wrote to the bishop of Rome, saying that the bishop was not to blame but the system in the church was. Though Luther was appalled at the church's condition, he said that it was precisely at this point that faith came to bear. Count Zenzendorf said in a lecture, "The first beginning of faith . . . is an effect of misery." He also said that the anxiety created by this distress forced him to cry out for help.

One of my seminary professors said that Christ's coming into his life tore him and his life into pieces. But then Christ helped him put it all back together again. Habakkuk believed that piety and prosperity were cause and effect. If a nation or an individual pleased God, then that nation or individual would prosper. But when Habakkuk sees the wicked prospering, he is puzzled. He struggles with this and asks, "How long shall I cry for help, and thou wilt not hear?" Then he agrees to take his stand and to wait.

How do we react in the face of robbery, violence, and other disturbances in our lives day by day?

Suggestion for meditation: *Do you recall a time when you were in distress or had anxious moments? What did you do? How would you act differently next time?*

Wednesday, October 18   Read Hab. 2:1-4.

We can be immobilized by conflict. But this was not the case with Habakkuk. In the face of violence, he said, "I will take my stand upon my watchtower . . . and watch to see what the Lord will say to me" (AP). This faith-in-distress is like the experience of giving birth. It is painful, yet even in the midst of the pain, there is hope and joyful expectancy. There is a faith that possesses patience and perseverance.

Faithful persons in distress need not be immobilized by what they see or hear. This was true of Habakkuk. He was going to watch and listen. Isaiah, like Habakkuk, spoke of God's promise to those who serve God's cause of justice: ". . . then shall your light break forth like the dawn" (Isa. 58:8, NEB). The yoke of oppression and the distress of violence would not overcome Habakkuk. Why? Because he waited for God's answer. The Chaldeans were fierce and hasty. Their horses were swift, "like vultures swooping to devour their prey" (Hab. 1:8, NEB). In view of this, what is the prophet to do? He is to write the message of the vision on tablets with large and clear letters: JUSTICE.

The vision has to do with faithfulness. "The righteous will live by his faith (faithfulness)" (NIV). This faithfulness is not an inherited creed. It is not a body of beliefs. It is not a rigid group of rules of do's and don'ts. This vision of faithfulness appears to a righteous person who sets out to right wrongs in God's way: "a way that starts in faith and ends in faith" (Rom. 1:17, NEB). This involves the faithful person in acts of mercy and retribution, making the crooked paths straight.

Suggestion for meditation: *Where do you see evidence that God's judgment comes to silence the oppressor? Are we keeping our faith in God that we may overcome our troubles?*

303

Thursday, October 19   Read Psalm 119:137-144.

As I read these words of the psalmist, I ask myself, How does this speak to me?

Alice Walker, author of *The Color Purple,* was asked in a television interview about a poem she had once written. The poem showed anger and bitterness. After she read the poem aloud, she was asked if she would write another that sounded that way. She shook her head and said no. Somehow her life had changed, and she was no longer so angry. Don't you think this is what the psalmist experienced? "I am speechless with resentment, for my enemies have forgotten thy words" (NEB). The following verse says, "Thy promise has been tested." God's promise has proved valid. And the writer, now with resentment gone, can say, ". . . and thy servant loves it" (NEB). And so it is with us. Sometimes it takes years for us to understand that God's promise is fulfilled. Righteousness and justice will prevail. Thus we can delight in God's precepts. Our resentment and hatred can be forgotten. We can move into the future with faith, knowing that God's commandments are right.

As we meditate on the scriptures daily, we can begin afresh. The Lord does vindicate troubled and oppressed hearts. The past night with its dreams of difficulties does not overwhelm us, because the Lord is faithful to those who call for help.

The psalmist says to me that my heart can be changed, my soul refreshed, my sins forgiven.

Prayer: *O God, we would put resentment and hatred aside and leave them there. Cleanse the thoughts of our hearts by the inspiration of thy Holy Spirit so that we may perfectly love thee and worthily magnify thy name. Amen.*

Friday, October 20   Read 2 Tim. 3:14–4:5.

Paul remembered sitting at the feet of Gamaliel, being educated according to the "strict manner of the law of our fathers, being zealous for God" (Acts 22:3).

Paul reminds Timothy and us to remember those who have taught us, saying, "Continue in what you have learned and have firmly believed." We can recall Sunday school teachers, pastors, and parents who taught us. I remember a teacher from my public-school days. His name is Nevin Neal. His teaching stimulated students' interest in current events. My thoughts turn to another teacher, Dr. Albert E. Barnett. Even though his New Testament class was at 8 a.m., we listened intently and asked questions fervently. Dr. Barnett's teaching appealed to our minds and to our consciences and inspired faithfulness to be steady.

Sound teaching of the holy scripture helps us to continue "in season and out of season." Today, some people have stopped listening to sound teaching and have sought to "accumulate for themselves teachers to suit their own likings." These prosper for a while, but commitment to a just society lingers and God continues to beckon. We may not see God's just society realized in our lifetime (for God's timetable is different than humans'), but we are to "endure suffering, do the work of a preacher of the Good News, and perform [our] duty as [servants] of God" (TEV).

Prayer: *Lord, we pause now in your presence to remember teachers, family members, pastors—all who have taught us. They are ever present in our thinking, our doing, and our admiration. We are grateful that we had the opportunity to sit at the feet of these whose names we call before you. Amen.*

Saturday, October 21　　　Read Hab. 2:1-4; Luke 18:1-8;
　　　　　　　　　　　　　　　　　　Psalm 119:137-144.

Perhaps too often today the media, as well as some of our church leaders, look at numbers and are ever impressed by large crowds. But in today's readings it is individuals who make impressions. "I will take up my position . . . I will watch" (NEB). "I may be despised and of little account, but I do not forget thy precepts" (NEB). "In the same town there was a widow who constantly came . . . demanding justice" (NEB).

Soren Kierkegaard, in his book *Purity of Heart,* writes, "Do you now live so that you are conscious of yourself as an individual?" Kierkegaard goes on to add that the individual is eternally responsible to God. It is important for us to be aware of our individuality, for often we are overly conscious of what the crowd is doing. But often the crowd possesses no conscience, hears no still small voice, and runs far afield of truth.

Today, we seem impressed by bigness. We are always counting. Yet it is the individual who hears, and it is the one who hears who can make a difference. We remember from our study of the Old and New Testaments that God spoke to the individual. Some listened, and these became God's leaders in history. God speaks to individual hearts, and it is the individual who influences the crowds. Today the individual is still God's channel. The Lord speaks to me and to you. And when the Son of Man comes, will you and I be found among the faithful? Have we listened?

Prayer: *Lord, help me to listen to you and pass your message on to those who feel lost and alone. Amen.*

Sunday, October 22   Read Hab. 2:1-4; Ps. 119:141.

We have been reading this week in Habakkuk, Second Timothy, Psalm 119, and Luke 18. This has led us to recall godly parents and teachers and to be aware of the injustices about us. The quest for a just society has been in the forefront of our minds and hearts.

The United States' Declaration of Independence declares that the colonies are breaking away from Great Britain to throw off the tyranny of a despot. The preamble to the United States Constitution reads, "In order to establish justice . . . promote the general welfare (we) . . . do ordain and establish this Constitution." Like the leaders of Israel of old, the leaders of our new nation held to a high purpose—to establish justice. We dare not forget this high purpose.

What is God up to in this continuing creation? The writer of Psalm 119 reminds us that little and weak though we may be, God's precepts surround us. And as we are aware of God's precepts, we realize that we as individuals and as nations can make a difference in living out God's purposes. The story is told that St. Francis of Assisi asked a young friend in the monastery to go with him for a walk through the streets and up and down the hills of the village until they came back to where they had started. Puzzled, the young friend exclaimed, "I thought you said we were going out to preach today." Francis replied that they had been noticed by the townsfolk, that they had been preaching even as they were walking.

What are we preaching by our lifestyle?

Prayer: *O God, give us your peace so that our lives will show its beauty and draw others into your kingdom. Amen.*

307

October 23-29, 1989   **Martha E. Chamberlain†**
Monday, October 23   Read Zephaniah 3:1-5.

We can choose to grow through criticism

Or, we can resent so deeply that we strangle the ragged, fragile relationships of our lives. Zephaniah spoke of those who cannot accept correction. Although painful, confronting our error produces change and growth.

"Admit it," our thirteen-year-old foster daughter screamed at me. "Say 'I am mad at you.' Don't say you're upset. You're as mad as I am!"

She was right. But why should I take correction from her? She could lie, curse, disregard all kindness and advice, and then dare to tell me what I felt, and furthermore, that I was dishonest.

Although hard to swallow, her reprimands taught me to identify and name my feelings honestly. Now, more than twenty years later, I am thankful that I chose to listen. I feel only the deepest love for her today.

Although not responsible for another's reactions, we are accountable for our own attitude in both giving and receiving rebuke. Whether it is a child or a cantankerous co-worker, each person has a right to courteous criticism.

Unfortunately, we all at times inflict as well as suffer unjust criticism. And when erroneously chastised ourselves, we need to forgive as we have been forgiven.

Prayer: *Anoint me with wisdom and love, O Lord, that I may choose both to give and receive correction in the spirit of humility. Amen.*

---

†Former missionary nurse in Zambia; free-lance writer and author (*Surviving Junior High*), Springfield, Virginia.

Tuesday, October 24   Read Zephaniah 3:6-9.

We can choose to change through cleansing

I recently heard a story that had been told by Robert Schuller which illustrates the tragedy of outward change rather than inward transformation. It seems that a great brown bear in a European zoo had been confined over a long period of time in a 12-foot square cage. When it was decided that greater freedom would enhance his well-being, the bear was placed in an outdoor area with trees and rocks and water. But for the remainder of his life, he continued to pace twelve feet in one direction, then twelve feet in another.

Although we may welcome new beginnings by adding to light-hearted New Year's Day resolutions or kneeling in humility at a private altar, permanent change may elude us because we do not experience inward cleansing.

"I will purify the lips of the peoples, that all of them may call on the name of the Lord and serve him shoulder to shoulder." This beautiful picture of God's intervention conjures up an idyllic scene where the purified worship together and work toward one purpose.

But unfortunately we are all too much like the ancient Israelites—or even the bear—who often returned to their former ways. Warring, idolatry, and sinful alliances strongly tempted the ancient Hebrews. Our temptations are much the same, but the cleansing love of our Lord Jesus Christ can set us free from the bondage of sin.

Prayer: *Could it possibly be that even though I am set free, I fail to choose abundant life, O Lord? Help me to choose the life you offer. Amen.*

Wednesday, October 25 · Read Psalm 3:1-4.

We can choose to praise God when discouraged

Twenty-six-year-old Mike disappeared while flying an F-18. I wondered how his family and friends and fiance would bear the pain. But when his parents visited us four months later, although our young Marine friend had not been found, they radiated peace and victory. I wondered, Was this simply their means of denial? As we talked, however, his mother told of her discovery that the intentional, paradoxical "sacrifice of praise" (Heb. 13:15) had produced hope and peace.

Sacrifice does not connote ease and comfort. Rather, in the presence of pain, we can choose to focus on who God is—on God's nature, purpose, love, and presence. Then, although the *choice* to praise God in those circumstances is difficult, its result is peace.

Praising God in a maze of discouragement and pain seems preposterous. Yet the sacrifice of praise bridges the gulf from despair to hope. Fearful and heartbroken, David wrote this psalm while fleeing from his own son, Absalom (2 Sam. 15). But he chose to focus on the "Glorious One," rather than on his circumstances.

The often repeated pattern of despair and hope is not confined to the ancient poetry of the Psalms. We see the pendulum swing from the depths of anguish in Genesis to the ultimate culmination of God's plan in Revelation. And sooner or later, we, too, walk with disease, disaster, and depression. But having experienced the depths of despair, we may choose God's way to the heights through intentional praise.

Prayer: *O gentle, loving God, may I continually choose to "offer a sacrifice of praise" rather than focus on my pain. Amen.*

Thursday, October 26 · Read Psalm 3:5-8.

We can choose to commit the outcome to God

Although we sometimes do not see how God is working in our lives, we can commit everything to God, assured of God's commitment to us.

In Rembrandt's painting, *Danae,* (1636) the artist, though hidden from the eye of the viewer, is actually central to the picture. One sees only the wife of Rembrandt, waiting in bed for her lover. Committed to his wife's well-being and love, the artist actively, though not visibly, participates in the whole picture.

The psalmist sleeps—because God is in charge. He faces the new day—because God's strength is his own. He relinquishes fear—because God fights his battles.

When we intentionally offer our lives to God, our ongoing, daily choices, though not necessarily more simple, can result in peace.

We can choose to commit to God those circumstances over which we have no control, those difficult choices between two equally good options, and those decisions of great import, whether they be choosing friends in high school, or a college major, or a spouse, or a career change.

We can also give to God our emotions and temperament, even when depression or illness or pressure has created a hard-to-live-with person. God is ready to work the miracle of new life even when we least expect it.

Prayer: *May we choose to recognize your present, active involvement in our lives, even though we do not see you, as we commit everything to you, O God. Amen.*

Friday, October 27   Read Luke 18:9-14.

We can choose to see ourselves through the scriptures

Looking at ourselves through the mirror of God's word may reveal depravity, vulnerability, deviousness, pride—things we would rather not see.

Therefore, although we spend a lifetime and sometimes a fortune, trying to discover who we are, we forego the plumbline in our searching. We ignore the mirror in our looking. Or, like my friends, we use the wrong pattern.

Starting with one paper pattern, the group of women cut and sewed several hundred cloth bags to fill with toys for Mexican children. But dozens of completed bags actually measured several inches smaller or larger than the original pattern. Pieces had been cut from numerous copies of copies of the original.

We do not like to acknowledge it, but we, too, have followed wrong models. We have even prayed as the Pharisee did, "I am not like other [persons]." To discover and admit the common denominator of our human condition is a lifetime process.

Even the disciples gathered around Jesus at the Passover meal registered sadness and disbelief at Jesus' announcement that one of them would betray him, "and one by one they said to him, 'Surely, not I?' " (Mark 14:19, NIV)

"Finding oneself" in the most helpful and healthful sense starts with looking in the right place. In the scriptures we confront the self for whom Jesus lived and died. Then change begins and continues a lifetime.

Prayer: *O God, give me courage to see the worst and grace to choose the best: change, cleansing, and growth through Jesus Christ. Amen.*

Saturday, October 28   Read 2 Timothy 4:6-8.

We can choose to persevere until death

In 1988 Christians in the Soviet Union celebrated the 1,000th anniversary of Christianity in that country. They understand perseverance. By choice. By grace.

Evelina Ahukovskaya serves a five-year term for teaching Sunday school to Russian children. Others from two Christian charities suffer in prison for supplying food, clothing, and conscience. A Baptist pastor and his three sons have suffered torture, beatings, imprisonment, isolation, and constant surveillance since January 1986 because they are Christians.

Aging Saint Paul wrote today's words of scripture to encourage young Timothy to endure. Timothy had begun to understand, observing the life of his mentor, that serving God does not make one immune to human problems such as loneliness or aging. In addition, his friend Paul suffered deprivation, imprisonment, danger, persecution, hunger, torture, and humiliation, just because he called himself a follower of Jesus Christ.

How much do we know of personal suffering as a result of our faith? Oh, perhaps a momentary embarrassment may have been associated with some thought of "suffering" for righteousness' sake. But even that admission causes us to blush with shame when memory searches out Saints Paul and Stephen, or those in *Fox's Book of Martyrs,* and the hundreds of thousands—even to this day—who suffer for their faith. Their ability to endure is enhanced by their active, intentional choice to persevere.

Prayer: *O God, may I choose to persevere even when my own human endurance gives out. And may I participate through prayer with those who truly suffer for your sake. Amen.*

Sunday, October 29   Read 2 Timothy 4:16-18.

We can choose to serve in spite of handicaps

Or, we can run like Jonah, refuse like the rich young ruler, complain like Moses, or legitimately beg off for our own good reasons.

Eleanor has a good reason not to be involved. She is paralyzed on one side. But she drives the community's handicapped wherever they need to go, and welcomes with a hug those who enter the church door. She looks for troubles and needs—then works to try to solve them as the "shepherd" of her neighborhood care group.

Pat and Carl's eight-year-old son is blind and deaf, both physically and mentally handicapped. But their three-year-old niece sometimes stays with them because her mother has cancer. Pat also brought our family dinner after my surgery, as she does for so many others. Recently she packed her car with three heavy boxes of food and a large turkey for Thanksgiving dinner for a needy family. Sunday mornings they teach a class, and at night lead kids' Bible Bowl.

Saint Paul in today's lesson was not only still suffering in old age from a bodily handicap but also other continuing difficulties. In prison again, saddened by the desertion of co-workers and working through the pain of persecution, he encouraged Timothy by writing, "But the Lord . . . gave me strength."

Prayer: *Lord, you profoundly illustrated the meaning of power through service as you chose to kneel at the feet of twelve friends with a towel and a basin. Whatever our circumstances, may we choose to serve as well. Amen.*

It's God's Fault

October 30–November 5, 1989   **David J. McNitzky**†
Monday, October 30   Read Psalm 65:1-4; 51:1-9.

One of my favorite games is "Whose fault is it?" When milk is spilled on the floor or a lamp is broken, my first concern is not with cleaning or repairing but with finding out who is to blame. This particular game has no real redeeming value for me, and my suspicion is that others who play this game are not helped either. Why? Probably because all of us who play this game have a tendency to put the blame on someone else.

Blaming others is not a particularly attractive or healthy trait. For example, you could almost feel sorry for the one-talent servant in Jesus' parable, except for the fact that he actually blames the master for his own failure to produce (see Matt. 25:24-25). Some psychotherapists suggest that the only persons who are not helped by therapy are those who continually blame others for their problems.

That is why I find the psalmist so refreshing. The psalmist admits to sin and, thereby, accepts part of the blame for life's problems. Psalm 51:3 states, "For I know my transgressions, and my sin is ever before me." Our psalm for this week is no different: "When our transgressions prevail over us . . ." John the Baptist's call to repentance, echoed by other great New Testament figures, only makes sense to persons who are willing to admit to sin and know that they are at least partially responsible for where they find themselves in life.

Suggestion for meditation: *For what problem in my life do I ordinarily take no responsibility? Is it possible that I could have some responsibility for it?*

---

† Pastor, Helotes Hills United Methodist Church, Helotes, Texas.

Tuesday, October 31   Read Psalm 65:3-8.

It is one thing to admit sin and mistakes; it is quite another to wallow in guilt over them. We've all known people who seem to get pleasure out of constantly feeling guilty for sins, both real and imagined. I also know some whose guilt makes them run around trying to make amends for past mistakes. They "can never do enough for others," it seems. In reality, they can never do enough for themselves, as they cannot really seem to achieve the desired peace and forgiveness.

It appears that both types of persons, tortured by their willingness to admit sin and accept blame, have the same problem—they cannot accept help. When my son, Mark, was two years old, his favorite phrase was, "Markie do it." He wanted, like any other two-year-old, to do things for himself. Unfortunately, the "Markie do it" approach does not work when sin is involved. When we sin, we need salvation; we need forgiveness.

Forgiveness, like respect and love, can never be earned—it can only be received. I once heard a minister speak on the subject of "what keeps us separated from God." I expected him to catalogue different types of sin; instead he said that it was simply our inability to receive grace that keeps us from God.

Fortunately, the psalmist had no such problem. While verse 3 begins, "When our transgressions prevail over us," the psalmist adds, "thou dost forgive them." The psalm confidently speaks about the power of God over the seas, mountains, and people, probably because the psalmist had experienced the power of God over that most demonic force in the life of God's people—guilt.

Suggestion for meditation: *Are there any sins for which I have not allowed God to forgive me?*

316

Wednesday, November 1   Read Haggai 2:1-3.

I was proud of our new education wing at the church; the $80,000 facility was a tremendous asset to the church's ministry. At a preachers' meeting, the district superintendent called on some of us for reports on the progress of our building programs. As I eagerly awaited my turn, I heard reports of a $1.1 million sanctuary, a half-million dollar gym, and a $2.3 million sanctuary. Quickly I calculated in my head and realized that I had an $.08 million building—I decided not to mention the cost!

What was the problem? I had perceived that our new building was nothing compared to the others about which I had heard. Of course, I had never seen those other buildings. Haggai addressed a people with a similar problem. They had been called on by God to rebuild Solomon's Temple, which had been destroyed about 70 years earlier. Only a short way into the rebuilding, Haggai's people were discouraged. God sensed it and asked, "Who is left among you that saw this house in its former glory? How do you see it now? Is it not in your sight as nothing?" Obviously, most of the people were not alive in the days of Solomon's Temple, and could not have seen it. The source of their discouragement was the distance between their perceptions of what the Temple might have been and the reality of what it currently was.

However, perceptions can be deceiving. But how do we check our perceptions if they can be deceiving? I go to the One whom I can trust, the One who truly defines "reality." Haggai thought the same thing was needed. He, too, asked how we can consider a building as "nothing" when God has called us to build it. Similarly, how can our lives ever be "nothing" when they are created and redeemed by God?

Prayer: *Loving God, help me to see myself and the world through your eyes. Amen.*

Thursday, November 2   Read Haggai 2:4-9.

A friend called me about a relative who was just found to have cancer. Whether or not the sickness was as bad in reality as she perceived it to be was not the issue. It also did not matter to what causes the cancer could be traced. My friend was in pain, and all I could offer her were words and the promise that I would be with them. I felt so helpless. "Words can never hurt me," say the children, but it also seems sometimes that they cannot help.

I guess I would not be a preacher if I did not believe in the power of words. Haggai also believed in the power of words. To the situation of discouragement that he found among his people, he offered the words of the Lord, "for I am with you." Funny, these words given to those discouraged folks are the same words Jesus offered to an overwhelmed group of disciples on the mountain, who had just heard the Great Commission: "Lo, I am with you always" (Matt. 28:20).

Of course, it was not only the words; it was who spoke them that really counted. My friend said, "Since you're a preacher, I thought your words and prayers might carry more weight." I doubt that. But what is beyond doubt is that God's words carry great weight and power. Haggai knew this. God had promised to be present with the people, and if God had spoken, that made all the difference.

In moments of desperation or discouragement, we would do well to remember the promise, "Take courage . . . for I am with you." It is even more crucial to remember who spoke the promise. Whose words are these? So take courage; the Lord *is* with you.

Prayer: *Gracious God of Haggai, in times of discouragement and despair help me to hear your promise, "I am with you." Then, help me to believe it. Amen.*

Friday, November 3   Read 2 Thess. 1:1-12.

Sometimes we can honestly answer the question, "Whose fault is it?" by pointing to someone other than ourselves. The church at Thessalonica was having great problems with "persecutions and afflictions," yet they had not done anything wrong.

One of the things that bothers me about this passage is that in answer to the question of "whose fault is it?" Paul points in the direction of God! Paul does not exactly say that God caused it, but he does say that the persecution is making the Thessalonians worthy of the kingdom of God "for which you are suffering." It stands to reason that if God brings you into faith, and faith brings persecution, then God must be somehow partly responsible for the problem.

Another thing that bothers me about the passage is how God plans to end the persecution. God is going to heap some mighty vengeance and eternal destruction upon those "who do not know God." They will be excluded from the "presence of the Lord."

Excluded from the presence of the Lord? That's a terrible fate. But maybe that is the key to this whole passage. Paul seems to indicate that those facing problems and persecution are not excluded from the Lord's presence. Paul seemingly says, "Yes, God knows about your suffering; God got you into it in the first place." Furthermore, by pointing to the eternal destruction of those "who do not know God," Paul is saying that God not only knows about our suffering, God is planning to do something about it!

Paul is saying that God is there at the beginning and at the end. That's good news because God most surely will be with us in the "between time." God is working in our lives from start to finish!

Prayer: *O God, you helped to get me to this point in my life; now, help me the rest of the way until I am in your heavenly kingdom. Amen.*

Saturday, November 4   Read Luke 19:1-10.

Zacchaeus "sought to see who Jesus was, but could not." Whose fault was it? Perhaps it was his parents and grandparents; something in his genes had made him "small of stature." He was not tall enough because a crowd had lined up (several persons deep, presumably) to see Jesus. So, maybe it was the crowd's fault. After all, none in the crowd offered to allow Zacchaeus to come through to the front because Zacchaeus had turned against his own people to collect taxes for Rome. Not only that, but to make a living he had to collect more taxes than were due to the government. Obviously, he had gotten good at stealing from people, for he was rich. In view of this, it could have been his own fault that he could not see Jesus.

This same combination of factors works against many who wish to see Jesus today. Perhaps their parents prevented them by never taking them to church or "burned them out" by beating them over the head with religion. It could be the fault of the "crowd" in church. They are so busy trying to do their thing with Jesus or with trying to be seen or heard in the church, that there is little concern for those on the outside. Maybe it is their own fault as well. They have not really made an attempt to participate in worship, Bible study, prayer, or any other means of grace.

In spite of the obstacles, Zacchaeus did not give up. He ran ahead and climbed a tree. No one can exactly tell why he went to this effort. Whatever the reason, he wanted to be with Jesus.

Many things prevent me from being with Jesus—interruptions, busy schedules, activities with children, tennis dates, financial concerns. Maybe the real problem lies in a lack of real desire—a desire that overcomes all obstacles—to be with him.

Suggestion for meditation: *What things prevent us from being with Jesus? Will we continue to let them?*

Sunday, November 5   Read Luke 19:1-10.

When Zacchaeus went off with Jesus, the crowd complained. No doubt they wondered "whose fault it was" that Jesus would go to be with a sinner. At first glance, it appears to be Zacchaeus' fault. He ran ahead and he climbed the tree in order to see Jesus. However, the crowd knew better; they were probably not as upset with Zacchaeus as they were with Jesus! "He has gone in to be the guest of a . . . sinner," they murmured. As much as Zacchaeus desired to see Jesus, Jesus desired to be with Zacchaeus even more than that.

Even if Zacchaeus had not run ahead and climbed that tree, Jesus would have still called him out of the crowd. After all, did Jesus not already know Zacchaeus' name even before they got together to eat? I say this with some confidence, because I believe it is Jesus' job "to seek and to save the lost." Whether up a tree or in a crowd, Zacchaeus was lost. My fantasy about this passage is that the one who ate with Jesus that day was the only one willing to admit to being lost.

When I think of this, I see what a lot of time I have wasted in my life. I have run ahead so often and climbed so many trees in the hope of being seen by Jesus. I have prayed, acted kindly, participated in Bible studies, and endured long sermons. Maybe I even became a pastor in order to get that attention from God. Maybe it was not all a "waste," as I have surely been edified from these activities. However, they did not gain me what I needed—acceptance and salvation.

Salvation can only come from God, and it is offered to all. Zacchaeus never would have to climb a tree again! Neither will I. Blame God for that!

Prayer: *God, help me to give up trying to gain your love and learn to accept that I already have it. Amen.*

THE LORD OF LIFE

November 6-12, 1989   **Mary Michael, S.S.M.**
Monday, November 6   Read Luke 20:27-28.

In our Gospel reading from this week's lectionary we learn that the Sadducees did not believe in resurrection. Christians (unlike the Sadducees of old) have the New Testament, which is God's revelation to us of Christ's birth, life, death, and resurrection. We can thank our Lord Christ for his church, with its life-giving and life-transforming sacraments and its Bible. And we can thank him for its ordinary sinners (like us) in every generation who inspire our hope—the hope that like them we might be transformed into great saints in response to his love, forgiveness, acceptance, and trust.

No matter what any of us may have sacrificed for the love of Christ, the blessings we have received are surely far greater. When Christ was here on earth, he told his closest friends how blessed they were to have seen the things they were seeing and to have heard the things they were hearing (Matt. 13:16). All the prophets of the Old Testament looked forward to the day of the Messiah's coming. Christ's friends then and now have the privilege of knowing, loving, and serving him—a privilege which the Sadducees could have had but did not recognize.

Suggestion for meditation: *I have been offered the pearl of great price (Matt. 13:45). What has been my response?*

---

†A sister of St. Margaret living at St. Margaret's House and working at St. Luke's church, Germantown, Pennsylvania.

Tuesday, November 7   Read Luke 20:1-40.

In each of the Gospels the chief priests, scribes, and elders questioned Jesus' authority for his teachings. In chapter 20 of Luke's Gospel, we see them trying to trick him into difficulty with government officials or with his own people. Spies ask him craftily whether or not it is lawful to give tribute to Caesar. They marvel at the God-given wisdom of his answer and become silent (Luke 20:26).

In our Gospel reading from this week's lectionary (Luke 20:27-38), Jesus silences the Sadducees. Not believing in resurrection, they ask him a question which, they think, will show the absurdity of belief in resurrection. Whose wife would a woman be who had married seven brothers one after the other? Jesus' reply makes it clear that he thinks it is far more important to live life now in such a way as to become worthy of resurrection than it is to waste time worrying about what such life will be like in the future.

Suggestion for meditation: *What do I believe about resurrection? How does my hope for the future influence my living in the present?*

Wednesday, November 8 Read Ephesians 1:1-20.

Unlike the Sadducees, Christians believe that Christ was raised from the dead by the almighty power of God and that he lives forevermore. Those who have been raised to the new life of Christ by baptism do not spend time arguing about such doctrine, nor do they try to prove it. Our Christian life is the response we make to the living God through our faith in the person of Jesus Christ.

When Jesus replied to the Sadducees' question about the resurrection in our Gospel reading from this week's lectionary, he did not talk about the nature of life after death except to say that it is very different from earthly life. His main point is that God is the God of the living—here and after death. That is why we need never be afraid again. God does not want any creatures made in his divine image to come to ultimate destruction. Resurrection is the gift of life restored to those who before death have given their time, their talent, their money, their very selves to Christ for love of him.

Prayer: *Teach us, heavenly Father, to become more worthy of the blessings you have poured upon us. Amen.*

Thursday, November 9   Read Ephesians 2:19-22.

Christians can thank God for having called, redeemed, and forgiven us. We are "no longer strangers and sojourners, but . . . fellow citizens with the saints and members of the household of God, built upon the foundation of the apostles and prophets, Christ Jesus himself being the cornerstone, in whom the whole structure is joined together and grows into a holy temple in the Lord."

Because of faith in Christ and his love, Christians have always been filled with tremendous, unshakeable joy. The gnawing fear of annihilation, nothingness, meaninglessness has been lifted from us by Christ's resurrection. The hearts of believers are filled with Job's great affirmation: "I know that my Redeemer lives" (Job 19:25). Because of our faith in Christ and his resurrection, we know that all shall be well even beyond death. All shall forever be well. That belief is what makes all the difference in life—the difference between a dismal, futile, meaningless existence and the fullness of life and joy which our Lord Christ desired for his friends. Thanks be to God that we believers can count ourselves among his friends.

Because of all the love and care Christ shows us daily in the beauty of his creation, his people, his church, his Eucharist, his Bible, surely we have no need to fear tomorrow. Christ is Lord of the living—here and beyond death.

Suggestion for meditation: *"Jesus Christ is the same yesterday and today and for ever" (Heb. 13:8).*

325

Friday, November 10　　　　　　　Read Zechariah 7:1-10.

In our Old Testament reading from this week's lectionary, Zechariah gives us the heart of all the moral teaching of the prophets: "Render true judgments, show kindness and mercy each to his brother, do not oppress the widow, the fatherless, the sojourner, or the poor; and let none of you devise evil against his brother in his heart." We hear echoes of Amos, who told the people of Israel that God hated their kind of offerings and urged them to "let justice roll down like waters, and righteousness like an ever-flowing stream" (Amos 5:21-22, 24). A century before, Jeremiah had told the people to amend their ways and their doings (Jer. 7:5), and Micah had put God's basic requirements clearly and succinctly several centuries before that: "What does the Lord require of you but to do justice, and to love kindness, and to walk humbly with your God?" (Mic. 6:8) Isaiah, a contemporary of Micah, warned that God wanted the people of Israel to "cease to do evil, learn to do good; seek justice, correct oppression; defend the fatherless, plead for the widow" (Isa. 1:16-17).

All these prophets tell us that God has a special concern for the poor, the oppressed, and the unjustly treated. How lovingly, compassionately, and justly we treat all God's children here and now will determine whether we are counted worthy to attain to the resurrection from the dead (Luke 20:35).

Suggestion for meditation: *"What does the Lord require of you but to do justice, and to love kindness, and to walk humbly with your God?" (Mic. 6:8)*

Saturday, November 11   Read Psalm 9.

"The Lord is a stronghold for the oppressed" and he "does not forget the cry of the afflicted" so the psalmist tells us in Psalm 9. He has "rebuked the nations" and "sits enthroned for ever." All the nations that forget God shall be destroyed, for God is not only Israel's God of old but the creator of us all, the ruler of heaven and earth. Even those of us who do not know or are unwilling to acknowledge that we are God's creatures can be used by God as instruments in the divine plan for the salvation of all people.

In light of our pursuit of more and more money, material things, and power; in light of our sexual freedom; and in light of our apparent indifference to the estimated millions of homeless people within our own borders—should not the psalmist's words send a chill through all those of us who live in such an affluent country as the United States? And should those words not chill to the bone those of us who claim to be members of Christ's Body on earth?

The apostle Paul once wrote that everything on earth is worth absolutely nothing compared to the joy of loving and serving Christ and of being loved by him. "I count it so much garbage, for the sake of gaining Christ and finding myself incorporate in him," he said (Phil. 3:9, NEB). Have we lost Paul's great vision of what Christianity really is? Have money, power, and pleasure become our idols?

Suggestion for meditation: *I count everything as so much garbage compared with gaining Christ and finding myself incorporate in him.*

Sunday, November 12   Read Philippians 3:10-11.

Paul once wrote: "All I care for is to know Christ, to experience the power of his resurrection, and to share his sufferings, in growing conformity with his death, if only I may finally arrive at the resurrection from the dead" (Phil. 3:10-11, NEB). Because of our baptism we have become members of the Body of Christ. The Word has become flesh within us, and we are called to lose ourselves in our Lord Christ's life. This means dying to our own selfishness and self-centeredness and finding our true Christlike selves in following him who is the way, the truth, and the life (1 Cor. 12:27; John 1:14; 14:6).

Empowered by Christ's life, light, and love, we are to carry him to all the world. We have become his flesh and blood alive on earth. In baptism we have been given the Holy Spirit's gifts of faith, hope, and love. These gifts within us need to be nourished, fed, and constantly renewed by the sacraments, by hearing and paying attention to God's word, and by trying to put into practice all that we learn from God's word about doing God's will.

From beginning to end, the story of the scripture is the story of God's love for us all. It is the story of our sin—our fears, our rebellion, our turning our backs upon God—and the two great commandments of love. And it is the story for each one of us of our restoration to God, to one another, and to ourselves. It is the story of our growth toward healing, wholeness, and holiness. "All I care for is to know Christ . . . if only I may finally arrive at the resurrection from the dead."

Prayer: *Thank you, Lord Christ, for calling, redeeming, and forgiving us. Amen.*

I AM SENDING MY MESSENGER

November 13-19, 1989 **James W. Holsinger Jr.†**
Monday, November 13 Read Malachi 3:1-5.

My messenger

God is sending a personal messenger! In Malachi 1:1, the messenger is identified as the prophet Malachi. However, in its Hebrew form Malachi is a title—my messenger or my angel—and not a personal name. The identical Hebrew form is found in Malachi 3:1, but here the title is always used and not the proper name.

Sending a messenger to prepare the way for the king was the custom in the ancient world. The duty of the messenger was not only to arrange for an appropriate reception for the king, but to prepare the highway, to build a road if necessary, to smooth the pathway and level the obstacles. The words of Malachi quickly bring to mind Isaiah 40:3-5. But here the messenger is coming to announce the arrival of God, bringing judgment to a people who have had the temerity to ask, "Where is the God of justice?"

Malachi later (4:5-6) identified the messenger with Elijah. Some interpreters have believed that Elijah would be sent at the time of the final judgment. In the New Testament the Christian interpretation establishes the forerunner as John the Baptist, who has been seen as the messenger sent to prepare the way for Jesus Christ. With the approach of Advent, we can be particularly grateful for the voice of John crying in the wilderness, "Repent, for the kingdom of heaven is at hand" (Matt. 3:2).

Prayer: *Lord God, send your messenger to prepare the way in order that we may confront the needs of your people, and in confronting their needs deal justly with all. Amen.*

---

† Director, McGuire Veterans Administration Medical Center, conference lay leader, Virginia Conference, The United Methodist Church, Richmond, Virginia.

Tuesday, November 14   Read Malachi 4:1-3.

The wicked will be destroyed

With this exclamation "Behold," Malachi introduces divine proclamations. Malachi did not doubt either the nearness or the certainty of the coming of the day of judgment. Behold, the day comes!

Malachi compared the day of judgment to an oven in which the wicked would be consumed. The Hebrew word for oven is *tannur,* a word which means a fire-pot or a clay oven. Even today in modern Palestine such ovens are used to bake bread. First a large hole is dug and the sides are plastered. Then a fierce fire is built in the lined hole using grass, thorns, or "stubble." Once embers have been produced and removed, the flat cakes of bread are stuck to the plastered sides of the holes and very quickly baked.

Malachi continued the development of his metaphor by comparing wicked people to the twigs and "stubble" which would be consumed when the day of judgment was come. Jesus himself used this metaphor when in Matthew 6:30 he spoke of "the grass of the field, which today is alive and tomorrow is thrown into the oven." The wicked on the day of judgment would be so completely destroyed that "it will leave them neither root nor branch."

Yes, God will send a messenger! God's messenger may take the form of the day of judgment in which the wicked will no longer prosper; a time when he "shall distinguish between the righteous and the wicked" (Mal. 3:18).

Prayer: *Righteous God, we come to you today praying that we might be among the righteous when you send your day of judgment. Amen.*

Wednesday, November 15   Read Malachi 4:1-3.

The sun of righteousness shall rise

As Malachi develops his imagery, he moves from searing heat to the gentle rays of the morning sun. He promises that for those who reverence and respect (fear) the Lord, the sun of righteousness will rise with healing in its wings. The wings of the sun are its shining rays. The sun is a symbol of blessing and protection. Isaiah (60:1-3) also declared that God's people would have their darkness dispelled and their sorrow and suffering banished by the light of God's glory.

Malachi does not expect that the sun of righteousness is to be taken as God personified. It is a term which represents righteousness. He speaks of a time when righteousness will shine on the lives of the people of God as the sun shines on the earth with all its splendor. It will be a time of vindication and victory.

Christians since the birth of Jesus have found the answer to Malachi's hopes in the Son of God. As so vividly expressed in the great Christmas carol "Hark, the Herald Angels Sing," God indeed sent a messenger in the form of the "sun of righteousness." The Son was sent to those who sit in darkness allowing them to see a great light. Paul expresses the idea most vividly when he says: "It is the God who said, 'Let light shine out of darkness,' who has shone in our hearts to give the light of the knowledge of the glory of God in the face of Christ" (2 Cor. 4:6). The righteous will sit in the glow of God's presence, and instead of consuming, the heat will bring healing.

Prayer: *Lord, bring to each of us the healing of the wings of the sun of righteousness, that we may see your glory shining in the face of your Son, Jesus Christ. Amen.*

Thursday, November 16   Read Malachi 4:4-6.

I will send you Elijah

In this brief passage, Moses and Elijah appear together and will not do so again in the Bible until they stand together on the Mount of Transfiguration with the Son of God. Verse 4 calls for remembrance, but the rest of the passage looks to the future and calls for watchfulness. Here the mysterious messenger of the preceding chapters of Malachi is identified with the prophet Elijah. Elijah's mission will be to "turn the hearts of fathers to their children and the hearts of children to their fathers." Here the prophet may be speaking of the fathers as the godly ancestors of Israel while the children are Malachi's contemporaries. Elijah will be commissioned to restore the faith of the children and bring about a reconciliation between the generations. Elijah was felt to be uniquely qualified for the assignment since he had once before succeeded in turning the people's hearts back to God.

At this point in the history of the people of Israel, the last of the prophets is moved to confess that the long line of prophecy is exhausted and their message to Israel is finished. Prophecy can do no more for the people of Israel than has already been accomplished. But the grand news of God sending Elijah once again is that prophecy will summon up old energy and fire with the return of God's great prophet. One last great effort will be made to bring the people into a right relationship with God before they are struck with judgment. A grim fate awaits those who persist in their rebellion against God. But the people of God will have no need to fear God's judgment as it will bring them healing and renewed strength.

Prayer: *Holy Father, bring us, too, into a right relationship with you as we struggle each day of our lives to live in our world as your people. Amen.*

Friday, November 17   Read Psalm 82.

Arise, O God

Years ago Michelangelo painted the ceiling of the Sistine Chapel at the Vatican. To do so he lay on his back, and it is well known that the best view of these great paintings comes to those who lie on the floor of the chapel and look up at Michelangelo's magnificent work. The psalmist in a very real sense is lying on his back gazing at the sky above him. He provides us with a picture of what he saw through the eyes of faith. In his vision, the psalmist saw God standing among the assembly of gods in heaven delivering divine judgment. God was exercising authority over all of the universe. The psalmist saw the whole earth rushing to its doom, and he calls on God to arise and judge his people.

We, too, are like the psalmist as we look around God's good earth. The world as we know it is surely rushing to its doom! With the madness of apparent never-ending warfare, the pain of the AIDS epidemic, the horror of hunger and starvation, the breakdown of family ties, the greed that grips so many, and the hurt that is represented by a soaring divorce rate, surely God will arise and come and judge the stewardship of humankind. Like the psalmist, we have waited to feel the presence of God in our world. Indeed, how long, how long, O God, must we wait?

But to all of us who wait on the coming of God as judge, the Bible also proclaims the good news. We hear from many voices the same thing that Jesus said to all who have ears to hear: "Be of good cheer, I have overcome the world" (John 16:33).

Prayer: *Lord, we come to you listening for the sound of your coming to judge your creation. Most of all, we know that you have overcome the world. Amen.*

Saturday, November 18   Read Luke 21:5-19.

Many will come in my name

Jesus and his disciples were standing in the temple precincts when Jesus felt moved to speak of what was to come. All around them was the splendor of the great Herodian temple. The Jewish historian Josephus described the temple in glowing phrases: "The natural magnificence, and excellent polish, and the harmony of the joints in these cloisters, afforded a prospect that was very remarkable." It was in this setting that Jesus tells his disciples that they will not be required to meet their tribulations alone. He will be with them through all that is to come.

But at the same time Jesus warns the disciples and he warns us today, "Many will come in my name, saying, 'I am he.' " He is explicitly warning against anyone who causes another to wander away from Jesus, anyone who deceives us as to what to expect. Even as late as the time of Origen (c. 250) individuals were still making such claims as Jesus describes in verse 8. The early Christian centuries were filled with the activities of heretics and false prophets. Instead of following false messiahs, Jesus' disciples and we as well are called by Jesus to persevere. "By your endurance you will gain your lives."

We are assured of a safety which surpasses the threats of this world. "Not a hair of your head will perish." It was during World War I that Rupert Brooke penned these lines:

> War knows no power. Safe shall be my going,
>   Secretly armed against all death's endeavour:
> Safe though all safety's lost; safe where men fall;
> And if these poor limbs die, safest of all.

Prayer: *Father of us all, though we know that we may lose our life as we walk with you, yet we know that our souls are forever safe with you. Amen.*

Sunday, November 19   Read 2 Thessalonians 3:6-13.

The Lord give you peace

Paul speaks to the church at Thessalonica in explicit terms condemning idleness. Some of the new converts apparently were waiting in idleness for the second coming of the Lord. By so doing they were placing a real burden on their fellow Christians who were continuing to work for the good of the entire group. Paul even invokes "the name of our Lord Jesus Christ" in an effort to demonstrate the urgency of his command.

Paul himself, although having the claim of an apostle to be supported by the young church, renounced his claim and worked in order not to be a burden on the Thessalonian Christians. Since Paul patterned his life after that of Jesus Christ, by imitating him the Thessalonians would be imitating the Lord himself! Paul did not loaf at Thessalonica, and he did not expect anyone else to do so. Instead he exerted himself tirelessly and at great cost. By working for his living he chose a path of fatigue and the necessity of overcoming the obstacles that this placed in the way of accomplishing the Lord's work. But rather than accepting a place of privilege, Paul was determined to leave behind an example to be imitated.

After airing all his complaints, Paul closes his letter with a prayer. Paul recognizes that ultimately only God can bring these people into compliance. God's peace alone can bring harmony to those who believe in the Lord. This peace which comes is first and foremost peace with God, and it alone provides the basis for peace between one Christian and another.

Prayer: *May the peace which passes all understanding be with each of us this day, O God. Amen.*

November 20-26, 1989 **Ellen A. Brubaker†**
Monday, November 20 Read 2 Samuel 5:1-5.

Signs from within

If we have learned not to look to the trees to find money growing, we must also learn not to look to the sky for great leaders—even saviors. God's sign in David arises in the midst of the people. "It was you that led out and brought in Israel." Martin Luther King, Jr., became God's sign for inclusive justice when those among whom he lived and worked recognized his gift and called it forth for the community.

The Christian family must be wary of those who with tears flowing and phony joy point beyond earthly time and space to a Super Savior who will fly in one day to right the wrongs and save the people. Remember the wonderful Pogo line, the effect being that we have met the enemy and the enemy is us. True enough. We have also met the Savior and "he is us." God has raised again and again leaders who have become signs of God's love and grace, justice and mercy. They have always been raised from within—from the people of God—from you and me. Even the one Savior, the Christ, was born of Mary and lived among us in the fullness of humanity. God would become a sign in each of us. Christ returns in those who bear his name. God, with us, will save the people.

Devotional exercise: *What does God offer to us through you?*

---

† District Superintendent, Grand Rapids District, West Michigan Conference, The United Methodist Church, Grand Rapids, Michigan.

Tuesday, November 21   Read Psalm 95:1-7*a*.

Signs in creation

In May of 1987 I held in my arms our first grandchild. Life from life. Jessica is God's child. In her smile is the sign of God's joy in creation. We are born to be at home in God's world of earth and sky. We are born to praise God for the gift of life and time. Time to grow, to become, to share, to give back to life from the abundance that has gifted us.

Only occasionally are most of us able to abandon our frailty, our guilt, our self-obsession, our slavery to schedules, even our struggle for meaning or purpose. The days when we step out in grace are our best days. We find ourselves free to act out our uniquely precious role in God's creation. On these days we know ourselves to be one with all that God has made; we know that it is good. There is no doubt that we are the people of God's pasture, the sheep of God's hand.

Most of us have to allow into our lives the space to praise. We do it some in worship, but we need to plan the alone times to give ourselves space to experience the Creator God. Your place to be alone with God may be a mountain, a desert, a beach beside a timeless sea, the backyard, a noisy city street, or a quiet room. Please go there often. Let there be the silence into which God moves and speaks, reminding you that everything, including you, is held in the hollow of God's loving hand.

Devotional exercise: *Spend time praising God for the gifts given to you.*

Wednesday, November 22   Read Psalm 95:7*b*-11.

Is there a word from the Lord?

Is there any word from God? Oh, for the courage to listen to God—and to each other when the sacred word is shared.

I remember many times laughing with other parents over our children's ability to "listen selectively." They could hear well enough when they wanted to. Are we different? Do we want to listen—to hear what God has to say to us? I sat in the Cathedral of St. John the Divine on the first Sunday of 1988. I sat there numb with grief. My husband, Bob, had died of cancer the previous November. There had been a whole year of losing him. I wondered at the beginning of the service, *Would there be a sign, any word from the Lord to me?* The preacher gently led us to image the past year—good or bad. Then he told us that it was time to let go, time to move with God into the future. I felt a stubborn resistance. A response formed within my shattered spirit: *I might like very much to let go of last year, but last year is not finished with me—not yet.*

But in my heart of hearts I knew the word from God had come. Ours is a God of creative vision moving from death to life, from darkness toward light and always, always into the future. Only as I would become willing to walk that path would the healing of my broken being begin to happen. The way for me would be painful; it could be measured in inches. It was up to me. God did speak. Response was my choice. It is always our choice. God speaks—who will hear?

Prayer: *Dear God, grant me the courage to hear you. Amen.*

Thursday, November 23   Read Colossians 1:11-14.

Signs from saints

Saints in light—a marvelous phrase. Who are they who light your path? Who continues with you as witness and model even though they may be gone?

One concept of immortality is the impact of a life that continues to influence and inspire as new generations hear the story. It is necessary that we tell the stories of God's saints. One U. S. visitor to Russia worshiped in an Orthodox service and noticed following the service a Russian grandmother holding her grandchild before an icon of one of the saints. She was telling the story of the saint to the child. After a while the child's attention began to wander. The American observer watched the grandmother gently turn her grandchild's head back toward the icon. She continued to tell the story. It is no wonder that the grandmothers of Russia perpetuate the faith in that country.

We have stories to tell of our personal saints. They are the ones who encourage us on our journeys. Or as one of my saints used to say, they are our balcony people. They are up there supporting, applauding, as we act our "hour upon the stage."

Whether the great saints of the church and of history—or personal saints—these women, men, and children have in some way borne for us the image of Christ in what they said or what they did; in the way that they touched or loved or fed the hungry or stood for God's justice. While they continue to shine for us, the scripture is quite clear. We are called to their inheritance. We are called to be like them.

Devotional exercise: *Visualize one who is a saint for you. Call to memory his or her impact on your life. Be willing to claim the inheritance your saints have passed to you.*

Friday, November 24   Read Colossians 1:15-20.

The sign of the cross

The cross is the ultimate signpost for personal faith. The human journey culminates in the cross of Christ. Gazing at the crucified one we know in an instant how far we have fallen. This Jesus walked among us and fulfilled God's vision for human life—"for in him the fullness of God was pleased to dwell." We observe him and become aware of the way it should be. Christ is complete integrity, complete love, complete forgiveness, complete peace, complete justice. He loved the gift of life and gave back to life in full measure. In Jesus is both laughter bubbling up from internal joy and tears from the depths of his soul for a friend and for a city. We are sometimes dismayed at the length of the journey to our fullness in God's love. We have so woefully missed the mark. We grow discouraged or angry or terribly sad for the failures.

But there it is. The love that is in God and is God beckons us back, calling us home. God, who is eternally patient, reminds us, once again, that love is finally victorious and will win in the end. Reconciliation is superimposed upon the cross. The defamed sign of death becomes a sign full of life, signaling the persistence of a God who will not let us go. The resurrection is the crown. The reign of God's shalom is set loose in the world. All things—all of us—are held together by the cross. Grace and peace in the person of the Christ bring us home again.

Suggestion for meditation: *Practice the acceptance of the love offered to you. Live in the strength of it.*

Saturday, November 25   Read John 12:9-19.

Choose your sign

In *Les Miserables* the policeman Javert cries to the stars that are for him the symbol of the orderliness of the universe. They are constant; they seemingly move unchanging. Without law and order, reward and punishment, Javert cannot live. His whole purpose has been to pursue the lawbreaker, Jean Valjean, so that order might be restored to his universe. Jean Valjean at last is given the upper hand. Retribution and revenge are his to command. But Jean, to whom mercy has been shown, chooses also to show mercy. He pardons his enemy. Javert cannot live in such a world. He cannot be excused for his crime. He jumps into the Seine in defiance of a God who breaks the rules.

The chief priests cannot live with the raising of Lazarus. They plot to kill him, this time to stay dead. They can't live with the ambiguity of miraculous life from death. The rules have been broken. They are afraid of what this will do to the flock. The sounds of hosanna stick in their throats.

Must we not also confront the very honest need for order, neatness, consistent rules in our own lives? Wouldn't it be so much easier if the answers to our questions of life and faith were not so elusive? Why do the innocent suffer? Why is violence so often the choice? Why do I find it so difficult to believe that I am loved? In the raising of Lazarus is not an answer but a direction. God pours life into death; hope into despair; turns weeping into hosanna, asking only that we choose the challenge of life over the nothingness of death—and promises to go with us.

Suggestion for meditation: *Consider with thanks the powers of life-giving love that give you strength.*

341

Sunday, November 26   Read John 12:9-19.

When the world goes after him

The vision of shalom, heaven on earth, an oasis in a desert place. Such are the signs of "God with us," the reign of God in this world. The Pharisees said they could do nothing because "the world had gone after him." The skeptic in us is prone to cynicism. Look at the wars, the poverty, the hunger, the continuous ways in which humanity uses and abuses. And yet, every now and then, the vision becomes real in our midst. Christ lives in you and in me. In these moments we walk through the world as bearers of Christ. And where we pass there is healing of hurts. There are children whose stomachs are filled and whose faces grow rosy, who run and play as they were meant to do. When we go after him, we are able to encourage those who don't believe that they are precious people. Because we believe in them with the love of God, they begin to believe in themselves.

Bit by bit the heavenly vision becomes a part of earth. The soldiers lay down their guns and go home to the arms of their families. Leaders of nations dare to negotiate alternatives to war. The streets of the cities of our world cease to be home to those who have no other place to lay their heads. Each life is lived in the fullness of its gifts. The warmth of God's loving arms enfolds each child, each man, each woman. No one need be afraid—ever again. The joy of God is complete.

Only now and then does the world go after Christ. But one day . . . one day—"on earth as it is in heaven."

Prayer: *O God, may your shalom be in me. May I share your love always. Amen.*

342

An Audience with the King

November 27–December 3, 1989   **Wightman Weese†**
Monday, November 27   Read Psalm 122:1-5.

Coming to Jerusalem was a time of gladness. This psalm was to be sung as the pilgrims approached the massive East Gate of the city. The city gates, within which the judges sat, symbolized the justice drawn from the righteous statutes of Israel. The people came without fear before the judges. Their coming was, in the fullest sense of the word, to celebrate God's true shalom.

Within its three rings of walls stood the temple, the place where the people of God came year after year to pay their tithes and to offer their sacrifices. They came to stand together as God's people to worship and praise God, to express their gratitude for God's sustenance, protection, and blessing.

The very thought of coming together with the people of God, to worship in concert within the temple courts brought joy to the psalmist's lips. Those who despise the company of God's people choose for themselves a double tragedy. They miss not only the fellowship with God but also the fellowship of other believers.

Part of the psalmist's joy came from knowing that where people praised God, there was God in their midst. As long as praises flowed from their lips and the love and reverence for God's statutes remained, God was being worshiped in spirit and in truth.

Prayer: *Dear God, may your peace rest upon us as we lift our praises to you. Amen.*

---

† Minister, free-lance writer; book editor, Tyndale House Publishers, Wheaton, Illinois.

Tuesday, November 28   Read Isaiah 2:1-3.

In David's day, the people of God were exclusively the people of Israel, or so they chose to think of themselves. From all the peoples of the world, God had chosen Abraham's line. God had brought the nation of Israel to the fullness of blessing in David's throne. But from the beginning it was God's plan for a greater king, greater even than David, to arise, a true Prince of Peace to whose throne the whole world would come to worship.

It was this vision of the temple that Isaiah saw. Jerusalem was a fearful huddle of people cowering under the threat of Assyria and rumors of war. The kingdom of Judah was in disarray, surrounded by enemies on all sides. Justice and righteousness no longer reigned within its gates, and the lamps within the temple grew dim.

To such troubled people, the words of God's prophet came with this promise of a new temple to which everyone could come. Isaiah's invitation was offered as David's psalm had been —as a call for God's people everywhere to come and meet God at the foot of God's throne. God is faithful. No matter how dark and threatening the world may be, God always makes known the place where we might find God and the peace God gives.

Prayer: *O Lord, we come before you surrounded with troubles. We seek peace before your throne. Amen.*

Wednesday, November 29 Read Psalm 122:6-9.

The house of the Lord, the temple, which stood secure within the citadels of Jerusalem, was a place where believers came to meet and commune with God. It was a place where the righteousness of God was satisfied as the people brought their sin offerings.

Tied up in the hearts of the Israelites was the knowledge that as long as the city was secure, Israel and all it stood for and held to be sacred was secure. To prosper they must continue in the teachings of Moses. The pilgrimages were for sacred transactions, physical and spiritual, to pay what was due to God, to bring God their praise as well their offerings, tokens of their thanksgiving.

The truth was there to see. But the people who came to the temple failed to see that the house of the Lord and the One who dwelt among them needed no protection, but was, and is, the Protector. We are secure only before God's throne, safe from all our enemies. The once-for-all offering for sin has bought for us what the psalmist sought—our peace, the privilege of coming before God without fear. The holy place has now become the throne room of our hearts. God dwelling within us is our hope of eternal life.

Prayer: *Our God, we thank you for the peace you have brought within our hearts through Jesus, the Prince of Peace, the once-for-all sacrifice. Amen.*

Thursday, November 30   Read Isaiah 2:4-5.

The weary, hungry laborer longs for food and rest. Troubled and tear-filled midnight hours make the joys of morning seem an eternity away. The heart is made ready for relief by the pain that it endures.

The troubled, fearful people of Judah were losing hope. Even during the reigns of the best of their kings, Uzziah and Jotham, wickedness reigned. Despite some victories over the Ammonites and the unsuccessful siege on Jerusalem by Israel and its allies, a greater threat from Assyria loomed over them. Sooner or later, judgment from God was bound to come, for God had promised peace and blessing only as they continued in his ways.

Isaiah's words were part of that great Advent story God had been preparing—the promise of a King who would, once and for all, judge between the nations, settle disputes for all people and, best of all, bring true peace to Israel and the whole world. But the people of Judah could not understand and fully appreciate the peace of God until they had known the terror of war, the fear of death, and the pain of loss. Those who will not accept the peace of God must accept the consequences, the constant fear of God's judgment. Wars make necessary the preparation for war, costly as the war itself. In all our struggles for peace, both inward and outward peace, God's peace flows out from the mountain of the Lord's temple, that place where we bow in worship before him. It is peace bought by the Prince of Peace, the One before whom the whole world will one day worship.

Prayer: *Dear God, we rejoice at another Advent season, awaiting the true Prince of Peace. Amen.*

Friday, December 1   Read Matthew 24:36-41.

Advent season brings again deep thoughts of the King who came first as a tiny child. With the children, we count the hours till the Christ candle is finally lit. We remember with gratitude during this season the Son God sent from heaven to be God with us. His time on earth went so quickly. It seems he spent only a few short days at his mother's knee and with his earthly father in the carpentry shop, then three short years of teaching and preaching. Finally he offered to us the ultimate Christmas gift, his sacrifice on the cross. Resurrected and ascended, the child is now the Savior King, sitting enthroned in heaven's glory. But the story is not yet over.

Advent seasons come and go. Each year, as the season ends, the world soon goes back to its old ways of eating and drinking, marrying and giving in marriage, making no preparation for the final advent of the King from heaven. The world seems almost unaware of the building project that has been underway for centuries. The kingdom of God is not building with noisy hammers and saws but in quiet preparation, and no one knows the day or hour when it will be complete.

We who await Advent enjoy his coming in truth and see in our minds' eye beyond the Bethlehem manger to the throne he will occupy on that day. We watch for his coming again.

Prayer: *Our God, who sent the Child to Bethlehem, prepare us for that day when he, enthroned here on earth, receives our worship. Amen.*

Saturday, December 2   Read Matthew 24:42-44.

The watchman on the city wall was the first to see the advance of attacking armies. The safety of the entire city depended on his careful vigilance. But now the waiting is not for attackers but the return of the king and his army who have been out in the battle. Soon the eyes of the watchman catch a glimpse of movement. First it is just a speck, then a column of marching people wavering on the horizon. Then the victory banners can be seen, and a mighty cheer goes up from those on the wall who were anxious for their return.

We are the watchers to whom Christ was speaking. One day he will be coming back again to claim the throne he has conquered through his victory over Satan, won on the cross and the open, empty tomb.

The thief about whom Christ spoke gained advantage not by stealth but by speed and surprise. If the victim had been alert, he would not have been caught off guard. So it is with the return of the King at his next coming. When it happens, the drama will unfold quickly and no one knows when, despite all the prophecies the world has heard.

We do not wait on a wall. Rather, our preparation for the King's coming takes the form of patience, steadfastness in good works, and unrelenting efforts to prepare a lost world to receive the gospel and the offer of citizenship into the kingdom of God.

Prayer: *Dear Lord Jesus, our bodies grow weary, but our hearts are aglow as we wait for your return. Come quickly, and claim your throne. Amen.*

December 3 (First Sunday in Advent)
Read Romans 13:11-14.

When the King's victory procession breaks into sight it is too late to prepare for his return. The apostle Paul set an excellent example for the churches for whom he labored. Tracing the life of Paul through the New Testament, we see that it seems he rested only when fatigue or illness felled him. He lived every moment as if it were his very last. He truly fought a good fight.

Some say that the King is coming soon—any day now. Others point to certain Old and New Testament prophecies that are yet to be fulfilled. But one thing about his coming is certain—his coming will be one day sooner than it was yesterday. Although we don't know how much sand is yet in the hourglass, we know that time will one day run out. On that day, the work we have neglected will forever remain undone. Today is the day, and now is the hour, to begin preparing if we haven't already done so. Those who await the kingdom of life and light should waste no time in works of darkness. We are children of the light.

Jesus once told a parable about a man who was unprepared, without a wedding garment, on the day the bridegroom arrived. Paul tells us here that it is the Lord Jesus Christ himself that we are to put on. The throne awaits the King and Bridegroom, and he seeks a spotless bride, one he himself has cleansed and for whom he has prepared a spotless robe, his own righteousness.

Prayer: *Matchless King, grant that we may be vigilant and that we may welcome you with clean robes and with ready hearts. Amen.*

HOPE

This psalm speaks of the hope the Hebrew people have for a leader who can offer them justice, righteousness, prosperity, deliverance, protection. One can sense the people's hope for immediate relief as well as peace and prosperity over a long period of time. The people saw a necessary connection between strong moral order within national leadership and the continued prospects of peace, justice, and righteousness. And they hoped such a long-range moral foundation would endure as the moon in the heavens.

The very fact that the psalm begins, "Give the king thy justice, O God, and thy righteousness to the royal son!" says that they saw these wonderful characteristics of justice and righteousness in the nature of their God, and they desired that their earthly leader would be blessed with these same qualities.

Has anything changed? Can we enjoy the benefits of justice, righteousness, and peace here on earth unless earth be wed with heaven, unless "the kingdom of the world . . . become the kingdom of our Lord and of his Christ"? (Rev. 11:15)

There is indeed a connection between lasting moral values of earth being founded upon those values of the kingdom of God. Therefore, let us pray, "Thy kingdom come, thy will be done, on earth as it is in heaven." Therein lies our hope.

Prayer: *Our God, we do sincerely pray this day for thy kingdom to come and thy will to be done, in earth as it is in heaven. Amen.*

---

† District Superintendent, East Jackson District, Mississippi Conference, The United Methodist Church, Jackson, Mississippi.

Tuesday, December 5   Read Isaiah 11:1-5.

The hopes and dreams mentioned in yesterday's royal psalm express themselves time and again in the Old Testament, as men and women dream of that ideal point in history when God will intervene and establish the kingdom through Israel. They never lose that sense of hope, that sense of "some day."

Such hope was beautifully put by Isaiah when he said, "There shall come forth a shoot from the stump of Jesse, and a branch shall grow out of his roots."

As I write here in southern Mississippi, it is spring. Stumps, branches, and trees that looked lifeless from the devastating cold of winter are now beginning to put forth shoots of new growth. Green is now taking the place of dead browns and grays. Anxiously, we await these signs of kept promises, promises that keep hope alive, that let us know God is at work restoring life to that which appeared dead.

If God can do that in nature, can God not also bring life through the stump or remnant of Jesse? Can God not take what is left of a people in captivity and through them, someday, bring about the social, political, and economic changes whereby justice, peace, and righteousness can grow and flourish? Can God not take the life of any individual who feels as though he or she has little to hope for in this world—or in the next—and bring forth new shoots of hope?

The secret is in whom we place our hope. Peter said it best, "Blessed be the God and Father of our Lord Jesus Christ! By his great mercy we have been born anew to a living hope through the resurrection of Jesus Christ from the dead, and to an inheritance which is imperishable, undefiled, and unfading" (1 Pet. 1:3-4).

Prayer: *Stir us with thy power, O God, that once again we may experience the resurrection of hope. Amen.*

Wednesday, December 6   Read Isaiah 11:6-9.

Who among us doesn't hope for peace? One of humankind's desires in all generations is ultimately to have peace. Granted there are always persons among us who, for whatever reason, like to stir up trouble. But, generally speaking, the majority of earth's people would like to beat their swords into plowshares and their spears into pruning hooks.

This passage depicts hope for such a day when conditions will be made right between God, humankind, and nature. Isaiah's dream seems too good to be true, like a fairy tale.

It seems that way because we and God are working with different agendas. God calls us to set our eyes upon the kingdom and to have a value system that is kingdom-of-God oriented. Christ commands us to "seek first the kingdom of God."

Yet, we continue to see the solution to our problems in materialism. Peace and security come, we say, by increasing our nuclear arms arsenal, having more money, enacting better welfare and pension programs, increasing job security.

How long does it take us to learn that the lion and lamb dwell together—when each better understands the values of the other, when trust has relaced fear and hatred, when security depends upon vulnerability and not walls, when, as Paul says, we have made love our aim? (see 1 Cor. 14:1)

When God's agenda becomes ours, then the peace and harmony hoped for by Isaiah, and the kingdom of God preached by Christ, will stand a real chance of becoming a reality.

Prayer: *In hope that sends a shining ray far down the future's broadening way; In peace that only thou canst give, with thee, O Master, let me live.* Amen.*

---

*Washington Gladden, "O Master, Let Me Walk with Thee."

Thursday, December 7   Read Romans 15:4-6.

Christians are the recipients of hope. Our Judeo-Christian tradition has favored us with literature from a people of hope—people who hoped for a promised land; people who hoped for kingly leadership that was divinely inspired and whose system of values would benefit all peoples; people who, having experienced a king like David, dreamed that someday God would send David's son as messiah; people whose hopes soared because of the Resurrection; people who hoped because they believed, good would triumph over evil; people who hoped because their trust was in a God who had covenanted to be their God and whose promises could be believed and trusted.

We live in troubled times when it is quite easy to give way to discouragement, to succumb to our fears, to believe the worst, to lose faith. But Paul reminds us that the hope of God's people has been preserved for us in the writings of our ancestors of the faith. He urges us to read the scriptural evidence and see that those who went before us didn't have it easy either, yet they refused to give up.

The Book of Revelation is the story of a writer named John. He wrote to the members of seven churches in Asia Minor lending them encouragement, calling them to be steadfast and immovable, urging them to keep faith. He reminded them that in spite of their tribulation, God would triumph over evil and reward those who remained faithful and kept hope alive.

God has set before us in scripture examples of encouragement and hope for this and every generation. "Thanks be to God, who in Christ always leads us in triumph, and through us spreads the fragrance of the knowledge of him everywhere" (2 Cor. 2:14).

Prayer: *Thy word is a lamp to our feet, O God, and a light to our path. Help us to walk in it. Amen.*

Friday, December 8   Read Romans 15:7-12.

As we are the recipients of hope, so are we also the dispensers of hope. We are they through whom God dispenses hope to a world in need of hope. In this passage, Paul speaks of the kind of courteous and hospitable climate the recipients of hope should consciously and deliberately establish in order to attract the Gentiles to God's glorious message, that they too might have reason to praise and glorify God.

During this second week of Advent we are very conscious of the hope of God's gift to us in Jesus Christ. We who have stood for 2000 years this side of the incarnate gift of God know that the One for whom our Hebrew ancestors yearned has come in Christ. We know that he came as a Jew, grew up in a Jewish family, was subject to Jewish law and tradition. In him was the fulfillment of all to which Jewish prophecy had pointed. He was given by God as the fulfillment of their hope.

But ours is not a provincial God, and therefore God's gift of hope and love was not just for Jews. It was for the Gentile world as well—for you and me. You and I are fortunate because we have heard and experienced God's good news of hope through the One whose birth we shall soon celebrate.

Our responsibility, therefore, is the greater, for as recipients of God's mercy and hope, we have much to share. We have been given a gift. We must also share our gift.

Prayer: *Hope of the world, who by thy cross didst save us from death and dark despair, from sin and guilt; we render back the love thy mercy gave us; take thou our lives, and use them as thou wilt.* Amen.*

---

*Georgia Harkness, "Hope of the World."

Saturday, December 9   Read Romans 15:13.

Paul now brings us to the very crux of the matter. The foundation of any hope we have is in "the God of hope." In this concluding benediction Paul prays for his friends and fellow believers in Rome that "the God of hope fill you with all joy and peace in believing, so that by the power of the Holy Spirit you may abound in hope."

How good it is to know we do not face life alone, nor is our hope based upon wishful thinking. Paul presented Christ to the church at Rome in the most systematic of all his letters. He made his readers aware, then as now, that the thing separating Christians from nonbelievers is that Christians have hope—not hope founded upon more and better education, or upon scientific and technological developments, or upon economic and political stability, or upon anything that humankind alone is capable of. We have hope because we believe in and trust the God of hope. In Jesus Christ we see what God has done for all of us. We have hope not only in life but also in death and beyond. Our God has claimed ultimate victory over sin and death. Therefore, no matter what may happen to us, we have full confidence that we are in good hands.

Likewise, our faith in the God of hope is buoyed by the presence and power of the Holy Spirit, without whom we would not "abound in hope." It is God, through the Holy Spirit in us, who continually enlarges our hope and causes us to experience a deep and wonderful sense of joy and peace. Praise God from whom all blessings flow!

Prayer: *God of hope, we praise you for giving us the gift of your Son, Jesus Christ, for in him we know we are loved. Amen.*

355

Sunday, December 10   Read Matthew 3:1-12.

John the Baptist had come to the crossroads of his career. It's hard to imagine what might have been going through his mind. Though he appears in the New Testament, John was basically an Old Testament person. His work was that of getting people ready to receive the Messiah, Israel's long-awaited hope. He had done his work well through baptism and the call to repentance, but his work was over. John knew his cousin Jesus was the one whom he had helped prepare people to hear and receive.

Jesus' beginning in ministry had to be a moment of mixed feelings for John—similar to what Moses must have felt as he had to remain behind and watch Joshua lead the Hebrew people into the promised land.

But like Moses, John the Baptist knew the goal at hand was larger than his personal feelings, and so we see John speak of his own unworthiness in comparison to Christ. In the Gospel of John, it is John the Baptist who points his disciples and the crowd to Jesus, and exclaims, "Behold, the Lamb of God, who takes away the sin of the world! This is he of whom I said, 'After me comes a man who ranks before me, for he was before me' " (John 1:29-30).

John shows us that the hope of the world does not depend upon our own careers or personal feelings, as imporant as these matters are. The hope of the world is Jesus Christ. He is that "branch of Jesse"; the messianic king upon whom "the spirit of the Lord shall rest"; the one who shall usher in a new kingdom; the one who announces that our sins are forgiven; the one through whom the blind see, the lame walk, the prisoners are free. Now is the acceptable time of God.

Prayer: *God of hope, help us to see, even as John, that Jesus Christ is the hope of the world. Amen.*

December 11-17, 1989   **Marie Livingston Roy**†
Monday, December 11   Read Psalm 146:5-10.

It is possible for us to live out our lives on many levels. For instance, we meet the least resistance by remaining on the surface of things. There we find no need to question the meaning of our existence—life on the surface is conveniently defined in black and white, and we, ourselves, are at the center of it.

But the very nature of Christianity calls us, even compels us, to live life at a deeper level—to experience in daily events the mysterious and wonderful interconnectedness of the whole of creation. When this happens, when we live deeply, life is no longer black and white, but various shades of gray. The implications of our daily decisions become more far-reaching, more intimately connected with our call to servanthood as followers of Jesus Christ.

Having left the world of easy answers and self-centeredness behind, we come face to face with the reality of our human need and recognize within ourselves the oppressed, the hungry, the prisoner, the blind. Beneath the surface we are no longer able to sustain the illusion that we are in control of our lives, that by willing it we can achieve that which we desire. We discover that we are an intimate part of creation, a creation that belongs not to us but to a loving God.

Suggestion for meditation: *Prayerfully reread today's scripture, applying it to your own life experiences. In what ways are you living on the surface? In what ways have you learned to live deeply?*

---

† Free-lance writer and editor, Nashville, Tennessee.

Tuesday, December 12   Read Isaiah 35:1-10.

Advent is traditionally a time during which we are encouraged to delve deeply into the spiritual dimensions of our humanity. The scripture passages associated with Advent reflect the longing of the human soul for the coming of the Messiah—the merging of divine grace with human existence. The imagery which gives voice to that longing is vivid—the flowering of the desert, the release of captives, the healing of the blind. No watered-down wishful thinking here, but powerful expressions from the depths of the human soul—fulfilled by the birth of the Child in Bethlehem.

Compare these scriptural images of longing with the anticipation with which we approach Christmas. While there are many for whom the holidays are a painful time, most of us look forward to get-togethers with family and friends, to the giving and receiving of gifts, to the beautiful music and liturgies associated with the season. These are important facets of our celebration of this holy time.

But we are also called to ponder the deeper significance of Advent—the significance of longing. Longing describes a strong desire, a wishing for something with one's whole heart. When we move beneath the surface of life into its deeper dimensions, we find our anticipation merging with a heart-felt longing. The symbol always points to a meaning beyond itself—the joy with which we anticipate the celebration of Christmas may be on the surface of our lives; the powerful longing for the redemption of life, of which it is the symbol, occurs at a deeper level.

Prayer: *Jesus, whose divinity and humanity we now celebrate, teach us to long again for your coming. Amen.*

Wednesday, December 13   Read Psalm 146:5-10.

Longing is a vital aspect of human life and an integral part of Advent. It is not possible to remain on the surface of life and experience longing—it is associated with living from the depths of our humanity. It is through action motivated by longing that the noblest of human endeavors are achieved. Without longing—desiring something with the whole of one's being—there would be no great art or literature, no great poetry or music. It is only from longing to express the inexpressible that the instinct to create arises. It is from a sense of longing to see humanity achieve its potential for compassion that we strive for peace, for justice, for freedom.

It is the longing for a mysterious something beyond ourselves that initiates our journey of faith, and our longing prompts us to seek a relationship in which we may come to know and be known by God. Longing is that divine spark within us to be all that we were created to be and to achieve the highest of which human-kind is capable.

But this longing within us can also unleash the destructive aspects of our human nature. If that for which we long is centered upon ourselves, we become the source of injustice, of war, of the basest of which the human heart, filled with pride, is capable.

Our introspection during Advent gives us an opportunity to look closely at those things for which we long, by examining them prayerfully in the presence of the loving God whose coming we celebrate.

Suggestion for meditation: *Spend some quiet time identifying the deepest longings of your heart. Ask God to guide you in discovering which of them arise from God's Spirit within you and which may spring from self-centeredness and pride.*

Thursday, December 14
Read Isaiah 35:3-6;
Psalm 146:7-9;
Matthew 11:4-5.

Today's scripture readings reflect the miracles associated with God's chosen Messiah. On the surface, these miracles belong to someone else, not only in Jesus' time but in our own as well. The blind, the prisoner, the oppressed are those to whom we are called to minister in Christ's name.

However, when we journey inward, these Advent scriptures are no longer comfortably connected with someone else. We come face to face with the reality of our human need and recognize within ourselves the oppressed, the hungry, the prisoner. But we find that we are powerless to help ourselves, and we long for the coming of the Messiah.

Many times those things which wound or imprison us are legitimate in themselves—building a successful career, establishing a home and family, becoming actively involved in ministry. The goals are different for each of us. But if the attainment of these goals takes precedence over our spiritual lives or diminishes our capacity to be compassionately involved in our world, they become the means of our oppression.

During Advent we have an opportunity to make that deliberate inward journey—to examine our consciences and to make ourselves available to Christ's healing, freeing power.

Suggestion for meditation: *Prayerfully consider the following questions: Is my drive to excel so strong that I am blind to the effect that it is having on others? Are my own opinions so firm that they prevent my hearing the opinions of others? Is my indecision robbing me of my ability to act? Is my concern over what others may think causing me to be mute when I should speak? Ask God to guide you on this inward journey.*

Friday, December 15   Read Isaiah 35:1-10.

When we live our lives at a deeper level, we become keenly aware of our need for daily guidance. When our mask of self-sufficiency has been stripped away, we learn to perceive and to trust in God's presence with us. But this does not mean that we become puppets. We are responsible for our choices, our actions—and they become increasingly Christ-centered. This is a time of growing, of maturing in living in the Spirit.

However, there may be times when we seek God's guidance in our lives and experience instead a mysterious silence. In contrast to the comforting presence upon which we have come to rely, we are faced with an overwhelming absence, an experience often described as spiritual dryness, being in the desert, or the dark night of the soul.

Whatever it is called, in feeling deprived of the comforting presence of God we are able to understand the longing of the Hebrew people in captivity. We long for the coming again of the Christ into our lives—the very essence of the Advent season.

Advent bids us to continue to hope, to long for the rebirth of Christ within us, even in the desert, even in the dry times when the absence of God seems painfully more real than the presence of God. The desert has long been a symbol of perseverance and longing and hope for those on a spiritual journey. Deprived of consolation, our faith becomes stronger and more mature as we learn to believe without seeing immediate fruition of that belief. The words of the writer of Isaiah become our heartfelt prayer.

Prayer: *O God, strengthen our feeble arms and steady our tottering knees. Say to the anxious, "Be strong and fear not." Amen.*

Saturday, December 16   Read Matthew 11:2-6.

Today's scripture reading is especially pertinent to our inner journey during Advent. John sends his followers to ask Jesus if he is the Promised One, or should they look for another. On the surface, this appears to be a strange question, for it was John who, at Jesus' baptism, first recognized him as the Messiah. However, Jesus' ministry had turned out to be one of servant-hood and compassion rather than one of God coming with a vengeance. For generations, the Hebrew people had awaited a powerful Messiah who would free them. It was difficult for a people who had longed for the coming of a particular type of savior to understand or accept one who did not meet their firmly-held expectations.

Jesus' response was to call attention to what they themselves had seen and heard—miracles which had traditionally been associated with the promised savior. Instead of giving a direct yes or no, he challenged each one to decide for himself or herself—to receive him in faith or to reject that which did not meet their expectations.

We are faced with the same question as we seek to live life from the depths. Is the suffering servant who merged with human life the Messiah whom we are expecting and are willing to follow, or are we waiting for one who, rather than transform-ing life from within, controls it from without? Do we recognize the miracles around us as signs of God's presence, or do we dismiss them as everyday events?

Suggestion for meditation: *Spend some quiet time pondering the kind of Messiah you are waiting for. Ask God to help you recognize the redeeming Presence in your life.*

Sunday, December 17   Read Matthew 11:7-11.

The questions Jesus asked are as penetrating today as they were two thousand years ago. In today's reading, Jesus, referring to John the Baptist, asks the crowd what it was that they went out into the desert to see. John was not swayed from his prophetic task by public opinion, like a reed swayed by the wind. Neither did he succumb to the lure of comfort, fine clothing, good food. John's role was to announce the coming of God's chosen one, and in the fulfillment of that role he held himself accountable only to God.

John's role in history is unique. However, there is much we can learn from him in examining our own spiritual journeys. Each of us has unique opportunities to prepare the way for Christ to come into the lives of those whose lives we touch. We are uniquely gifted by the very nature of who we are to fulfill God's call to us.

Do we, like John, cooperate with God at work in and through us, regardless of the cost, or do we bend with the prevailing wind and opt for the more comfortable route?

Our call may not be as dramatic as was John's, but God prepares us for that call as carefully as John was prepared for his. Make no mistake, our role can be as pivotal in someone's life as John's was in the revealing of the Messiah. John was the bridge between the longing and the fulfillment of God's promise. In our individual ways, we, too, are bridges between a hurting world and the redeeming presence of God.

Prayer: *O God, who came to us to heal and set free, come to us again in these days, making us instruments of your grace to others. Amen.*

GOD WITH US

December 18-24, 1989 **Charles W. Maynard†**
Monday, December 18 Read Isaiah 7:10-16.

Susan's family called me to be with them at the hospital. Susan was going into a coma. She was only semi-conscious when I arrived. Her daughter talked to her as she gently stroked her hand. There was no response from Susan. The daughter spoke louder, "Mother, can you hear me?" Again there was no response. The daughter persisted, "Mother, if you can hear me, squeeze my hand." Susan gently squeezed her hand. We all breathed a little easier. It was very important for us to have some sign, some little signal that she was still there.

Things did not look good in Isaiah's day. Syria and Israel were invading Judah to force an alliance upon King Ahaz at Jerusalem. King Ahaz did not know what to do. Isaiah said that God would give Ahaz a sign. However, in a show of false piety, Ahaz refused the sign. God offered the sign anyway. The sign was to be a baby called "Immanuel," which means "God with us."

God knows the need that we have for reassurance, whether we ask for it or not. God offers signs of God's continued presence with us. The sign may be the gentlest of squeezes, or a baby, but the message is always "God is with us."

Suggestion for meditation: *Reflect on your need for reassurance. Where do you need to be assured? How does God give you a sign?*

---

† Pastor, Seymour United Methodist Church, Seymour, Tennessee.

Tuesday, December 19   Read Isaiah 7:14;
                                            Matthew 1:18-25.

On a visit to my grandparents when I was six years old, my grandfather and I walked to church together. I remember it for two reasons. The first is that we crossed a creek by crawling on a log in our Sunday clothes. The other is that he told me what my first name meant. I was the fourth generation to have that name, and he told me to live up to it.

Names are important. Names shape individuals as much as individuals shape names. We did not name our daughters certain names because of people and memories that were associated with those names. The baby that comes as a sign is called "Immanuel," which means "God with us." Joseph and Mary were told to name their child "Jesus," which means "Yahweh will save." God does not act through some nameless force but comes as a person with a name.

Isaiah proclaimed one called "Immanuel." Joseph and Mary called their baby "Jesus." In both cases, God lived up to the name. God stood with the people of Judah in the face of the enemy. God worked through Jesus to save the people. God still lives up to the names of Immanuel and Jesus.

When we hear that a baby has been born, one of the first questions is, "What is her name?" At Christmas we shout and sing about the birth of a baby. His name is Jesus, "Immanuel."

Prayer: *O Lord, we are thankful that we can call upon you by name and that you live up to that name. Amen.*

Wednesday, December 20   Read Psalm 24:1-2.

The earth is a planet of contrasts. Ocean and desert, mountain and plain, mountain stream and river delta. There is a wide variety of life on the earth. Flowers, trees, vegetables, fruits, shrubs, though all plants, are very different. Birds, reptiles, fish and mammals are all animals, but none is the same. Even among people there are many differences. Each individual is unique down to the tiny lines on each finger. The variety is unending.

The psalmist proclaims that all earth and its richness of life is the Lord's. It is not the product and territory of some committee of gods. Nor is it the possession of one god among several. The earth is the Lord's.

This Lord is the one who made a covenant with Abraham, with Moses, and with David. God created and sustains the earth. It is to the earth and its diversity that God comes in all fullness and variety. The psalmist sings of that entry of God, the King of Glory.

God did not set the universe in motion to back away. We are not left to our own devices but are touched by the One that made the earth and all that is in it.

Suggestion for prayer: *Today, notice the wide variety of the earth and the life in it. Thank God for the diversity, and watch for God's coming.*

Thursday, December 21   Read Psalm 24.

Psalm 24 is an entrance song. It was used to begin worship in the temple. It may originally have been sung when the Ark of the Covenant was brought into the temple at the head of a great procession. The priests and people sang it as a litany of praise.

When we began to clean the house recently, our daughters asked, "Who is coming?" We laughed at the thought that we only cleaned up for guests. But we do make special efforts when we know someone is going to visit.

The psalmist speaks of being prepared for the entrance of the King of Glory by being clean, pure, honest, and faithful. There is the understanding that one's life must be in order to welcome the King. Even the doors and gates are a part of the welcome of the King of Glory.

God comes into our lives at all times, not just at Christmas. However, in this Advent season we are particularly mindful of God's entrance. It was not a grand parade down the streets of Jerusalem but a humble birth in a back-lot stable.

Advent is a time of preparing for God's entrance into the world. Psalm 24 can be chanted as we make ready to celebrate "God with us."

Suggestion for prayer: *Pray the 24th psalm as you prepare your house for the season. Make your work an "entrance psalm."*

Friday, December 22   Read Romans 1:1-7.

Every year we receive numerous Christmas cards. In many of them are notes from family and friends. Some catch us up on happenings. Others simply give greetings or bear a signature. We enjoy the cards and display them in the living room of our house.

When Paul sent his personal greetings to the church at Rome, he was writing to a group he had not met. He introduced himself in the first words of the epistle. Paul did not tell who he was as much as he told whose he was. He identified himself as a servant of Christ Jesus. This Jesus was the Son of God and a descendant of David. Paul summarized the gospel message as he understood it. The recipients of the letter were also identified as to whose they were.

God works in and through individuals. God worked in Paul, a servant and apostle. Isaiah and other prophets were messengers for God. Jesus was Immanuel, "God with us." God comes to us personally. It is not some nameless power that says, "Hey you!" We are addressed by name by One who comes to be with us.

Paul sent greetings of grace and peace to the believers at Rome. We send and receive Christmas cards and notes with season's greetings. But God sends us the most personal of greetings in the Baby of Bethlehem. It is such a personal message that it is entrusted to no one. God brings it. God is the message. "God with us."

Suggestion for prayer: *As you write and open cards, send and receive God's gifts of grace and peace. Remember your family and friends by name.*

368

Saturday, December 23   Read Matthew 1:2-11, 20;
Romans 1:2-4.

The name of David is a common thread that runs through this week's selections. It appears in each passage as a reminder. The name "David" connects the time of each writer with another day in which the kingdom of Israel was at its peak. It speaks of God's activity among God's people.

The name "David" speaks of humanity, royalty, and promise. Jesus comes through the power of the Holy Spirit but as a descendent of a human being. David, as idealized as he was, made mistakes. Matthew reminds us of one of those mistakes in the genealogy. David's affair with Uriah's wife produced Solomon. Matthew points the reader to Jesus' humanity, to his being like we are.

Jesus is identified as royalty due to his descent from David, the king. Jesus is *the* king, God's chosen one. He is *the* Messiah, just as David was a messiah, an anointed one. Jesus is also the fulfillment of God's promise to David to establish David's throne forever.

"David" also serves to fix God in this time and in this place. God is active in history as God was in the time of David. God came to be with David's descendents through a descendent of David. God is with us today, just as God has always been with his people.

Suggestion for prayer: *Reflect on your own family and its heritage. Be thankful that God comes to us in family to work his purposes.*

Sunday, December 24   Read Matthew 1:18-25.

"God with us" does not always arrive as the King of Glory of Psalm 24. The first Christmas, God did not come "strong and mighty" or "mighty in battle." Instead, God came amid fear, shame, and pain. Joseph was ashamed that Mary, his promised, was pregnant. He was going to have nothing to do with her until told in a dream about all that was to happen. He could not see that God was in those embarrassing events.

Our younger daughter was with me when we made a visit to a home in the community. Our church was trying to help this family get water lines into their house. The house was a small cinder block building with a rickety wooden front porch. As we were leaving, Anna said, "Look, Dad, it's Christmas!" She pointed to the house. I could not see anything Christmas about the poor dwelling of so many people. She insisted, "It's Christmas," and pointed to the front porch. Then I saw the string of Christmas lights under the eaves. She saw Christmas beauty where I could see only poverty and ugliness.

God as Immanuel does not come only in our strongest moments. God also comes in our most trying times, when we are our weakest. God gave a baby as a sign to King Ahaz in Isaiah's day. A baby was how God chose to come so long ago on an evening in Bethlehem.

Suggestion for prayer: *Pray that you might see Immanuel however God may appear on this Christmas Eve.*

LIGHT IN OUR DARKNESS

December 25-31, 1989   **Jo Carr†**

Monday, December 25 (Christmas)

Read Luke 2:1-7;
Isaiah 9:6-7.

Christmas is a miracle. It was miracle enough then that the Lord of Hosts should choose to come to dwell with humanfolk, should become incarnate as a baby in a Bethlehem manger. It is miracle all over again that it should be for us . . . to us . . .

Unto us a child is born. Unto *us* the Christ is come. Not just to Mary and Joseph, a handful of shepherds, and three Middle Eastern sages. Not just to the disciples, running to keep up with him. Not just to Mary Magdalene and Peter and Mary and Martha. Not just to Matthew, Mark, Luke, and John.

To us. That's the message of Christmas. To us. Here in this town. Here in this house. Here in this body where I live, in this mind and heart, the Christ is born. Light comes; and the darkness will not, cannot, put it out. I can turn my back. I can squinch my eyes shut—but some of the light seeps in, creeps in anyway . . . reminding me that I am not alone. For unto *me* the Christ is born.

Prayer: *God of Jesus Christ, for this, above all, I give thanks: that Christmas is not just a historic event that happened a long time ago . . . that Christmas is not just something that happens to other folks . . . but that unto me the Christ is come. It is into my darkness that Christ's light shines. Amen.*

---

† United Methodist minister, author, former missionary to Zimbabwe, Levelland, Texas.

371

Tuesday, December 26   Read Luke 2:8-20.

The shepherds saw the light, all right. And they heard the heavenly music—and it scared them speechless. It would me, too, I think: if all glory broke loose, right in my own backyard. They were "sore" afraid, the King James Version puts it.

This was no ordinary fear, like the fear they knew on other nights: fear of wolves . . . fear of bandits . . . fear of the owners of the sheep if one of the animals was lost . . . fear of the dark (for some of them) . . . or even the vague fear that another age would call *existential anxiety*.

None of those. They were filled with a great fear of that very thing the angel was announcing: that the Lord God Almighty would reveal himself. And in dreadful awe, the shepherds were afraid . . . deeply afraid to stand in God's presence.

It is to that great fear that the angel speaks. "Fear not: for behold, I bring you good tidings of great joy"(KJV). The Lord God reveals himself to us as a Savior . . . not as the one who will shatter us, but as the one who will restore us. God comes as light in our darkness.

Prayer: *Lord God, Awesome One: I guess I've always been afraid to ask for very much of your presence in my life. "Fear not?" Then I pray that you would come, Lord, and bring your light into the darknesses of my daily life. Amen.*

Wednesday, December 27   Read Isaiah 9:2.

Only once have I experienced genuine and total darkness. Years ago, down in the depths of Carlsbad Caverns, seated near a mighty formation called "Rock of Ages," having been properly prepared for it, I was given the experience of total darkness. All the lights were extinguished. No fragment of sunlight filtered down into those very innards of the earth. It was totally, totally dark.

But I have felt like that other times. Even in broad daylight I have felt a darkness of the spirit, felt like one who dwells in a land of deep darkness.

Darkness is not comfortable, so it is my inclination to try to solve the problem myself. To study enough, maybe, that I can map my own way out of the darkness . . . to learn enough that I can see answers in the dark. To rub two sticks together, maybe, and make a little fire to see by. To solve it, fix it. And then to cry in the dark, in impotent frustration, when I cannot make it light.

Sometimes, in the darkness of my spirit, I forget that we are a Christmas people. On us has Christ's light shined. We don't have to solve the darkness, for God has already done so through Christ.

Prayer: *Lord, help me remember in the darkest times of my soul . . . help me remember Christmas. Amen.*

Thursday, December 28   Read Isaiah 9:2-7.

I seem to have this problem with accepting the wattage of the light God gives me, here in the darkness of my dailiness. I'd like a floodlight—one of those megawatt affairs that sweeps the skies to announce the opening of a new supermarket. I'd like that kind of a light to see by!

Isn't that what Isaiah promised? "The people who walked in darkness have seen a great light." Sounds like megawatts to me.

But what if "great" has to do with the quality of that light, and not its wattage? What if "great" means a noble, pure, wondrous, steady, enduring, guiding, totally trustworthy light . . . but it's more candle-sized than sun-sized? Not a light that blinds us, but one that enables us to see.

A candle-sized light is enough to take the next few steps by. And it's not as though we walk away from the candle into the darkness, but that we take the candle with us. We have God's light of guidance with us, so we can see to take the next few steps. And the next.

Prayer: *Dear God, keep me content with the light I do have, for you are with me. Amen.*

Friday, December 29   Read Isaiah 9:2;
                                            John 1:1-5.

It was 10 P.M. at the Christmas Eve service in a church in Houston. The lights in the sanctuary were fairly subdued. People came in from their various Christmas Eve preparations and found their seats by families and little clusters and groups until it was time for the service to begin.

Then the lights began to dim . . . and grew steadily dimmer until they were out altogether . . . until the sanctuary was in darkness, and in total quiet. There was a long, expectant pause in the quiet blackness—and then the sound and the flame of a struck match . . . and the Christ candle was lighted: the white, center candle of the Advent wreath.

And the people who sat in darkness saw that light.

We understand sitting in darkness. We know what despair and poverty and injustice and disease and emptiness and frustration are like.

But one evening God struck a match across the dark sky of earth and lit the eternal flame of Christ-among-us, of God-with-us. And no darkness can extinguish that light! Christ is with us, with me, forever.

Prayer: *I give thanks, O God, that I can walk in your light and know your fellowship of love. Amen.*

Saturday, December 30

Read Psalm 111.

> *Almighty God, Master of the universe,*
> *Beneath whose wings we all take refuge,*
> *Care, oh care for us continually!*
> *Day after day we come to thee,*
> *Ever reminded by our own falling short,*
> *Frustrated by our own "teaberry shuffles," . . . but . . .*
> *God-lured back to God . . .*

That's what today's psalm was written like: the first letters of each line being the listed letters of the Hebrew alphabet. Odd, isn't it, that the psalmist should try to do that: should tax his brain to praise God in acrostic . . . as some creative sorts praise God in poetry, and others in song.

And I—I am only able to praise God in ordinary prayer. Oh, and in thoughts that turn toward God. And in deeds done for these others around me whom God so loves. And in kindnesses passed on, and bigotries resisted, and beauty appreciated. When I think about it, I guess there are really quite a few ways in which I can praise God.

Prayer:

> *Almighty God, Master of the universe,*
> *Beneath whose wings we all take refuge,*
> *Christmas day is gone, and I am needing comfort.*
> *Dismal is the corner without the tree;*
> *Empty the shelves without the trappings.*
>
> *Forgive my needing the manger; it is thee I need.*
> *Give me the head and heart to praise thee, today.*
> *Holy Lord, be thou with me throughout the year,*
> *Illumining my often-denseness with thy light.*
>
> *Amen.*

Sunday, December 31   Read Isaiah 9:2;
Psalm 96.

Year's end. Good day for reflecting.

I wonder, in the presence of God, where growth has happened this year . . .

Of the things I hoped to do, have I completed a reasonable number of them? (Of the letters I had hoped to write, the friends I had intended to visit, perhaps the list of "haven't yet" stretches longer than the list of "yes, I did do that.")

I can list quite a number of *unanticipated* things done, burdens undertaken, tasks accomplished. And I usually forget to count those.

I can list some pain survived, some worries resolved, some relationships strengthened, some risks dared. I usually forget to count those, too.

But today is for *reflecting,* not for adding up sums on some hypothetical end-of-year exam.

Today is for reflecting, for being grateful, for taking a winter walk, for reading one of those end-of-the-book psalms . . . the praise-and-thanksgiving ones . . .

And for realizing that there has been light for my path all the year, even during those periods when I thought there was none.

Prayer: *Dear Lord, I give thanks for the year, and for the joys and sorrows and dailiness that it has contained. I give thanks most of all for your presence with me, your light on my path all the way. Safely through another year, you have brought me. I entrust the new year into your hands. Amen.*

New Common Lectionary, 1989
(*Disciplines* Edition)

January 1

1 Samuel 2:18-20, 26
Psalm 111
Colossians 3:12-17
Luke 2:41-52

January 2-8
Epiphany

Isaiah 61:1-4
Psalm 29
Acts 8:14-17
Luke 3:15-17, 21-22

January 9-15

Isaiah 62:1-5
Psalm 36:5-10
1 Corinthians 12:1-11
John 2:1-11

January 16-22

Nehemiah 8:1-4a, 5-6, 8-10
Psalm 19:7-14
1 Corinthians 12:12-30
Luke 4:14-21

January 23-29

Jeremiah 1:4-10
Psalm 71:1-6
1 Corinthians 13:1-13
Luke 4:21-30

January 30–February 5

Exodus 34:29-35
Psalm 99
2 Corinthians 3:12–4:2
Luke 9:28-36

February 6-12
Ash Wednesday

Deuteronomy 26:1-11
Psalm 91:9-16
Romans 10:8b-13
Luke 4:1-13

February 13-19

Genesis 15:1-12, 17-18
Psalm 127
Philippians 3:17–4:1
Luke 13:31-35

February 20-26

Exodus 3:1-15
Psalm 103:1-13
1 Corinthians 10:1-13
Luke 13:1-9

February 27–March 5

Joshua 5:9-12
Psalm 34:1-8
2 Corinthians 5:16-21
Luke 15:1-3, 11-32

March 6-12

Isaiah 43:16-21
Psalm 126
Philippians 3:8-14
John 12:1-8

March 13-19
Passion/Palm Sunday
Isaiah 50:4-9*a*
Psalm 31:9-16
Psalm 118:19-29
Luke 19:28-40

March 20-26
Holy Week
Isaiah 52:13–53:12
Psalm 22:1-18
Hebrews 4:14-16; 5:7-9
John 18:1–19:42
Isaiah 65:17-25
Psalm 118:14-24
1 Corinthians 15:19-26
Acts 10:34-43
John 20:1-18

March 27–April 2
Acts 5:27-32
Psalm 2
Revelation 1:4-8
John 20:19-31

April 3-9
Acts 9:1-20
Psalm 30:4-12
Revelation 5:11-14
John 21:1-19

April 10-16
Acts 13:15-16, 26-33
Psalm 23
Revelation 7:9-17
John 10:22-30

April 17-23
Acts 14:8-18
Psalm 145:13*b*-21
Revelation 21:1-6
John 13:31-35

April 24-30
Acts 15:1-2, 22-29
Psalm 67
Revelation 21:10, 22-27
John 14:23-29

May 1-7
Acts 16:16-34
Psalm 97
Revelation 22:12-14, 16-17, 20
John 17:20-26

May 8-14
Pentecost
Acts 2:1-21
Psalm 104:24-34
Romans 8:14-17
John 14:8-17, 25-27

May 15-21
Proverbs 8:22-31
Psalm 8
Romans 5:1-5
John 16:12-15

May 22-28
Isaiah 55:10-13
Psalm 92:1-4, 12-15
1 Corinthians 15:51-58
Luke 6:39-49

May 29–June 4
1 Kings 8:22-23, 41-43
Psalm 100
Galatians 1:1-10
Luke 7:1-10

June 5-11
1 Kings 17:17-24
Psalm 113
Galatians 1:11-24
Luke 7:11-17

June 12-18

1 Kings 19:1-8
Psalm 42
Galatians 2:15-21
Luke 7:36–8:3

June 19-25

1 Kings 19:9-14
Psalm 43
Galatians 3:23-29
Luke 9:18-24

June 26–July 2

1 Kings 19:15-21
Psalm 44:1-8
Galatians 5:1, 13-25
Luke 9:51-62

July 3-9

1 Kings 21:1-3, 17-21
Psalm 5:1-8
Galatians 6:7-18
Luke 10:1-12, 17-20

July 10-16

2 Kings 2:1, 6-14
Psalm 139:1-12
Colossians 1:1-14
Luke 10:25-37

July 17-23

2 Kings 4:8-17
Psalm 139:13-18
Colossians 1:21-29
Luke 10:38-42

July 24-30

2 Kings 5:1-15*ab*
Psalm 21:1-7
Colossians 2:6-15
Luke 11:1-13

July 31–August 6

2 Kings 13:14-20*a*
Psalm 28
Colossians 3:1-11
Luke 12:13-21

August 7-13

Jeremiah 18:1-11
Psalm 14
Hebrews 11:1-13, 8-19
Luke 12:32-40

August 14-20

Jeremiah 20:7-13
Psalm 10:12-18
Hebrews 12:1-2, 12-17
Luke 12:49-56

August 21-27

Jeremiah 28:1-9
Psalm 84
Hebrews 12:18-29
Luke 13:22-30

August 28–September 3

Ezekiel 18:1-9, 25-29
Psalm 15
Hebrews 13:1-8
Luke 14:1, 7-14

September 4-10

Ezekiel 33:1-11
Psalm 94:12-22
Philemon 1-20
Luke 14:25-33

September 11-17

Hosea 4:1-3; 5:15–6:6
Psalm 77:11-20
1 Timothy 1:12-17
Luke 15:1-10

September 18-24

Hosea 11:1-11
Psalm 107:1-9
1 Timothy 2:1-7
Luke 16:1-13

September 25–October 1

Joel 2:23-30
Psalm 107:1, 33-43
1 Timothy 6:6-19
Luke 16:19-31

October 2-8

Amos 5:6-7, 10-15
Psalm 101
2 Timothy 1:1-14
Luke 17:5-10

October 9-15

Micah 1:2; 2:1-10
Psalm 26
2 Timothy 2:8-15
Luke 17:11-19

October 16-22

Habakkuk 1:1-3; 2:1-4
Psalm 119:137-144
2 Timothy 3:14–4:5
Luke 18:1-8

October 23-29

Zephaniah 3:1-9
Psalm 3
2 Timothy 4:6-8, 16-18
Luke 18:9-14

October 30–November 5

Haggai 2:1-9
Psalm 65:1-8
2 Thessalonians 1:5-12
Luke 19:1-10

November 6-12

Zechariah 7:1-10
Psalm 9:11-20
2 Thessalonians 2:13–3:5
Luke 20:27-38

November 13-19

Malachi 4:1-6
Psalm 82
2 Thessalonians 3:6-13
Luke 21:5-19

November 20-26

2 Samuel 5:1-5
Psalm 95
Colossians 1:11-20
John 12:9-19

November 27–December 3
1st Sunday in Advent

Isaiah 2:1-5
Psalm 122
Romans 13:11-14
Matthew 24:36-44

December 4-10

Isaiah 11:1-10
Psalm 72:1-8
Romans 15:4-13
Matthew 3:1-12

December 11-17

Isaiah 35:1-10
Psalm 146:5-10
James 5:7-10
Matthew 11:2-11

December 18-24

Isaiah 7:10-16
Psalm 24
Romans 1:1-7
Matthew 1:18-25

December 25-31
Christmas

Isaiah 9:2-7
Luke 2:1-20
Isaiah 63:7-9
Psalm 111
Hebrews 2:10-18
Matthew 2:13-15, 19-23